Exposing the Antichrist

A Fresh Look at Who He Is

by
Larry Booth

JHM
Publishing

Unless otherwise indicated, all Scripture quotations in this volume are from the King James Version of the Bible and marked KJV. *The Holy Bible: King James Version* (Electronic Edition of the 1900 Authorized Version.). Used by permission.

Scripture quotations marked HCSB are taken from the Holman Christian Standard Bible®, Used by Permission HCSB ©1999,2000,2002,2003,2009 Holman Bible Publishers. Holman Christian Standard Bible®, Holman CSB®, and HCSB® are federally registered trademarks of Holman Bible Publishers.

Scripture quotations taken from the Amplified® Bible (AMPC), Copyright © 1954, 1958, 1962, 1964, 1965, 1987 by The Lockman Foundation. Used by permission. lockman.org.

Most charts and illustrations are owned by Joyful Harvest Ministries except where noted which are used by permission. Some maps come from free sources like Wikimedia commons. Original photo on cover by pxhere.com. Finished cover by Larry Booth.

Exposing the Antichrist-
A Fresh Look at Who He Is
By Larry Booth
First Printing 2023

ISBN 979-8-9877431-0-2 & 979-8-9877431-1-9
(Hardback) Copyright registered

Joyful Harvest Ministries Publishing
P.O. Box 367
Ironton Mo. 63650

Content

Forward

When a friend wrote me with a question about eschatological timing concerning dates that just didn't seem to add up, I was totally stumped. Even after checking several resource books, I couldn't find an answer since none of them even addressed the issue. At that point, I decided, "This is a 'Larry Booth question.'" Almost as quickly as my email went out, his reply with a full, logical explanation landed in my inbox. It is this kind of expertise concerning end-time prophecy that I have come to expect from the author of the volume you are holding in your hand. With some thirty-five names and titles given to the Antichrist in the Bible, it is no wonder that the average believer finds himself at a loss to unravel all the biblical clues concerning the identity of this important end-time figure. Therefore, it is encouraging that an astute scholar of biblical prophecy has taken up the task for us. However, I must warn you – <u>Exposing the Antichrist – A Fresh Look at Who He Is,</u> is no "easy read." With so many mysteries and puzzles to solve and "dots to connect," you will find it challenging to wonder if you'll ever "find your way out of the maze." However, trust Pastor Larry that he knows where he's taking you. At the same time, give him credit for not jumping to unfounded and poorly reasoned conclusions. You'll read the words "probably," "possibly," and "perhaps" enough times to know that Pastor Larry is cautiously guarding against "stepping across the line" into speculation rather than solid research and sound analysis.

May the extent of your encounter with this mysterious – yet key figure – in the not-too-distant events of the destiny of human civilization be limited to what you read in <u>Exposing the Antichrist – A Fresh Look at Who He Is</u> and not from personal experience with him!

Dr. Delron Shirley

Dr. Delron Shirley is founder and president of Teach All Nations Mission, an evangelical educational ministry. He is also an adjunct faculty member at Charis Bible College in Colorado Springs and serves as a consultant for Every Home for Christ in their discipleship department. Before moving to Colorado, Delron served for twenty-five years as dean of World Harvest Bible College and Indiana Christian University and worked as a chaplain in Yosemite National Park.

Dedication

I dedicate this book to my wife Joy. Nobody has given more to its creation than her. Without her love and devotion to our ministry, I would be nothing. Thank you for all the personal hours with me you lost while I was studying, writing, and preparing this work. Thank you for believing in God's call on my life. I love you.

Preface

I hope you have a love for the Word of God. It has its own mystery and intrigue and is full of the answers we seek, especially about this man. Why write a book about the Antichrist? For one, the Bible has so much to say about him. So much so, we examine him and try to understand what kind of person he will be. In these uncertain times, many are turning to the wrong places to find answers about the future. I see a lot of theories out there that are not founded in Scripture. We must look at where the story begins first before we may inject some theory into a subject. God's Word must be our primary source.

The Antichrist is obviously an egotistical psychopath worse than Hitler, bent on destroying God's people. Jesus stated that the Tribulation would be worse for the Jewish people than at any other time in history. At some point, this once-insignificant man will think he is God himself and replace all religion with worship of himself.

Maybe, instead of trying to find out who the Antichrist is in the world and naming names, we should be studying who he is in Scripture first. We do this so that when he does appear on the world scene, others will recognize him. As believers, I don't think we will know his name yet. Although there are some in the shadows today who work to bring about his start, the Devil wants us to tremble at his beginning and get lost in fear, suspicion, and naming names.

An antichrist may be alive today, and probably is. I believe Satan is prepared in every generation for when Christ removes the restrainer, to make his move. While there were many "types" presented earlier in Scripture, the Emperor Nero was no doubt one of his first attempts in the New Testament.

This study was one of three that the Lord gave me during the time of COVID (2020). I believe that there is so much in the Word of God that we pass over to our detriment in understanding a subject. Especially about the end-times events. We read too quickly and miss the details. This is a study of the details. Let's go back and study every verse again that could be a reference to the Antichrist and uncover him. Let's see what makes him tick and maybe reveal a bit of his personality. At the end of our study, I have compiled the facts about the Antichrist that I have uncovered, so that we might expose everything about him.

This book took many months to finish, and I hope it brings a blessing to you in your understanding of this subject. In some of the Scripture references, to emphasize certain things, I have underlined, and my comments sometimes are preceded by an "LB-" The Scripture references are in **bold**, and my comments are in parenthesis and not in bold.
God bless you as you study with all of us who want to know and uncover the truth.

A great number of verses are used from the Old Testament prophets in this work. I thought it would be beneficial to list the prophetic books in the divisions of time that they represent based on Israel's history. We could see a middle point as being during the Babylonian captivity or exile in their history.

Understanding the Prophets in Relation to Israel's History The Kingdom of Messiah, Israel's Kingdom, the Millennial Kingdom, and the nations related to each				
Pre-Assyrian	**The Assyrian**	**Transitional**	**Chaldean Period**	**Persian Period**
Prior to the Assyrian invasion & captivity of Israel		Spanning from the end of the Assyrian into the Babylonian	During the Babylonian exile era	From the restoration down to the close of prophecy
(Elijah/Elisha)	Amos	Nahum	-Jeremiah	-Daniel
Obadiah	Hosea	Zephaniah	Ezekiel	Haggai
Joel	Isaiah	Habbakuk	Daniel-	Zechariah
Jonah	Micah	Jeremiah-		(Ezra/Nehemiah)
				Malachi

Chart by Larry Booth

Hidden amidst the Old Testament prophetic books are the future events of "things to come." All speak of a future kingdom when the Messiah will come to judge the earth, rule, and restore Israel fully to her lands. With the New Testament, we see a clearer picture of what lies ahead for Israel, the Church, and the nations of the earth. Below is a chart I borrowed and further edited from Mark Martin. I added to it the future judgments as they relate to the end times.

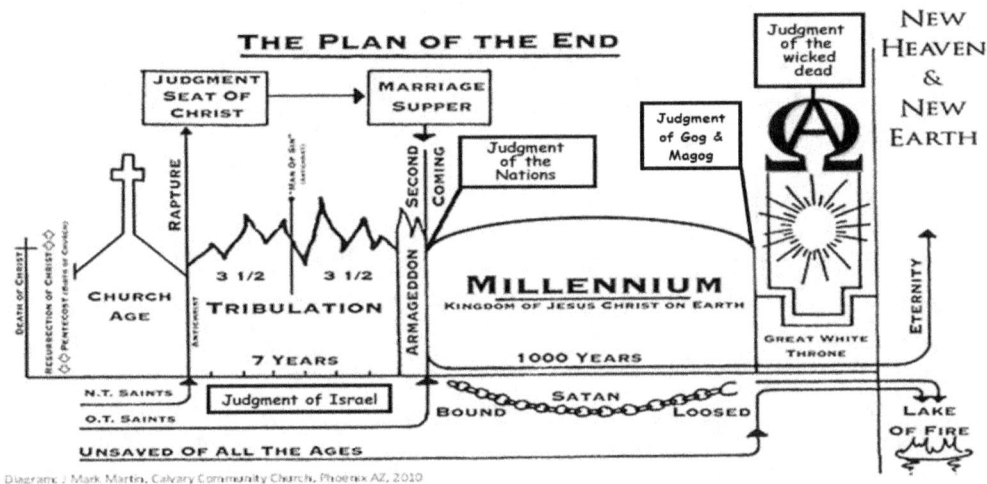

Maranatha,

Larry Booth

1/14/23

Chapter 1
Introductions

You might think this book is about a subject that would be more appropriate for those who have already entered the Tribulation period. If you are reading this and this is true, then maybe this book will help guide you over the next few years. If you are a believer and want to know more about this subject, then keep reading. I wrote this with both of you in mind. We would never try to sensationalize this subject, beyond the massive degree to which it has already been taken. I do not want to add to the madness. So much of what we have come to believe about the Antichrist is myth and conjecture, and is not founded soundly in Scripture. Someone once stated that over 100 passages mention this person. I hope a fresh look at many of these passages will help you find a balance about this future terrible man.

Before we jump headlong into this important subject, we need to first make sure we have a common understanding of a few words and concepts. When we study a prophetic viewpoint, we are generally looking to the future of things. The study of *eschatology* is the study of "things to come." It is a study of the end times. Here is a simple chart to help us understand future events.

The End Times

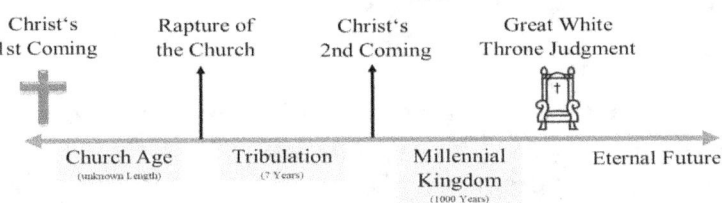

After our Lord and Savior Jesus Christ came and gave His life for us, He resurrected from the dead and was victorious over death and the grave. This also proved that He is the Son of God, sent to save us. Paul the Apostle stated that our faith in Christ and our belief in this resurrection is how we are saved in Romans 10:9. While all of His life was predicted by the Old Testament prophets many hundreds of years before, like His virgin birth, His death, and His purpose (Isaiah 7:14; 9:6-7; Isaiah 53; Psalm 22; Micah 5:2; Daniel 9:24-27), many of the Jews focused on the passages that spoke of the "Day of the Lord," when the Messiah would deliver them from the bondage of Gentile rule (Psalm 2:7-9; Isaiah 13:9-11; Ezekiel 30:3-4; Joel 3:12-14; Zephaniah 3:8).

Hundreds of Old Testament verses speak of this event for the Jews. The disciples even thought at that time after the resurrection, that Jesus as the Messiah, would usher in this "Day of the Lord" and then the Millennial (1000 year) kingdom when He would personally rule the world from Israel. Israel was under Roman rule at the time of Jesus's first coming. Jesus stated that it wasn't the proper time yet in Acts 1:6-7.

A promise to return

He rose into the clouds to leave the earth 40 days later after spending time with His disciples (Acts 1:3, 9). At the time Jesus left, two angels promised that He would return to the earth just like He had left-*visibly* in a cloud from the sky. Before Jesus was even crucified, He had promised the disciples that He would come back briefly and take the church back to Heaven to be where He was. This is found in John 14.

John 14:2-3 (KJV)
² In my Father's house are many mansions: if *it were* not *so*, I would have told you. I go to prepare a place for you.
³ And if I go and prepare a place for you, I will come again, and receive you unto myself; that <u>where I am, *there*</u> <u>ye may be also.</u>

The "place" that Jesus was going to prepare for us was our Father's house in heaven, and He promised the Church that He would take us there in the future. This event is called the Rapture of the Church. Those who belong to Christ Jesus will one day be "caught up" in the clouds to be with Him. In that event, Jesus will not touch the ground. This is when Christ comes *for* His saints. There are two parts to His return in the future, separated by a seven-year period of time. One is the Rapture, when the believers will be caught up in the air and Christ will not touch the ground, and the other is the "Day of the Lord" event, when Jesus's feet will touch the Mount of Olives and He will establish His throne there in Jerusalem. This is when Christ comes *with* His saints and is visibly seen. The Church is taken up in a moment of time (1 Cor. 15:52), but when Jesus comes to conquer every eye will see Him (Rev. 1:7).

RAPTURE EVENT

1 Thessalonians 4:16-17 (KJV)
[16] For the Lord himself shall descend from heaven with a shout, with the voice of the archangel, and with the trump of God: and the dead in Christ shall rise first:
[17] Then we which are alive *and* remain shall be <u>caught up together with them in the clouds</u>, to meet the Lord in the air: and so shall we ever be with the Lord.

1 Corinthians 15:52 (KJV)
[52] In a moment, in the twinkling of an eye, at the last trump: for the trumpet shall sound, and the dead shall be raised incorruptible, and we shall be changed.

Notice that this Rapture event happens in a moment of time. When Jesus does this, it will be in an instant of time and will not be a prolonged event. Then He takes the believers away with Him back to heaven. The earth will not see this event. They are spared the next events on the earth and will be rewarded in Heaven at the judgment seat of Christ (1 Peter 5:4). At the same time, the earth will go through seven years of tribulation. Some of this time will be marked with a sense of false peace and some with great wrath.

DAY OF THE LORD EVENT

Jude 1:14-15 (KJV)
[14] And Enoch also, the seventh from Adam, prophesied of these, saying, Behold, <u>the Lord cometh with ten thousands of his saints,</u>
[15] <u>To execute judgment</u> upon all, and <u>to convince all</u> that are ungodly among them of all their ungodly deeds which they have ungodly committed, and of all their hard *speeches* which ungodly sinners have spoken against him.

Revelation 19:11-16 (KJV)
[11] And I saw heaven opened, and behold a white horse; and he that sat upon him *was* called Faithful and True, and in righteousness <u>he doth judge and make war.</u>
[12] His eyes *were* as a flame of fire, and on his head *were* many crowns; and he had a name written, that no man knew, but he himself.
[13] And he *was* clothed with a vesture dipped in blood: and his name is called The Word of God.
[14] And <u>the armies *which were* in</u> heaven followed him upon white horses, clothed in fine linen, white and clean.
[15] And out of his mouth goeth a sharp sword, that with it he should smite the nations: and he shall rule them with a rod of iron: and he treadeth the winepress of the fierceness and wrath of Almighty God.
[16] And he hath on *his* vesture and on his thigh a name written, KING OF KINGS, AND LORD OF LORDS.

When Jesus comes back to the earth the second time after seven years, He comes to save Israel, to judge, and to make war. In the Rapture, He comes to take the believers back to heaven for a time, but in the "Day of the Lord" or "Second Coming" event, He comes with *armies* that "were in heaven." The Bible says we will be with Him when He comes back to judge the earth.

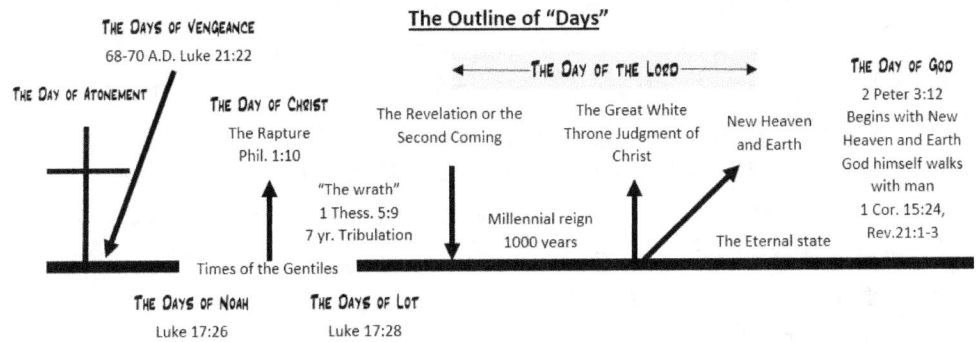

Chart by Larry Booth

The seven-year Tribulation period

In the book of Daniel, we find that there is a future seven-year period that relates to Israel's future judgment that has never yet been fulfilled. We call this period "the Tribulation." This is a human term and not directly scriptural. This is a set time that is described as containing great tribulation for those left on earth. The time period itself is not called "THE Tribulation" in the Bible, but it is more correctly a *description* of that period of time. You can see this clearly in Deuteronomy 4:30.

Deuteronomy 4:30 (KJV)
30 When thou art in tribulation, and all these things are come upon thee, *even* in the latter days, if thou turn to the LORD thy God, and shalt be obedient unto his voice;

Jesus stated that in the last half of this period there would be "*great* tribulation" for the Jewish people. He used the adjective "great," which means "big as in a very wide application." Perhaps this is why most use this term.

Matthew 24:21 (KJV)
21 For then shall be great tribulation, such as was not since the beginning of the world to this time, no, nor ever shall be.

My young grandson, while on a trip with his mom and my wife, asked them, "What is the apocalypse?" He had seen something on the internet and wanted to understand what it was. My wife explained in simple terms that it was when the Lord would judge the world. His next question became the right one to ask, "Why is the Lord going to do this?" This answer took a little more discussion about how men in the world have chosen to rebel against God's ways and will get worse and worse until Christ intervenes.

John in the book of Revelation spoke of this time period in detail and properly titled the end of days as the "Apocalypse of Jesus Christ." All that is in the future will come down to one thing: the revelation of Jesus as the supreme ruler of this world, who rules with majesty and power. First, this period of time is to finish God's punishment of Israel as foretold by Daniel. Second, it is to deal with the wickedness that prevails in the world today, which is being led by the future Antichrist. These seven years are to finish the time of punishment for Israel's rebellion against God and rejection of His Christ.

The Old Testament prophets used many names for this time period in Israel just before the Messiah's second return to the earth. Below is a short list of these names.

1. The last days or latter days- Gen. 49:1, Isa. 2:2, Micah 4:1, Num. 24:14, Deut. 4:30, 31:29, Jer. 23:20, Jer. 30:24, 48:47, 49:39, Ezek. 38:16, Dan. 2:28, 10:14, Hos. 3:5.

    Isaiah 2:2 (KJV)
    ² And it shall come to pass in the last days, *that* the mountain of the LORD'S house shall be established in the top of the mountains, and shall be exalted above the hills; and all nations shall flow unto it.

    The phrase "the last (latter) day" in the *singular* is used for the *one-day* event called the "Second Coming of Christ Jesus" or the "Day of the Lord," as in Job 19:25. Also, the phrase "day of vengeance" is used for that one day. (Isa. 34:8, 35:4, 47:3, 61:2, 63:4, Jer. 46:10, 50:15, 50:28, 51:11, 51:36, Micah 5:15, Nah. 1:2).

> **Isaiah 34:8 (KJV)**
> [8] For *it is* the day of the LORD'S vengeance, *and* the year of recompences for the controversy of Zion.

2. The time of trouble, the day of trouble, and the time of Jacob's trouble. (Ps. 27:5, 37:39, Isa. 33:2, Jer. 2:27-28, 11:12, 14:8, 30:7).

> **Jeremiah 30:7 (KJV)**
> [7] Alas! for that day *is* great, so that none *is* like it: it *is* even the time of Jacob's trouble; but he shall be saved out of it.

3. The time of God's wrath. (Ps. 21:9, Isaiah 65, 1 Thess. 5:1-10, Rev. 6-19)

> **1 Thessalonians 1:10 (KJV)**
> [10] And to wait for his Son from heaven, whom he raised from the dead, *even* Jesus, which delivered us from the wrath to come.

4. The indignation- Duet. 29:28, Ps. 110:5, 10, Isa. 10:5, 25, 26:20, 30:30; 13:5; Ps. 69:24; 78:49; 102:10; Jer. 10:10; 15:7; 50:25; Lam. 2:6; Ezek. 21:31; 22:24,31; Dan. 8:19; 11:36; Nah. 1:6; Hab. 3:12; Zeph. 3:8;

> **Isaiah 26:20-21 (ASV)**
> [20] Come, my people, enter thou into thy chambers, and shut thy doors about thee: hide thyself for a little moment, until the indignation be overpast.
> [21] For, behold, Jehovah cometh forth out of his place to punish the inhabitants of the earth for their iniquity: the earth also shall disclose her blood, and shall no more cover her slain.

5. Daniel's 70th week of years- the last "week" or seven years of Daniel's prophecy are what most people call "the Tribulation."

> **Daniel 9:24 (KJV)**
> **24 Seventy weeks** (LB- lit. seventy *sevens*) **are determined upon thy people and upon thy holy city, to finish the transgression, and to make an end of sins, and to make reconciliation for iniquity, and to bring in everlasting righteousness, and to seal up the vision and prophecy, and to anoint the most Holy.**

Daniel's Prophetic Weeks

Chart by Larry Booth

The Command to Restore

70 Weeks- 490 years to finish the transgression

1948- Jews return to Israel

7 Weeks	62 Weeks	Church Age	The Final Week
(49 Years)	(434 Years)	Pause in	(3 ½ Years- 3 ½ Years)
		Daniel's	Daniel 9:27
Daniel 9:25	Daniel 9:25	timeline	The Tribulation

Israel ceases After 3 wars- 136 AD

Treaty- Abomination- 1260 Days Of Desolation

The Decree of Artaxerxes
Nehemiah Ch. 2

The Messiah cut off
Daniel 9:26

The Catching away
1 Thess. 4:16-17
Romans 11:25

Jesus Returns
Rev. 19:11-21

The angel Gabriel gave the prophet Daniel a prophecy that there were seventy weeks of years (70 x 7 = 490 Jewish years of 360 days each) left for the nation of Israel to finish their punishment for rebelling against God. This period would begin after a future royal decree to restore and re-build the Jewish temple and Jerusalem, which was given by Artaxerxes, the Persian king, *upholding* a past written decree that Cyrus the Great had made (see Ezra 1:1-4, 6:3; 2 Chron. 36:32-33). This happened around 445-4 BC. And this is found in Nehemiah Chapter 2. The original decree by Cyrus was made in 539 BC. Amazingly 200 years before this happened, God told the prophet Isaiah that "Cyrus" would do it in Isaiah 44:28, 150 years before Cyrus was even born!

At the end of these "seventy-sevens," the Messiah would be ruling the world, and Israel would be brought back into a relationship with God. Daniel was also told before this of when the Messiah would come and even be "cut off" and killed. It would happen *after* 69 weeks of years (483 years) after the royal decree was made (7 x 7) + (62 x 7) = 49 + 434 which is 483 years total.

Daniel 9:26-27 (KJV)
26 And after threescore and two weeks (LB- 62 weeks plus the previously mentioned seven weeks) **shall Messiah be cut off, but not for himself: and the people of the prince that shall come shall destroy the city and the sanctuary; and the end thereof *shall be* with a flood, and unto the end of the war desolations are determined.**
27 And he shall <u>confirm the covenant with many</u> for <u>one week</u>: and <u>in the midst of the week</u> he shall cause the sacrifice and the oblation to cease, and for the overspreading of abominations he shall make *it* desolate, even until the consummation, and that determined shall be poured upon the desolate.

As Daniel predicts, Jesus the Messiah came and gave His life after the 483 years. Daniel was told that many events would happen up to and after those first 483 years, and that many years would fall into the "gap" in between until the last week of 7 years would be fulfilled, completing the 490 years. Proof of this is that the city and the sanctuary wasn't destroyed by the Romans as predicted by Verse 26 until almost 40 years after the Messiah was cut off, and that there was no seven year covenant made. Where did the last seven years get fulfilled? One last week of years (7 years) would mark the end when the Messiah would "finish the transgression." This last week was postponed until a time when God would work with Israel again in their own land. We exist now in this "gap" of time.

Notice above in Daniel 9:27 that a "he" would come and make a treaty or covenant with "many" and rule in that last week of years. This is the Antichrist, who will also cause an abomination in the newly rebuilt Jewish temple halfway through the seven years. The Tribulation will *begin* with a covenant being made with many for exactly seven years. Again, this last week has not happened yet, for it will conclude when Israel will be saved by Jesus the Messiah, and Jesus will return to the earth and defeat this Antichrist and his armies.

Daniel 12:1-3 (KJV)
¹ And at that time shall Michael stand up, the great prince which standeth for the children of thy people: and there shall be <u>a time of trouble, such as never was since there was a nation *even* to that same time:</u> and at that time thy people shall be delivered, every one that shall be found written in the book.
² And many of them that sleep in the dust of the earth shall awake, some to everlasting life, and some to shame *and* everlasting contempt.
³ And they that be wise shall shine as the brightness of the firmament; and they that turn many to righteousness as the stars for ever and ever.

Zechariah 12:9-10 (KJV)
⁹ And it shall come to pass <u>in that day,</u> *that* I will seek to destroy all the nations that come against Jerusalem.
¹⁰ And I will pour upon the house of David, and upon the inhabitants of Jerusalem, the spirit of grace and of supplications: and <u>they shall look upon me whom they have pierced,</u> and they shall mourn for him, as one mourneth for *his* only *son,* and shall be in bitterness for him, as one that is in bitterness for *his* firstborn.

This last week of Daniel is what is commonly called the Tribulation period. It is primarily a time for the judgment of Israel but also for all of the wicked people on the earth who will rise up against Christ and His followers.

Those who are saved will not go through the tribulation period

I believe that during this great time of tribulation, there is a focus on the salvation of Israel. At its close, the remaining Jews who survive will find the Lord, who saves them from their destruction. It is not a time for the church to be tested or tried. Israel and the Church of Jesus are on two different timelines to be fulfilled. During the Tribulation, the Lord will save millions of Jews and non-Jews. However, many will lose their lives. This will all happen after the departure of the Church.

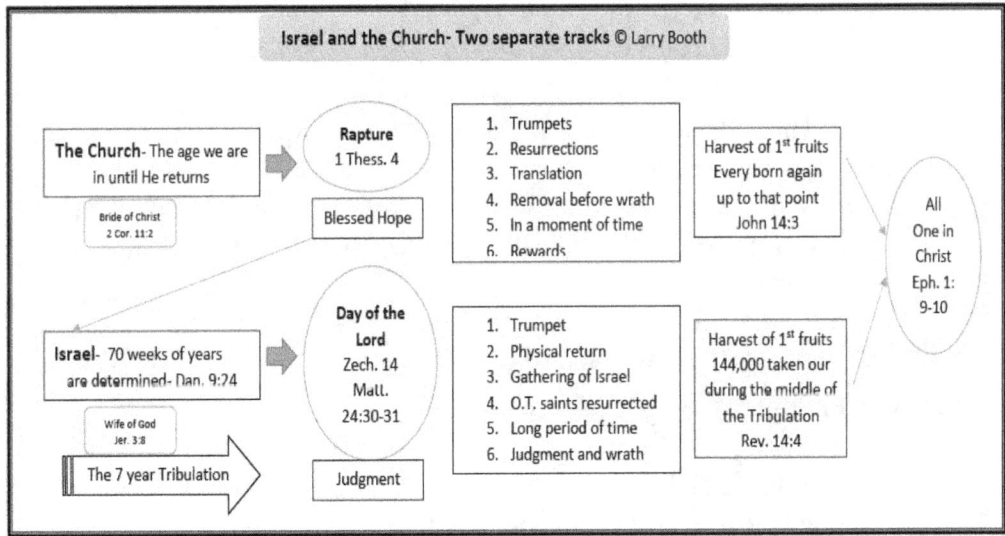

In Romans 11:1, Paul states that God has not cast off His people, the Jews. He then goes on to teach that the Church has not replaced Israel and that at the end of the Tribulation all living Jews will be saved by the Lord Himself. We see this outlined in Zechariah 12-14.

> **Romans 11:26-27 (KJV)**
> **²⁶ And so all Israel shall be saved: as it is written, There shall come out of Sion the Deliverer, and shall turn away ungodliness from Jacob:**
> **²⁷ For this *is* my covenant unto them, when I shall take away their sins.**

Jesus promised to keep His Church out of this time of tribulation. Look at Luke 21 concerning this period of time. Jesus first tells of what was going to happen in 70 AD when the Temple would be destroyed, and then He taught about the end of the age just before He comes back physically to the earth to judge (vs. 24-27). He told of the time of persecution for the Jews and the terrible things the Antichrist would do to them. Notice in Verse 28, Jesus says, "When these things begin to come to pass," "look up," for your redemption is about to happen. Not in the middle of these events, or at the end of these Tribulation events, but at the *beginning*.

> **Luke 21:27-28 (KJV)**
> **²⁷ And then <u>shall they see the Son of man coming</u> in a cloud with power and great glory.**
> **²⁸ And when these things <u>begin to come to pass</u>, then look up, and lift up your heads; for <u>your redemption draweth nigh.</u>**

It will be at the beginning of these great events that Jesus will come in the Rapture to take out His Church. Now look a few verses later what Jesus says:

> **Luke 21:35-36 (KJV)**
> **³⁵ For as a snare shall it come on all them that dwell on the face of the whole earth.**
> **³⁶ Watch ye therefore, and pray always, that ye may be accounted <u>worthy to escape all these things</u> that shall come to pass, and <u>to stand before the Son</u> of man.**

Jesus said if we watch and pray, we would be found worthy to escape everything that will come to pass and to "stand" before Him. The only way to escape all of those events and to stand before Him in Heaven is the pre-Tribulation Rapture of the church. One could *escape* an event to be safe, as many of the Jews will during the Tribulation, but here Jesus is referring to a time when we would escape *and* stand before Him *in* Heaven. The Church will leave this earth before these events take place, and we will stand in Heaven with the Lord till He comes to the earth to battle the Antichrist and the kings of the earth.

Jesus promises this to the Church of Philadelphia: "I will keep you FROM the hour of temptation," which is another name for those seven years.

Revelation 3:10 (KJV)
¹⁰ Because thou hast kept the word of my patience, I also will keep thee from the hour of temptation, which shall come upon all the world, to try them that dwell upon the earth.

Paul taught that all Christians would be kept from the time of wrath. Notice the "you" and the "they" statements in 1 Thess. 5. The time of wrath and the day of the Lord would come upon *them* like a thief in the night. But this is not the case for true believers who are of the day. These would all be kept from the time of wrath and saved from it.

1 Thessalonians 4:14 (KJV)
¹⁴ For if we believe that Jesus died and rose again, even so them also which sleep in Jesus will God bring with him.

1 Thessalonians 5:1-10 (KJV)
¹ But of the times and the seasons, brethren, ye have no need that I write unto you.
² For yourselves know perfectly that the day of the Lord so cometh as a thief in the night.
³ For when they shall say, Peace and safety; then sudden

destruction cometh upon them, as travail upon a woman with child; and <u>they shall not escape.</u>

[4] But <u>ye, brethren, are not in darkness</u>, that that day should overtake you as a thief.

[5] Ye are all the children of light, and the children of the day: we are not of the night, nor of darkness.

[6] Therefore <u>let us not sleep</u>, as *do* others; but let us <u>watch and be sober.</u>

[7] For they that sleep sleep in the night; and they that be drunken are drunken in the night.

[8] But let us, who are of the day, be sober, putting on the breastplate of faith and love; and for an helmet, the hope of salvation.

[9] <u>For God hath not appointed us to wrath, but to obtain salvation by our Lord Jesus Christ,</u>

[10] Who died for us, that, <u>whether we wake or sleep, we should live together with him.</u>

Now if the Rapture happened at the mid-Tribulation or post-Tribulation, how would it be a "thief" to the world? Every believer would be waiting, and even unbelievers would be waiting for the appearing of Jesus to go to war against him. Jesus' return will be a surprise.

According to Scripture, the Antichrist will come to rule during this seven year time period. As we will see in our future chapters, the details of these events in the prophecies of Daniel, Jesus, Peter, Paul, and John.

Jesus will come to punish the Antichrist and the rest of the world

The nations of this world will be united under one group and one man during the Tribulation. They will make war with the Lamb because their leader, Satan, wishes to overthrow Jesus and Heaven. He uses a man who we call the Antichrist to unite the nations against the Lord.

Revelation 17:12-14 (KJV)

¹² And the ten horns which thou sawest are ten kings, which have received no kingdom as yet; but receive power as kings one hour with <u>the beast.</u>
¹³ These have one mind, and shall give their power and strength unto the beast.
¹⁴ <u>These shall make war with the Lamb, and the Lamb shall overcome them:</u> for he is Lord of lords, and King of kings: and they that are with him *are* called, and chosen, and faithful.

Daniel 2:44 (KJV)

⁴⁴ And in the days of these kings shall the God of heaven set up a kingdom, <u>which shall never be destroyed:</u> and the kingdom shall not be left to other people, *but* it shall break in pieces and consume all these kingdoms, and it shall stand for ever.

Revelation 19:19-21 (KJV)

¹⁹ And I saw <u>the beast,</u> and the kings of the earth, and their armies, gathered together to make war against him that sat on the horse, and against his army.
²⁰ And <u>the beast was taken, and with him the false prophet</u> that wrought miracles before him, with which he deceived them that had received the mark of the beast, and them that worshipped his image. <u>These both were cast alive into a lake of fire burning with brimstone.</u>
²¹ And the remnant were slain with the sword of him that sat upon the horse, which *sword* proceeded out of his mouth: and all the fowls were filled with their flesh.

So we see that God has it all planned. The kingdoms of this world belong to Jesus and His saints, and we will all rule with Him for a thousand years after His second coming. This is commonly called the millennial reign of Christ.

Revelation 20:2-4 (KJV)

2 And he laid hold on the dragon, that old serpent, which is the Devil, and Satan, and bound him a thousand years,
3 And cast him into the bottomless pit, and shut him up, and set a seal upon him, that he should deceive the nations no more, till the thousand years should be fulfilled: and after that he must be loosed a little season.

4 And I saw thrones, and they sat upon them, and judgment was given unto them: and I saw the souls of them that were beheaded for the witness of Jesus, and for the word of God, and which had not worshipped the beast, neither his image, neither had received his mark upon their foreheads, or in their hands; and they lived and reigned with Christ a thousand years.

Micah 4:1-3 (KJV)
1 But in the last days it shall come to pass, *that* the mountain of the house of the LORD shall be established in the top of the mountains, and it shall be exalted above the hills; and people shall flow unto it.
2 And many nations shall come, and say, Come, and let us go up to the mountain of the LORD, and to <u>the house of the God of Jacob</u>; and he will teach us of his ways, and we will walk in his paths: for <u>the law shall go forth of Zion, and the word of the LORD from Jerusalem.</u>
3 And he shall judge among many people, and rebuke strong nations afar off; and they shall beat their swords into plowshares, and their spears into pruninghooks: nation shall not lift up a sword against nation, neither shall they learn war any more.

Israel and the Church are on two different timelines. At the end of Daniel's gap of time, Christ will come back for His bride, and the church age will be fulfilled. After the last week for Israel is accomplished, Israel's transgressions will be finished, and she will be restored by Christ on earth. The Church and the remnant of Israel will be one under Christ, reigning together on the earth.

Ephesians 1:9-10 (KJV)
9 Having made known unto us the mystery of his will, according to his good pleasure which he hath purposed in himself:
10 That in the dispensation of the fulness of times he might gather together in one all things in Christ, both which are in heaven, and which are on earth; *even* in him:

Chapter 2
Primary Names that Describe Him:

By now, who has not heard of the Antichrist? He will come in the last days during the time of the Tribulation and will oppose Christ Jesus, the Messiah. John and others stated that the believers, even in his day, had heard of him (1 John 2:18, Matt. 24:24, 2 Thess. 2:3, 4). This was of course, from Daniel and other prophetic books that mention a man who would resist the future Son of God, who is coming to rule the earth.

In this volume, we will work our way through the many biblical passages that describe in detail this man, who is the anti-Messiah, to unveil or make clear who he really is.

Is there a man alive today to fulfill all of these verses? Probably. Can we really have more than a clue about who he might be and where he is from? Yes. I must be honest, my goal is to uncover the truth that has been hidden for thousands of years about this person in Scripture. We want to get a clear picture of his ways, his purpose, and his personality. I really don't care what his name is today. Maybe this study will help us rule out who he isn't in the world. Do we really need to know his name in the world? Not really, for the Church should be gone before this name is revealed.

My goal also is not to fill in all of the blank spaces with words. It is your command by the Lord to study the Word of God for yourself, to be approved of God. Start with this small study and get an understanding of what God wants to teach you about this subject.

Why such a study about this infamous character? Because the Bible has so much to say about him. Should we just throw the verses and concepts to the side? Many might think this study places undue emphasis on Satan and his work. In no way do we want this, for this is a study that comes from the Word of God. There are so many passages that expose who this person is and what he does. It is a marvelous study about the final battle at the end of this age!

Satan is called the accuser and the father of lies. John 10:10 says he is a thief, a killer, and a destroyer. The Antichrist is also known by many names. As we discover his names we gain insight into who he is. Let's look at a few.

"Another" shall come-

John 5:43 (KJV)
[43] I am come in my Father's name, and ye receive me not: if another (Vines gr. *allos*- "another of the same sort") **shall come in his own name, <u>him ye will receive</u>.**

Vines Expository Dictionary:

"Original Word: ἄλλος, *allos*

Usage Notes: have a difference in meaning, which despite a tendency to be lost, is to be observed in numerous passages. *Allos* expresses a numerical difference and denotes "another of the same sort;" *heteros* expresses a qualitative difference and denotes "another of a different sort." Christ promised to send "another Comforter" (*allos*, "another like Himself," not *heteros*), John 14:16. Paul says "I see a different (AV, "another") law," *heteros*, a law different from that of the spirit of life (not *allos*, "a law of the same sort"), Rom. 7:23.

After Joseph's death "another king arose," *heteros*, one of quite a different character, Acts 7:18. Paul speaks of "a different gospel (*heteros*), which is not another" (*allos*, another like the one he preached), Gal. 1:6, 7."[1]

Jesus predicted this and was possibly speaking of the Antichrist, or at the very least another whom they would call a "messiah." The Antichrist is one of those who will come in his own name and work to deceive the Jews of Israel. In John 5:15, John states what group was speaking to Christ and says that it was "the Jews." It isn't just the "Pharisees" or "religious leaders" here, but the Jewish people *as a whole*, that is rejecting Jesus, and will one day accept *another*. This and other verses, have led many to teach that the Antichrist would be masquerading as the messiah of the Jews in the last days to deceive them and gain their trust. However, this verse may only predict that Israel would accept another as a false messiah and not necessarily be about the Antichrist.

"And just as eve's rejection of the word of God's truth laid her open to accept the serpent's lie, so Israel's rejection of the true Messiah, has prepared them, morally, to receive the false Messiah, for he will come in his own name, doing his own pleasure, and will "receive glory from men." Thus will he thoroughly appeal to the corrupt heart of the natural man."[2]

Some teach that the Jew's false messiah would be the Antichrist. I have a hard time with this concept, although I

---

[1] William E. Vine, *Vine's Expository Dictionary of Old Testament and New Testament Words*, (Nashville, TN: Thomas Nelson, 1940), WORD*search* CROSS e-book, Under: "Another".
[2] Arthur W. Pink, *The Antichrist*, (Swengel, PA: Bible Truth Depot, 1923), WORD*search* CROSS e-book, 24.

believed it as a young man. The Jews will pick a man who is a Hebrew with a perfect lineage to be the Messiah. He will work with the Antichrist during the beginning of the Tribulation. I do believe, out of sheer ego, the Antichrist will claim to be the Messiah eventually, and God, along with the titles of many other religions that claim their great one will return. He will say he is all of them. He will replace the recognized Jewish messiah.

In the Bible, there are many names that are used for the person who would, in the last days, oppose Christ. From these names, we get a better description of him and his character. There are perhaps as many as 38 names given to him, and we've already seen a few, including "the horn, the lawless one, the oppressor, wicked one, king of Babylon, Assyrian, and another that shall come." Let's look at a few more.

If this verse is about the Antichrist, we learn:

1. He will come in his own name or authority and not the Father's.

2. You (Israel) will receive him

The Antichrist

1 John 2:18 (KJV)
18 Little children, it is the last time: and as ye have heard that antichrist shall come, even now are there many antichrists; whereby we know that it is the last time.

It seems here that John was referring to the teaching of Daniel and possibly of Jesus that there would come a time when a future "antichrist" would come to oppose the messiah.

Matthew 24:23-24 (HCSB)
²³ **"If anyone tells you then, 'Look, here is the Messiah!' or, 'Over here!' do not believe it!**
²⁴ **False** (LB-lit. "christs") **messiahs and false prophets will arise and perform great signs and wonders to lead astray, if possible, even the elect.**

Jesus stated that toward the end of the Tribulation, false messiahs and prophets would emerge, Although Daniel never used this word in his text. This is the primary name we use for this person who works against Christ. Some Jewish traditions call him Gog. John stated that even during his time or up until his time, there were men who could be called antichrists.

> Vines: "*antichristos* (ἀντίχριστος, 500) can mean either "against Christ" or "instead of Christ," or perhaps, combining the two, "one who, assuming the guise of Christ, opposes Christ" (Westcott)." ³

Will the Antichrist be the Jewish Messiah?

It is popular to believe, that at first, the Antichrist will claim to be the Jewish Messiah. Keep in mind this word primarily means one who is "against the Messiah." Westcott suggests, as the Vine's Expository Dictionary states, that he might be "one who assumes the guise of Christ." While you may agree with this, based on my studies, I cannot agree with this right now. "Messiah" is a Jewish concept. The Jews will soon choose a man to be their physical Messiah. There are whispers of that even now. They would not choose a non-Jew to be their Messiah. I believe this Jewish Messiah will work with the Antichrist at first, as long as the Antichrist works *with*

---

³ Vine, W. E., Unger, M. F., & White, W., Jr. (1996). Vine's Complete Expository Dictionary of Old and New Testament Words (Vol. 2, p. 30). Nashville, TN: T. Nelson.

him. What we find in the Bible passages is that the Antichrist claims to be God and not the Jewish messiah.

It is possible that he will claim to fulfill many of the predicted future other religious "messiahs" all in one. Islam is looking for their Mahdi and their Muslim "Jesus," the prophet, to appear and to come and destroy the infidels. Catholicism has stated that Muslims believe in the same God as Christians and are also saved.

> **"CCC 841**, quoting the Dogmatic Constitution on the Church, *Lumen Gentium* 16, from Vatican II, declared:
>
> The plan of salvation also includes those who acknowledge the Creator, in the first place amongst whom are the Muslims; these profess to hold the faith of Abraham, and together with us they adore the one, merciful God, mankind's judge on the last day."

This article however goes on to say that Catholicism does not agree with the unethical type beliefs and behaviors of Muslims.

It is possible that the Antichrist during the first half of the Tribulation period claims to be the Mahdi, or the culmination of many others also. The Hindus await the Kalki tenth Avatar of Krishna,[4] the Muslims await the Mahdi, the Buddhists await the Maitreya Buddha, and the Zoroastrians await the Shah Bahram. Even many of the North and South American indigenous religions await a redeemer of the earth. After Christ Jesus raptures the true believers, the Antichrist will rally the world religions as one as a sign of unity, even with a false Christianity that will still exist on earth. He will do this through the work of the false prophet. It may be that the Jews never accept him as their messiah, and this is

---

[4] See article https://bahaiteachings.org/awaiting-hindu-messiah/

perhaps one of the reasons why he will choose to slaughter them after 3 ½ years (Rev. 12).

John coined the word "antichrist" to describe him, the future man of sin, and used it five times to mainly denote other corrupt powers and people that worked against the church and the true doctrine of Christ, some even in the church itself.

The Greek word "*Antichristos*" means "opposite of," or "opponent of Christ." According to Eisenmenger[5] the Jews had differing opinions of the one who would come to oppose their messiah based off of Daniel 11:36; 7:25; 8:25, and partly Ezekiel 38-39. John refers to this teaching and calls him the "Antichrist" for the first time. This is the first reference to this name. John states that because many antichrists were already in the world, it signified that they were already in the "last days." The Jews taught that according to the book of Daniel, one would come and oppose Christ himself and lose. Most of us today use this name primarily for this infamous character.

1 John 2:18-22 (KJV)
[18] Little children, it is the last time: and as ye have heard that antichrist (LB- Gr. *singular HCSB uses "Antichrist is coming"*) **shall come, even now are there many antichrists** (LB- Gr. *plural*)**; whereby we know that it is the last time.**
[19] They went out from us, but they were not of us; for if they had been of us, they would *no doubt* have continued with us: but *they went out,* that they might be made manifest that they were not all of us.
[20] But ye have an unction from the Holy One, and ye know all things.
[21] I have not written unto you because ye know not the truth, but because ye know it, and that no lie is of the truth.
[22] Who is a liar but he that denieth that Jesus is the Christ? He is antichrist, that denieth the Father and the Son.

---

[5] Eisenmenger, Entdecktes Judenthum, ii 704ff; See also Gesenius in Ersch and Gruber's Encycl. iv. 292ff, under the word Antichrist.

1 John 4:3 (KJV)
³ And every spirit that confesseth not <u>that Jesus Christ is come in the flesh</u> is not of God: and <u>this is that *spirit* of antichrist,</u> whereof ye have heard that it should come; and even now already is it in the world.

2 John 1:7 (HCSB)
⁷ Many deceivers have gone out into the world; they do not confess the coming of Jesus Christ in the flesh. This is <u>the deceiver</u> and <u>the antichrist.</u>

What we learn about the antichrist in these verses:

1. Through Scripture and Jewish teaching the church has heard about a man called Antichrist.

2. Because (the spirit of the) antichrist exists now, we are in the last days.

3. He denies that Jesus is the Messiah.

4. He denies the Father and the Son.

5. He denies Jesus came in the flesh.

6. Even in John's day, antichrists were in the world.

7. They came out from among us (the apostles, the believers, the Jews?).

"We are now living in the last times, which are characterized by the coming of the antichrist. Here John uses this word in the plural, as well as in the singular, and it is clear that he has heretics primarily in view. Antichrists are people who once belonged to the church in formal terms but who never shared its spirit and who eventually went off to proclaim their own beliefs. The most common of these was that Jesus was not the Messiah come from God to save us from our sins. The Fathers recognized that this denial of Christian orthodoxy could come in many forms, ranging from Judaism to the heresies of the fourth and fifth centuries, but the precise details were secondary. It was only to be expected that heretics would have confused and contradictory beliefs. All that mattered is that whatever they were, they were a departure from the faith once delivered by the apostles."[6]

8. They are deceivers, therefore he is a deceiver

9. They are liars, therefore he is the liar

The Liar/Denier- John's definition of the Antichrist-

1 John 2:21-22 (HCSB)
21 I have not written to you because you don't know the truth, but because you do know it, and because no lie comes from the truth.
22 Who is <u>the liar</u>, if not the one who denies that Jesus is the Messiah? This one is the antichrist: the one who denies the Father and the Son.

1. He is called "the liar."

2. Antichrist is one who denies Jesus is the Messiah.

---

[6] Stott, pp. 104-5; Alfred Plummer, *The Epistles of S. John*, p. 107.— Tom Constable's Notes on the Bible

3. Antichrist is one who denies the Father and that Jesus is the Son of God.

All false religions or cults of Christianity follow this principle: deny the Father and the Son.

"Islam- Quran Surah 19:88-89; 43:59

They say: "(Allah) Most Gracious has begotten a son!" 89 "Indeed ye have put forth a thing most monstrous!"

43:59 "Jesus was no more than a mortal whom Allah favored and made an example to the Israelites. They are unbelievers who say God is Messiah, Mary's son." Surat al Nisa 4:157-158 "And because of their saying: we slew the messiah Jesus son of Mary. Allahs messenger-they slew him not nor crucified"

Jehovah's Witnesses- Charles Taze Russell- "There is Scriptural evidence for concluding that Michael was the name of Jesus Christ before he left heaven and after his return." (WT 5/15/1969, p. 307) ..."Michael the great prince is none other than Jesus Christ himself." (WT 12/15/1984 p29) Michael the archangel is no other than the only begotten son of God, now Jesus Christ.."(New Heavens and New Earth pg.30-31).

The Moonies- "He can by no means be God Himself."— *Divine Principle*, pp. 210-211

Christian Science Christian Science (Mary Baker Eddy): "Jesus Christ is not God, as Jesus Himself declared, but is the Son of God." (Science and Health Key to the Scriptures p.361). Jesus is the name of the man who, more than all other men, has presented Christ, the true idea of God. . . . Jesus is the human man, and Christ is the divine idea; hence the duality of Jesus the Christ. (Mary Baker Eddy, Science and Health and Key to the Scriptures The

First Church of Christ Scientist 1934, p. 361.) " he was the first human to understand the Divine Mind." "Jesus means "the highest human corporeal concept of the divine idea. . ." (ibid. p. 589).

Unitarian Universalism: Unitarian Universalist minister Waldemar Argow states: "They [Unitarian/Universalists] do not regard him as a supernatural creature, the literal son of God who was miraculously sent to earth as part of an involved plan for the salvation of human souls.', (Waldemar Argow, Unitarian Universalism-Some Questions Answered (pamphlet) (Boston, MA. Unitarian Universalism Assoc., nd.), p. 6.)

Mormonism- Church of Jesus Christ of Latter day saints- "...That Lucifer, the son of the morning, is our elder brother and the brother of Jesus Christ." (Apostle B. McConkie *Mormon doctrine* p.163-164) "...Jesus, our elder brother, was begotten in the flesh by the same character that was in the garden of Eden, and who is our Father in Heaven," (Journal of Discourses, Vol. 1, pp. 50-51). Jesus got married at Cana and had many wives Martha, Mary and others he also had many children," (J & D vol.1 345-346 vol.2 79-82 vol.4:259-260 the seer p.172)

For a much larger list see:
http://www.letusreason.org/Cult13.htm

"Many of these cults use the name of Jesus (or Jesus Christ) in their own church names and in their teachings. They may even appear to believe in the Jesus of the Bible, but upon closer examination, you will see that their core beliefs deny Christ in one way or another, such as:

• Denying that Jesus is God,
• Denying that Jesus has existed eternally (i.e., Jesus was a created being, and that Jesus had a beginning),

- Claiming that Jesus is just "an angel" (e.g., Michael) or the "brother of Satan,"
- Claiming that God is "flesh and bones" (instead of spirit),
- Claiming that there are other ways to heaven,
- Claiming man can become "a god" (apparently, one of many gods),
- Or other heresies"[7]

> **Galatians 1:8 (KJV)**
> **8 But though we, or an angel from heaven, preach any other gospel unto you than that which we have preached unto you, let him be accursed.**

---

[7] https://eachday.org/part-vi-beware-the-wolves/6-47-cults-which-deny-christ/

Chapter 3
More Biblical names that are used

The "Seed" or "head" of the serpent

Genesis 3:14-15 (KJV)
[14] **And the LORD God said unto the serpent, Because thou hast done this, thou** *art* **cursed above all cattle, and above every beast of the field; upon thy belly shalt thou go, and dust shalt thou eat all the days of thy life:**
[15] **And I will put enmity between thee and the woman** (LB. Israel, the Church), **and between <u>thy seed and her seed</u>; it shall bruise** (Heb.-Gape, break open, crush**) <u>thy head</u>, and thou shalt bruise his heel** (Heb.- heal, footsteps, rear; fig., that which comes last-the remnant).

"Thy seed" or the "seed of the serpent," has in the past thought to be a title of the Antichrist because the "seed" of the women in this passage is obviously Christ. So, the seed of the serpent/Devil here must be the Antichrist. Jesus was the only true seed of the women and not of Adam or the seed of Adam, for no human male contributed to His birth. So some believed that the Antichrist man would naturally be the "seed" or offspring of Satan. This means that Satan himself would mate with a physical woman and birth an Antichrist son. I have a hard time with this concept and would say that "the seed" here refers to the "ungodly" in general. Maybe this reference is specific to the future man, the Antichrist, because

29

of the specific reference to the word "head" here and not to the word "seed." The seed of the woman, who is Christ, would crush the "head" of the serpent, the Antichrist. Perhaps the "head" of the snake is the Antichrist.

"Seed" here obviously has dual meanings because Satan cannot reproduce a person per se, but he does have a "seed" or offspring. Many have believed that the Antichrist has somehow come from Satan's loins himself. Maybe I'm wrong, but I can't see this happening. 1 John 3:10 refers to the "children of the devil," who are those who do not love righteousness or their brothers. Jesus said to some religious Jews in the treasury of the Temple, "You are of your *father* the Devil" in John 8:44. But these were not born of Satan through the flesh, but he *became* their father when the world fell into sin. Genesis 3:15 does predict that the seed of the woman (Christ) would break open, or gape, the "head" of the serpent. Perhaps this is another metaphor for the Antichrist in the future: "the head of the serpent." Also, the Antichrist is called the "son of perdition" in 2 Thess. 2:3. The late Arthur Pink, who wrote an amazing book on the Antichrist, was one who taught that Satan would father the Antichrist and that he would be a superhuman.

> "Is there a Holy Trinity, then there is also an Evil Trinity (Revelation 20:10). In this Trinity of Evil Satan himself is supreme, just as in the Blessed Trinity the Father is (governmentally) supreme: note that Satan is several times referred to as a *father* (John 8:44, etc.). Unto his son, the Antichrist, Satan gives his authority and power to represent and act for him (Revelation 13:4) just as God the Son received "all power in heaven and earth" from His Father, and uses it for His glory. The Dragon (Satan) and the Beast (Antichrist) are

accompanied by a third, the False Prophet, and just as the third person in the Holy Trinity, the Spirit, bears witness to the person and work of Christ and glorifies Him, so shall the third person in the Evil Trinity bear witness to the person and work of the Antichrist and glorify him (see Revelation 13:11-14).

Now the Antichrist will be a man, and yet more than man, just as Christ was Man and yet more than man. The Antichrist will be the 'Superman' of whom the world, even now, is talking, and for whom it is looking. The Wicked One who is to be revealed shortly, will be a supernatural character, he will be the Son of Satan. His twofold nature is plainly declared in 2 Thessalonians 2:3—"That man of Sin, the Son of Perdition."[8]

"That day shall not come, except there come a falling away (the Apostasy) first, and that Man of Sin be revealed, *the Son of Perdition*" (2 Thessalonians 2:3). Nothing could be plainer than this. Here the Antichrist is expressly declared to be superhuman—"the Son of Perdition." Just as the Christ if the Son of God, so Antichrist will be the son of Satan. Just as the Christ dwelt all the fullness of the Godhead bodily, and just as Christ could say "He that hath seen Me, hath seen the Father," so the Antichrist will be the full and final embodiment of the Devil. He will not only be the incarnation of the Devil, but the consummation of his wickedness and power."[9]

---

[8] Arthur W. Pink, *The Antichrist*, (Swengel, PA: Bible Truth Depot, 1923), WORD*search* CROSS e-book, 47.
[9] ibid, 51.

The spoiler, and extortioner

Isaiah 16:4 (KJV)
⁴ **Let mine outcasts dwell with thee, Moab; be thou a covert to them from the face of <u>the spoiler</u>** (Heb. verb)**: <u>for the extortioner</u> is at an end, the spoiler** (Heb. noun) **ceaseth, the oppressors are consumed out of the land.**

This Hebrew word *shadad (verb), shode (noun)* or "spoiler" means "powerful ravager," with the idea of "violently robbing" from someone. It was used of Babylon in Jer. 6:26 of the destruction of Jerusalem. "The ferocity of *šādad* is indicated by its coupling with <u>the activities of a wolf (Jer. 5:6) who pursues, attacks, and mauls its victim.</u>" [10]

"Extortioner" here means "squeezer," or "oppressor," i.e., one who causes trouble and hardship for another (Isa 16:4).[11] With these two words, we get the idea of a gangster who demands protection money and will tear to pieces the countries who do not fall in line.

1. He is a gangster like ravager who violently takes from others.

2. He is one who squeezes and oppresses people.

The terrible one, and scorner

Isaiah 25:5 (KJV)
⁵ **Thou shalt bring down the noise of strangers, as the heat in a dry place;** *even* **the heat with the shadow of a cloud: <u>the branch of the terrible ones</u> shall be brought low.**

---

[10] Hamilton, V. P. (1999). 2331 שָׁדַד. R. L. Harris, G. L. Archer Jr., & B. K. Waltke (Eds.), *Theological Wordbook of the Old Testament* (electronic ed., p. 906). Chicago: Moody Press.
[11] Swanson, J. (1997). Dictionary of Biblical Languages with Semantic Domains : Hebrew (Old Testament) (electronic ed.). Oak Harbor: Logos Research Systems, Inc.

Isaiah 29:20 (KJV)
[20] For <u>the terrible one</u> is brought to nought, and <u>the scorner</u> is consumed, and all that watch for iniquity are cut off:

Isaiah 29 relates specifically to Jerusalem in the future when they will be delivered from the Antichrist and calls him the terrible one and scorner. Read verses 17-19 for proof that this verse is about the end of the Tribulation and beginning of the Millennium.

1. He is "the terrible one," literally in the Hebrew it means "tyrannical mighty oppressor."

   "The verb *'āraṣ* denotes fear or terror; transitively, "to cause terror," or intransitively, "to be terrified." The Hebrew root may be compared with a Syriac root, "to come upon suddenly, violently," and the Arabic *'araṣa* "to quiver, flicker."[12]

2. He is a scoffer-(Hb. "Lîs"- pronounced "loots"). The Hebrew word "scorner" means:

   "(1) *to speak barbarously*, i.e. in a foreign tongue, from those who speak a foreign language appearing, to those who are ignorant of it, <u>as if they babbled and stammered senselessly</u>; see Hiphil.
   (2) *to deride, to mock* any one, prob. by imitating his voice in sport (compare Isa. 28:10, 11,… [13]

   "*a mocker, scoffer*, i.e. a frivolous and impudent person, <u>who despises scoffingly the most sacred</u>

---

[12] Allen, R. B. (1999). 1702 עָרַץ. R. L. Harris, G. L. Archer Jr., & B. K. Waltke (Eds.), *Theological Wordbook of the Old Testament* (electronic ed., p. 699). Chicago: Moody Press.
[13] Gesenius, W., & Tregelles, S. P. (2003). Gesenius' Hebrew and Chaldee lexicon to the Old Testament Scriptures (p. 435). Bellingham, WA: Logos Bible Software.

precepts of religion, piety, and morals (compare Lîs), Ps. 1:1; Pro. 9:7, 8; 13:1; 14:6; 15:12; 19:25; 22:10; 24:9; Isa. 29:20." [14]

2 Thessalonians 2- The Apostle Paul describes him as "the Man of sin," "son of destruction/perdition," and "that wicked"-

Paul said the Antichrist was a future man also, but he stated that 3 ½ years before Jesus comes back to the earth to reign, his true identity would be revealed. He will break the covenant with Israel and defile the Jewish temple. Paul also here calls him the "man of sin" and the "son of destruction."

2 Thessalonians 2:3-4 (KJV)
[3] Let no man deceive you by any means: for *that day shall not come*, except there come a <u>falling away</u> (LB- Lit. a "departure") first, and that <u>man of sin</u> be revealed, <u>the son of perdition</u>;
[4] Who opposeth and exalteth himself above all that is called God, or that is worshipped; so that he as God <u>sitteth in the temple of God</u>, shewing himself that he is God.

The second coming will not happen until:

1. The departure (I believe this means the "Rapture") happens first (departure from what? is debated).

2. The man of sin be uncovered as the son of destruction (doom, perdition).

3. He opposes and elevates himself above anything godly.

[14] Gesenius, W., & Tregelles, S. P. (2003). Gesenius' Hebrew and Chaldee lexicon to the Old Testament Scriptures (p. 435). Bellingham, WA: Logos Bible Software.

4. He sits himself *in the temple* as if to say he were god, in the middle of the 7 years (Daniel 9:27; Matt. 24:15, Rev. 13:5). Some say that he will do this at the dedication of the new temple in Jerusalem.

Finis Dake:

"Multitudes will soon be saved afterward through an awakening (Acts 2:16-21; Rev. 6:9-11; 7:1-17; 12:17). The rest will become so hardened as to seek to destroy these being saved in those days (Rev. 9:20-21; 16:2,9-11). The great whore of Rev. 17 will destroy multitudes of Christians during the first 3 1/2 years of Daniel's 70th week, while the Antichrist is coming to power over the 10 kingdoms inside the old Roman Empire (Rev. 6:9-11; 17:6). When Antichrist comes to full power over the 10 kingdoms in the middle of Daniel's 70th week, he, together with the 10 kings, will destroy the great whore, establish the worship of the beast, and kill multitudes who will not worship him and his image or take his brands (Rev. 7:9-17; 13:1-18; 14:9-13; 15:2-4; 16:6-11; Rev. 2-4; 17:16-17)." [15]

Judas was also called "the son of perdition" (see John 6:70; 17:12; and 2 Thess. 2:3) and may very well be a *type* of the Antichrist. As he broke covenant with Christ, so will the Antichrist break covenant with Israel (Isaiah 28:18; Daniel 9:27).

---

[15] Finis Jennings Dake, Dake's Annotated Reference Bible: Containing the Old and New Testaments of the Authorized or King James Version Text, (Lawrenceville, GA: Dake Bible Sales, Inc., 1997), WORDsearch CROSS e-book, Under: "Chapter 2."

The Wicked one

"The wicked" or "the wicked one" are two of the most popular Biblical names for the Antichrist. Read through these verses and see if you agree.

2 Thessalonians 2:7-10 (KJV)
[7] For the mystery of iniquity doth already work: only <u>he </u> (Greek personal pronoun- "He" meaning "the Holy Spirit") **<u>who now letteth</u> *will let*, until <u>he</u>** (Greek neuter pronoun "it"- meaning "the church") **<u>be taken out</u> of the way.**
[8] And <u>then shall that Wicked be revealed</u>, whom the Lord shall consume with the spirit of his mouth, and shall destroy with the brightness of his coming:
[9] *Even him*, whose coming is after <u>the working of Satan</u> with <u>all power and signs and lying wonders</u>,
[10] And with <u>all deceivableness of unrighteousness</u> in them that perish; because they received not the love of the truth, that they might be saved.

1. The mysterious workings of the Antichrist were already working in Paul's day.

2. The Holy Spirit will take the church out of the way first, and then the Antichrist will be uncovered.

3. He works just like Satan with all his energy, with powerful lies and signs and wonders.

4. He is called "the wicked," possibly a reference to Isaiah 11:4, 14:5; Psalm 9:17, 10:2, 4; Jeremiah 30:14, 23.

    Isaiah 11:4 (KJV)
    [4] But with righteousness shall he judge the poor, and reprove with equity for the meek of the earth: and he shall smite the earth with the rod of his mouth, and with <u>the breath of his lips shall he slay the wicked</u> (LB. Gk. singular).

5. He comes with supernatural manifestations.

6. With extreme deception toward the lost- They will believe a lie-He is extremely charismatic.

7. Jesus will kill him with the breath of His mouth.

8. Jesus will destroy all that he has done and is "by His appearing at His coming" -AMP.

> **1 John 2:13-14 (KJV)**
> [13] I write unto you, fathers, because ye have known him *that is* from the beginning. I write unto you, young men, <u>because ye have overcome the wicked one</u>. I write unto you, little children, because ye have known the Father. [14] I have written unto you, fathers, because ye have known him *that is* from the beginning. I have written unto you, young men, because ye are strong, and the word of God abideth in you, and <u>ye have overcome the wicked one</u>.
>
> **1 John 2:18 (KJV)**
> [18] Little children, it is the last time: and as ye have heard that (LB-the) antichrist shall come...

The spirit of the antichrist is who we overcome in the world. This includes those people who operate in that demonic realm.

> **1 John 4:3-4 (KJV)**
> [3] ... and this is that *spirit* of antichrist, whereof ye have heard that it should come; and even now already is it in the world. [4] Ye are of God, little children, and have overcome them: because greater is he that is in you, than <u>he that is in the world</u>.

Belial- Wicked one

Nahum 1:15 (HCSB)
[15] **Look to the mountains— the feet of one bringing good news and proclaiming peace!** (LB- Christ in the millennium Isa. 52:7) **Celebrate your festivals, Judah; fulfill your vows. For the wicked one will never again march through you; he will be entirely wiped out.**

This was at first speaking of Sennacherib, who invaded Judah in the days of Hezekiah (2 Ki. 18:13 – 2 Ki. 19:37; Isa. 36:1 -- Isa. 37:38). He was the king of Assyria, who was also a *type* of the antichrist. The actual Hebrew word is "Belial" here, which is translated in the KJV as the "Wicked One."

Baker defines Belial as "worthless" or "ungodly" as in 2 Cor. 6:15:

> "1100. בְּלִיַּעַל beliyya'al: A masculine noun of unknown origin meaning worthlessness. Often a strong moral component in the context suggests the state of being good for nothing and therefore expresses the concept of wickedness (Job 34:18; Prov. 6:12; Nah. 1:11). It is always used in reference to persons with only two exceptions, once for a disease and once for a nonspecific thing (Ps. 41:8[9]; 101:3). The term is applied to the hard-hearted (Deut. 15:9; 1 Sam. 30:22); perjurers (1 Kgs. 21:13; Prov. 19:28); and those promoting rebellion against a king's authority (2 Sam. 20:1; 2 Chr. 13:7) or God's authority (Deut. 13:13[14]). This word was not treated as a proper name by the Septuagint translators of the Old Testament, but it does appear in its Greek form

as a name for the devil in the Dead Sea scrolls and in the New Testament (cf. 2 Cor. 6:15)." 16

The foolish and idol-worthless shepherd

In Zech. 11:15-17, He is called a foolish and worthless shepherd who will eat the fat of the lambs. In context, this could also represent a false Messiah who comes after Christ-John 5:43. If this is the Antichrist: 1. His arm will one day be wounded and dried up 2. His right eye will be blinded.

A few more names to consider from Arthur W. Pink's book, *The Antichrist:*

The Bloody and Deceitful Man- Psalm 5:6

"Thou shalt destroy them that speak leasing: the Lord will abhor the *Bloody and Deceitful Man*" (Psalm 5:6). The Psalm from which this verse is quoted contains a prayer of the godly Jewish remnant, offered during the Tribulation period."[17]

The Man of the Earth- Psalm 10:18

"To judge the fatherless and the oppressed, that the Man of the Earth may no more oppress" (Psalm 10:18)."[18]

---

[16] Baker, W., & Carpenter, E. E. (2003). In The complete word study dictionary: Old Testament (pp. 140–141). AMG Publishers.
[17] Arthur W. Pink, *The Antichrist*, (Swengel, PA: Bible Truth Depot, 1923), WORD*search* CROSS e-book, P. 65.
[18] IBID P. 67.

The Mighty (immensely wealthy) Man- Psalm 52:1

"Why boasteth thou thyself in mischief, *O Mighty Man*" (Psalm 52:1). This is another Psalm which is devoted to a description of this fearful character. Here again we have mention of his boastfulness (v. 1), his deceitfulness (v. 2), his depravity (v. 3), his egotism (v. 4), his riches (v. 7). His doom is also announced (v. 5). This title, the Mighty Man, refers to his immense wealth and possessions, and the power which they confer upon their possessor. It also points a striking contrast: Christ was the Lowly Man…"[19]

The Liar- John 8:44, 2 Thess. 2:11

""Ye are of your father the Devil, and the lusts of your father ye will do. He was a murderer from the beginning, and abode not in the truth, because there is no truth in him. When he speaketh a lie, he speaketh of this own; for he is a liar, and the father of it" (John 8:44). Here is still another proof that the Antichrist will be superhuman, the offspring of Satan. In the Greek there is the definite article before the word "lie"—the lie, "the Lie." There is another passage in the New Testament where "the Lie" is mentioned, namely in 2 Thessalonians 2:11, where again the definite article is found in the Greek, and there the reference is unmistakable."[20]

2 Thessalonians 2:11 (NKJV)
[11] And for this reason God will send them strong delusion, that they should believe <u>the lie</u>,

---

[19] IBID P. 67.
[20] IBID P. 51.

Chapter 4
Comparisons and Differences of the Antichrist and Jesus

The picture above is the "Temptation of Christ" painted by Ary Scheffer in 1854.[21] It is no secret that the Antichrist will pose as some form of deity on earth. He is a deceiver and

[21] "Temptation on the Mount"; Ary Scheffer, After; 1858

a counterfeit. Just as the Godhead is three distinct personalities in one, Father, Son, and Holy Spirit- so also will Satan provide his religious estate with a trinity: Satan, the Antichrist, and the false prophet. In every way, it seems the Antichrist tries to imitate the true Christ, Jesus. Jesus came as the full expression of the Father, full of love, truth, and mercy. In this, we know the Antichrist cannot do. He is the opposite of this, as we shall see in every way.

Below are just a few of the many comparisons in Scripture between the two. Most of these can also be found in Arthur Pink's 1923 book called *The Antichrist.*

1. As Christ was prophesied of in the Old Testament, so also is the Antichrist- Genesis 3:15; Daniel 11:35-45.

2. Jesus was found as a "type" in many Old Testament characters like Abraham's sacrifice, Joseph, Moses, and David. The Antichrist is typified in many others like King Nebuchadnezzar, Antiochus IV, Nero, and others.

3. "Christ was revealed only at God's appointed time: such will also be the case with the Antichrist. Of the one we read, "But when the fullness of time was come, God sent forth His Son" (Galatians 4:4); of the other it is said, "And now we know what withholdeth that he might be *revealed in his time*" (2 Thessalonians 2:6)."[22]

4. Christ was a man, the most perfect man- "the man Christ Jesus." (1 Timothy 2:5). The Antichrist is also a man, "the man of sin." (2 Thessalonians 2:3).

---

[22] Arthur W. Pink, *The Antichrist*, (Swengel, PA: Bible Truth Depot, 1923), WORD*search* CROSS e-book, 86.

5. Christ will make a covenant with Israel (Hebrews 8:8); so will the Antichrist (Daniel 9:27).

6. Christ will be the true King of kings (Revelation 17:14); so will the Antichrist be over kings (Revelation 17:12, 13).

7. Christ wrought miracles: of Him it is said "approved of God among you by miracles and wonders and signs" (Acts 2:22); so also will the Antichrist, concerning whom it is written, "whose coming is after the working of Satan with all power and signs and lying wonders" (2 Thessalonians 2:9).

8. Christ's public ministry was limited to three years and a half; so also will the Antichrist's final ministry be (Revelation 13:5).

9. Christ will be the object of universal worship (Philippians 2:10); so also will the Antichrist (Revelation 13:4).

10. The followers of the Lamb will be sealed in their foreheads (Revelation 7:3; 14:1); so also will the followers of the Beast (Revelation 13:16, 17).

11. Christ has been followed by the Holy Spirit who causes men to worship Him; so the Antichrist will be followed by the Anti-spirit—the False Prophet—who will cause men to worship the Beast (Revelation 13:12).

These charts are great for quick references and comparisons.

In Their Respective Positions	
One is called the Christ (Matthew 16:16)	The other the Antichrist (1 John 4:3)
One is called the Man of Sorrows (Isaiah 53:3)	The other the Man of Sin (2 Thessalonians 2:3)
One is called the Son of God (John 1:34)	The other the Son of Perdition (2 Thessalonians 2:3)
One is called the Seed of woman (Genesis 3:15)	The other the seed of the Serpent (Genesis 3:15)
One is called the Lamb (Isaiah 53:7)	The other the Beast (Revelation 11:7)
One is called the Holy One (Mark 1:24)	The other the Wicked One (2 Thessalonians 2:8)
One is called the Truth (John 14:6)	The other the Lie (John 8:44)
One is called the Prince of Peace (Isaiah 9:6; Gen. 49:26)	The other the wicked, Prince that shall come (Daniel 9:27)
One is called the glorious Branch (Isaiah 4:2)	The other the abominable Branch (Isaiah 14:19; 24:5)
One is called the Good Shepherd (John 10:11)	The other is called the Idol Shepherd (Zechariah 11:17)
Christ came down from heaven (John 3:13)	Antichrist comes up out of the bottomless pit (Revelation 11:7)
One has for the number of His name (the gematria of "Jesus" in Greek) 888	The other has for the number of his name 666 (Revelation 13:18)

In Their Respective Purposes	
Christ came in Another's Name (John 5:43)	Antichrist will come in his own name (John 5:43)
Christ came to do the Father's will (John 6:38)	Antichrist will do his own will (Daniel 11:36).
Christ was energized by the Holy Spirit (Luke 4:14)	Antichrist will be energized by Satan (Revelation 13:4)
Christ submitted Himself to God (John 5:30)	Antichrist defies God (2 Thessalonians 2:4).
Christ humbled Himself (Philippians 2:8)	Antichrist exalts himself (Daniel 11:37)
Christ honored the God of His fathers (Luke 4:16)	Antichrist refuses to (Dan 11:37)
Christ cleansed the temple (John 2:14, 16)	Antichrist defiles the temple (Matthew 24:15)
Christ ministered to the needy (Isaiah 53:7)	Antichrist robs the poor (Psalm 10:8, 9)
Christ was rejected of men (Isaiah 53:7)	Antichrist will be accepted by men (Revelation 13:4)
Christ leads the flock (John 10:3)	Antichrist leaves the flock (Zechariah 11:17)
Christ was slain for the people (John 11:51)	Antichrist slays the people (Isaiah 14:20)
Christ glorified God on earth (John 17:4)	Antichrist blasphemes the name of God in heaven (Revelation 13:6)
Christ was received up into heaven (Luke 24:51)	Antichrist goes down into the Lake of Fire (Revelation 19:20)

Chapter 5

HOW IT ALL ENDS FOR THE ANTICHRIST-

The Judgment of the Antichrist and the False Prophet when Jesus Returns

Daniel 11:36 (KJV)
36 And the king shall do according to his will; and he shall exalt himself, and magnify himself above every god, and shall speak marvellous things against the God of gods, and shall prosper till the indignation be accomplished: for that that is determined shall be done.

Daniel 11:45 (KJV)
45 And he shall plant the tabernacles of his palace between the seas in the glorious holy mountain; yet he shall come to his end, and none shall help him.

1 John 2:18-22 (KJV)
18 Little children, it is the last time: and as ye have heard that antichrist shall come, even now are there many antichrists; whereby we know that it is the last time.

John goes on in the following verses in 1 John 2 to describe what an antichrist is and proclaims that many existed in his day. He states that an antichrist is one who opposes the Father and the Son and one who denies that Jesus is the Christ and God.

> "In the drama of human history all of John's readers including ourselves play our part in the last act. Throughout the New Testament the writers regarded the present age before the Lord's return as the last hour or the last days. This is the final period before the Lord Himself breaks into history again. Then the first stage of the new age will be judgment (the Tribulation) and the second stage blessing. In the second stage Jesus Christ will rule directly over human beings first in the Millennium and then in the new heavens and the new earth.
>
> The revelation concerning the appearance of the world ruler who will exalt himself against God had reached John's audience (Dan. 11:36-45; 2 Thess. 2:3-5; et al.). However even as John wrote many little antichrists, people who exalt themselves against God, had arisen. John saw this as evidence that the appearance of *the* Antichrist was not far away. Antichrists are those who oppose Jesus Christ and His teachings, not just people who profess to be the Messiah."[23]

Revelation 13:5-7 (KJV)
5 And there was given unto him a mouth speaking great

---

[23] Ancient Christian Commentary on Scripture. Gerald L. Bray, *New Testament XI: James, 1-2 Peter, 1-3 John, Jude,* (Downers Grove, IL: InterVarsity Academic, 2000), WORD*search* CROSS e-book, 185.

things and blasphemies; and power was given unto him to
continue forty and two months.
6 And he opened his mouth in blasphemy against God, to
blaspheme his name, and his tabernacle, and them that dwell
in heaven.
7 And it was given unto him to <u>make war</u> with the saints, and
to overcome them: and power was given him over all kindreds,
and tongues, and nations.

As we delve into the many scriptural names of the man,
the Antichrist, that reveal and define his varied and evil
character, we need to see his end and what is written of his
judgment. We do this because we must always know his end
before his beginning, lest we think he is any match for the
wonderful, mighty Son of the living God.

We learn here in Revelation that the Antichrist seems to
take power and be given a mouth to blaspheme more in the
last half of the seven years and attack the "saints" of the
Tribulation period. According to Rev. 12, after the middle
point of the seven years, he goes violently to slaughter the
Jews and the Tribulation saints of Jesus.

Notice that the Bible says that this "mouth" and "power"
were given to him by the dragon in vv.2-5. Also, we see even
his ability to "make war with the saints" was *given* to him.
These all are not from his abilities or powers, but they have
been given to him. We surmise that the Devil gives him his
power, and no doubt he thinks he does. However, even in this
passage, it infers that he is only allowed to be what he is,
because God has allowed it to be so. Much like God used the
king of Assyria to break Israel for a season so that His people
would repent (Isaiah 10:5-19), this pattern repeats itself.

Revelation 12:17 (HCSB)
¹⁷ So the dragon was furious with the woman (LB-Israel) and
left <u>to wage war</u> against the rest of her offspring—those who
keep God's commands and have <u>the testimony about Jesus</u>.

The woman is Israel, and here, the "rest" of her offspring are the remnant Jews and the saints who are saved during the Tribulation. While he rules through the ten kings mentioned in Daniel and Revelation, and conquers much of the world in the first three and a half years, it seems that he is eventually possessed by a great ranking demon controlled by Satan himself. Some say he is possessed by Satan himself. This happens perhaps at the midpoint of the Tribulation, and Satan begins to use him in a different way. The Antichrist demands to be worshipped at this point. So we see this man in various roles and characters, fully evil from the beginning of his start, but progressively worse at his end.

2 Thessalonians 2:4 (HCSB)
⁴ He opposes and exalts himself above every so-called god or object of worship, so that he sits in God's sanctuary, publicizing that <u>he himself is God</u>.

Daniel 9:27 (KJV)
²⁷ And he shall confirm the covenant with many for one week: and <u>in the midst of the week</u> he shall cause the sacrifice and the oblation to cease, and for the overspreading of abominations he shall make *it* desolate, even until the consummation, and that determined shall be poured upon the desolate.

Paul describes the Antichrist coming into the newly built Jewish temple and seating himself on the mercy seat in the Holy of Holies. This event is described by Jesus Himself as "the abomination of desolation," which happens in the middle point of the Tribulation (Matthew 24:15). One writer suggests he does this at the dedication of the temple.

What we learn from these verses:

1.   He exalts himself above anything that is worshipped.

2.   He sits in the sanctuary in Jerusalem, where no man is allowed, defying Jewish law.

3.   He publicizes that he now is God at this time.

4.   This happens in the middle of the Tribulation period.

His judgment foretold

Habakkuk 3:12-18 (HCSB)
[12] You march across the earth with indignation; You trample down the nations in wrath.
[13] You come out to save Your people, to save Your anointed. You crush (KJV- "wound") the leader of the house of the wicked and strip ⌊him⌋ from foot (Lit. Foundation) to neck. *Selah*
[14] You pierce his head with his own spears; his warriors storm out to scatter us, gloating as if ready to secretly devour the weak.
[15] You tread the sea with Your horses, stirring up the great waters.
[16] I heard, and I trembled within; my lips quivered at the sound. Rottenness entered my bones; I trembled where I stood. Now I must quietly wait for the day of distress to come against the people invading us.
[17] Though the fig tree does not bud and there is no fruit on the vines, though the olive crop fails and the fields produce no food, though there are no sheep in the pen and no cattle in the stalls,
[18] yet I will triumph in Yahweh; I will rejoice in the God of my salvation!

The leader of the house of the wicked

Here is a name for the Antichrist we often miss "the leader of the house of the wicked." He becomes fully in charge of all that is wicked and evil in this world. He is to lead the world into a worse than sinful state: fully wicked.

What we learn from these verses:

1. Christ will crush or wound the leader of the house of the wicked.
2. He will be stripped from "foot to neck."
3. Christ will "pierce his head with his own spears." This could refer to his leaders or battlements, or that the Antichrist will be judged by his own words.

The Antichrist and the false prophet will be "taken prisoner" at the battle of Armageddon, according to Rev. 19:20. There is a short time after when Christ begins to judge the nations of people.

> **Matthew 25:31-32 (KJV)**
> **31 When the Son of man shall come in his glory, and all the holy angels with him, then shall he sit upon the throne of his glory:**
> **32 And <u>before him shall be gathered all nations</u>** (Greek-*ethnos*, or non-Jewish peoples)**: and he shall separate them one from another, as a shepherd divideth *his* sheep from the goats:**

There, the Antichrist will proudly oppose Christ as if he were something to behold. This is not the final judgment for those who are in Hell; for that will come some time later at the Great White Throne Judgment.

Thrown alive into the Lake of Fire

Revelation 19:20 (HCSB)
²⁰ But <u>the beast was taken prisoner, and along with him the false prophet</u>, who had performed the signs in his presence. He deceived those who accepted the mark of the beast and those who worshiped his image with these signs. <u>Both of them were thrown alive into the lake of fire that burns with sulfur.</u>

According to Daniel 7:11 (see below), it appears he will present his case before Christ himself at the beginning of the Sheep and Goats Judgment of the Nations, and *his body* will be thrown into the burning Fire. In Heaven, God sits on His throne, and on earth, Christ comes to judge. The beast is killed, and his body is thrown into the heaps of fire like the rest.

We will see later that his body will be thrown out and "covered by those slain by the sword." These are probably those killed *after* Armageddon, and not those killed *at* Armageddon; those who die at Armageddon will die a different death. Many will die by the sword, even after Armageddon. Some earthly rulers will be allowed to live for a period of time. This is evidence that not all the kings or rulers of the earth will follow completely after the Antichrist.

The "horn," the "beast" is judged

Daniel 7:9-12 (HCSB)
⁹ "As I kept watching, <u>thrones were set in place</u>, and <u>the Ancient of Days took His seat</u>. His clothing was white like snow, and the hair of His head like whitest wool. His throne was flaming fire; its wheels were blazing fire.
¹⁰ A river of fire was flowing, coming out <u>from His presence</u>. Thousands upon thousands served Him; ten thousand times ten thousand stood before Him. <u>The court was convened</u>, and the <u>books were opened.</u>

> [11] "I watched, then, because of <u>the sound of the arrogant words the horn was speaking</u>. As I continued watching, <u>the beast was killed and its body destroyed</u> and given over to <u>the burning fire</u>.
> [12] As for the rest of the beasts, <u>their authority to rule was removed</u>, but <u>an extension of life was granted</u> to them for <u>a certain period of time</u>.

What we learn about the Antichrist in this verse:

1. The Ancient of Days takes his seat in glory.

2. The Antichrist called the "horn," stands before Jesus.

3. He speaks arrogantly.

4. The "beast," another name for the Antichrist, is killed.

5. His body is destroyed and put in the fire.

The lawless one is destroyed

2 Thessalonians 2:8 (HCSB)
8 and then the lawless one will be revealed. The Lord Jesus will destroy him with the breath of His mouth and will bring him to nothing with the brightness of His coming.

Another name is ascribed to the Antichrist, the "lawless one." This word carries the connotation "wicked one" without law. Arthur Pink wrote in his classic book on the Antichrist:

"Each of his names exhibits him as the antithesis of the true Christ. The Lord Jesus was the Righteous One; the Man of Sin will be the Lawless One. The Lord Jesus was "made under the law" (Galatians 4:4); the Antichrist will oppose all law, being a law unto himself. When the Saviour entered this world, He came saying, "Lo I come to do Thy will, O God" (Hebrews 10:9); but of the Antichrist it is written "And the king shall do according to his will" (Daniel 11:36). The Antichrist will set himself up in direct opposition to all authority, both Divine and human."[24]

What we learn about the Antichrist in this verse:

1. He sets himself apart from God's law and is wicked.

2. He will one day be revealed to the world.

3. He will be destroyed by the words of Jesus.

4. Nothing he will do will ever matter after Jesus returns.

The swiftly fleeing and twisting serpent

Isaiah 27:1 (AMPC)
1 IN THAT day [the Lord will deliver Israel from her enemies and also from the rebel powers of evil and darkness] His sharp and unrelenting, great, and strong sword will visit and punish Leviathan the swiftly fleeing serpent, Leviathan the twisting and winding serpent; and He will slay the monster that is in the sea.

The timing of this verse is the day of the Lord's return to the earth physically. The language here in Chapter 27 seems to be symbolic. "He will slay the monster." Leviathan, the

---

[24] Arthur W. Pink, *The Antichrist*, (Swengel, PA: Bible Truth Depot, 1923), WORD*search* CROSS e-book, 63.

monster in the sea of people mentioned here, is probably Satan, but it also could be the name of a powerful demon who possesses the Antichrist. Maybe even Leviathan *is* the Antichrist, as some have suggested. If so, Leviathan would be another name for him.

> **Job 41:1 (KJV)**
> ¹ **Canst thou draw out leviathan with an hook? or his tongue with a cord *which* thou lettest down?**
> **Job 41:34 (KJV)**
> ³⁴ **He beholdeth all high *things*: <u>he *is* a king over all the children of pride</u>.**

I only suggest this because this monster is *slain*. This is why I bring up this first verse. Again, I don't want to confuse the matter. Interestingly, ancient Jewish mythology states that the dragon will be eaten at a great feast after the Messiah sets up His kingdom. If this were literally true, then this monster is an enormous serpent in the sea.

Who then is the dragon?

In Revelation 12:3, Satan is pictured as a great red dragon with seven heads. He most definitely is a monster in the sea, and he is punished and bound in the pit at this time also.

> **Revelation 12:3 (KJV)**
> ³ **And there appeared another wonder in heaven; and behold <u>a great red dragon</u>, having seven heads and ten horns, and seven crowns upon his heads.**

> Revelation 12:9 (KJV)
> ⁹ **And <u>the great dragon was cast out</u>, that old serpent, called <u>the Devil, and Satan</u>, which deceiveth the whole world: he was cast out into the earth, and his angels were cast out with him.**

Who or what is the "beast?"

Revelation 16:13 (KJV)- The Antichrist
¹³ And I saw <u>three unclean spirits</u> like frogs *come* out of the mouth of the dragon, and out of the mouth of the beast, and out of the mouth of the false prophet.

Revelation 17:8 (KJV)- A kingdom
⁸ <u>The beast</u> that thou sawest was, and is not; and <u>shall ascend out of the bottomless pit,</u> and go into perdition: and they that dwell on the earth shall wonder, whose names were not written in the book of life from the foundation of the world, when they behold <u>the beast that was,</u> and is not, and yet is.

Revelation 11:7 (KJV)- A demonic spirit
⁷ And when they shall have finished their testimony, <u>the beast that ascendeth out of the bottomless pit</u> shall make war against them, and shall overcome them, and kill them.

We have to keep in mind that in the Apocalypse, the word "beast" could refer to three things:

<u>The beast in prophecy</u>

1. A supernatural fallen angelic spirit- Rev. 11:7; Rev. 17:8

2. A man-Rev. 13:18; Rev. 17:12; Dan. 7:11, 24

3. A kingdom-Rev. 17:9-17

There are three demonic hosts mentioned in Revelation 16:13. Satan, the Antichrist "beast" spirit who possesses him, and one that possesses the false prophet. There is a ranking demon who was bound during John's day and will ascend out of the pit during the Tribulation, reviving the sixth/eighth empire that the Antichrist will finally rule. This one called "the beast" is probably the one who possesses the Antichrist. Remember, he is a high-ranking demon named "Beast" released from the pit of Hell and he possesses a man.

How the Antichrist is destroyed

Isaiah 14:19 (KJV)
19 But thou art cast out of thy grave like an abominable branch, and as the raiment of those that are slain, <u>thrust through with a sword</u>, that go down to the stones of the pit; as a carcase trodden under feet.

Isaiah 14 is a reference to Satan and the Antichrist. As we will see in Revelation 19:15, the "sword" is the word that Jesus speaks out of His mouth. The Antichrist, possessed by a high-ranking demon, or some even say Satan himself, will die by Jesus's words, not a physical sword, like the KJV seems to read in Isaiah 14:19 (see our discussion on this whole chapter below). Newer translations correctly translate the Hebrew in this verse and declare that it is the *others* who are slain by the sword and not the Antichrist (see below, where both the HCSB and Amplified bear this out).

Keep in mind that Hell and the Lake of Fire are not one and the same. Hell itself will one day be thrown into the Lake of Fire. If Revelation 19:20 is speaking of the *literal* Lake of fire then this statement would have to be true: that *a human man* would go to the lake of fire before going to Hell itself, which would be unprecedented. No man has ever gone there *first*. God reserves the Lake of Fire as the *last* judgment after Hell (Rev. 20:14).

There may be another explanation here. Jesus spoke clearly of this physical "Gehenna of fire," that will one day

burn like the fires of Hell, near Jerusalem after His return
(Mark 9:47).

Mark 9:47 (KJV)
**⁴⁷ And if thine eye offend thee, pluck it out: it is better for thee
to enter into the kingdom of God with one eye, than having
two eyes to be cast into hell** (Note the Greek word used here is
Gehenna[25] not Hades.) **fire:**

Gehenna was a place during Jesus' day southeast of
Jerusalem where trash, sewage, and dead carcasses were
thrown and burned. During the Judgment of the Nations, dead
bodies will be thrown here and burned. Gehenna represents
the true Lake of Fire, where all evil men and demons will
eventually go. Remember, the Lake of Fire is not Hell, but *a
worse place* than Hell. It is the final judgment, where evil men
will one day go after Hell's confinement.

It makes more sense to me that the Antichrist will be
taken wounded, but not dead, and tried before Jesus, and his
personal *spirit,* will be thrown into Hell. His body will be
burned. I could be wrong, because the Bible does say the beast

---

[25] "The Greek word *gehenna*, the transliteration of the Hebrew phrase *ge hinnom* (lit. "Valley of
Hinnom"). This valley, just south of Jerusalem, is where the apostate Jews offered human
sacrifices to the pagan god Molech (cf. Jer. 7:31; 19:5-6; 32:35)." — Tom Constable's Notes on
the Bible

An aerial view of Hinnom

and the false prophet go to the lake of fire in this passage. But this "lake of fire" may be speaking of the earthly fires of Gehenna outside of Jerusalem, where the dead bodies will be burned in a deep ravine for some time. There is an *eternal* lake of fire where all evil men who will be resurrected out of Hell itself, (at the end of the millennial), will be judged and thrown- Rev. 20:11-15.

> **Revelation 20:14-15 (KJV)**
> [14] **And death and hell were cast into the lake of fire. This is the second death.**
> [15] **And whosoever was not found written in the book of life was cast into the lake of fire.**

As I said, Hell and the Lake of Fire are two different places. One is confinement/pre-punishment, and the other is final punishment. I ask carefully, shouldn't these two *human* men *also* spend time in Hell to wait and be punished before going to the final eternal Lake of Fire?

There is another possibility: Could this statement about the punishment of the Lake of Fire here in this verse be about the punishment of the *demonic spirits* that possess them, and be where *they* are thrown first? I ask, could it be that their physical *bodies* are thrown into Gehenna, their personal *spirits* go to Hell, and the *demons* who possess them are thrown directly into the Lake of Fire?

Maybe some of the angels will be thrown into the Lake of Fire at that time. Satan, however, will be bound in Hell's pit for a thousand years first, along with all those who have gone there before. Generally, according to Isaiah 24:21-22, angels and the kings of the earth will be thrown into Hell's pits on the Day of the Lord.

> **Isaiah 24:21-22 (KJV)**
> [21] And it shall come to pass in that day, *that* the **LORD** shall punish <u>the host of the high ones *that are* on high</u>, and the **kings of the earth upon the earth.**
> [22] And they shall be gathered together, <u>*as* prisoners are</u> <u>gathered in the pit</u>, and shall be shut up in the prison, and <u>after many days</u> shall they be visited (Gr. punished)

Hell and the Lake of Fire were originally created for demons, but even Satan will one day be thrown in the Lake of Fire too, later in Rev. 20:10. However, at this particular time, at the coming of Christ, Satan himself will be bound in the pit of Hell and not thrown in the lake of fire, until after one thousand years are finished.

> **Revelation 20:1-3 (KJV)**
> [1] And I saw an angel come down from heaven, having the key of the bottomless pit and a great chain in his hand.
> [2] And he laid hold on the dragon, that old serpent, which is <u>the</u> <u>Devil</u>, and Satan, and bound him a thousand years,
> [3] And cast him into <u>the bottomless pit</u> (LB- Even Satan has to go to the prison of hell for a time before being cast into the Lake of Fire), **and shut him up, and set a seal upon him, that he should deceive the nations no more, <u>till the thousand years should be</u>** <u>fulfilled</u>**: and after that he must be loosed a little season.**

> **Revelation 20:10 (KJV)**
> [10] And the devil that deceived them was cast into the lake of

fire and brimstone, where the beast (LB- The demonic spirit named "beast") **and the false prophet *are*, and** ("he" the Devil) **shall be tormented day and night for ever and ever.**

I'm suggesting that the "beast" and the "false prophet" here in the Lake of Fire are the ranking demonic spirits that possessed these human counterparts. The demonic "Beast," or the one who possessed the Antichrist, will be thrown into the lake of fire. This is why Revelation 20:10 uses the word "beast" and not "Antichrist." So we would know that he is referring to the demonic spirit here. As we shall see, according to Isaiah 14, the Antichrist's *human spirit* will go into Hell when he dies, although his physical body will burn up in Gehenna. He will wind up in the Lake of Fire as he is to be judged like other men at the Great White Throne Judgment (see Rev. 20:11-14). Let's look at this important chapter.

Isaiah 14- A spiritual king (Satan) and a physical king (Antichrist) are judged

In Isaiah 14, there is a *spiritual* king and a *physical* human king portrayed who meet their judgments. Here the *spiritual* king is *Satan* himself, who some say possesses the Antichrist[26] and will be thrown into hell's pit (the worst part of Hell) to suffer for a thousand years (vs. 12-15; Rev. 20:3). Because they are judged on the same day, both are mentioned in the scope of Chapter 14. The Antichrist, *the physical man* who is called the king of Babylon, will be judged by Christ himself at the beginning of the Judgment of the Nations (i.e. the "Sheep and Goats" judgment, after the Tribulation). The Antichrist's children will be cut off also.

---

[26] I generally disagree- because in the book of Revelation the identity of the dragon who is clearly Satan, is distinctly different from the Beast who is the Antichrist- Chp. 12 & 13)

Most of Isaiah 14 seems to be about the Antichrist and Satan because of certain phrases that are used, of which are clearly millennial in nature (Vs. 1-7) and speak about a final ruler. This sets the timing of most of this chapter to be fulfilled in the end time. Gaebelein and many others believed this (see below).

Isaiah 14:1-3 (KJV)
[1] **For the LORD will have mercy on Jacob, and will yet choose Israel, and <u>set them in their own land</u>: and the <u>strangers shall be joined with them</u>, and they shall cleave to the house of Jacob.**
[2] **And the people shall take them, and bring them to their place: and the house of Israel shall possess them in the land of the LORD for <u>servants and handmaids</u> (LB- see Isaiah 66:19-21): and they shall take them captives, whose captives they were; and <u>they shall rule over their oppressors</u>.**
[3] **And it shall come to pass <u>in the day that the LORD shall give thee rest from thy sorrow,</u> and from thy fear, and from the hard bondage wherein thou wast made to serve,**

The judgment of the king of Babylon:

Isaiah 14:4-6 (KJV)
[4] **That thou shalt take up this proverb against <u>the king of Babylon</u>, and say, How hath the oppressor ceased! <u>the golden city ceased!</u>**
[5] **The LORD hath broken the staff of <u>the wicked</u>, *and* <u>the sceptre</u> of the rulers.**
[6] **He who smote the people in wrath with a continual stroke, <u>he that ruled the nations in anger</u>, is persecuted, *and* none hindereth.**

Isaiah 14 is probably about the Antichrist, the future king of Babylon. Babylon was never fully destroyed, like Isaiah prophesied it to be. It continued on for centuries and just faded away. Nothing like Isaiah 13 or Revelation 18 describes.

So we see the future resurrection of the city of Babylon in Iraq, being used by the Antichrist as his headquarters, until he moves toward Jerusalem.

> Isaiah 13:19-20 (KJV)
> 19 And Babylon, the glory of kingdoms, the beauty of the Chaldees' excellency, shall be as when God overthrew Sodom and Gomorrah.
> 20 It shall never be inhabited, neither shall it be dwelt in from generation to generation: neither shall the Arabian pitch tent there; neither shall the shepherds make their fold there.
>
> Revelation 18:10 (HCSB)
> 10 They will stand far off in fear of her torment, saying: Woe, woe, the great city, Babylon, the mighty city! For in a single hour your judgment has come.

Babylon and its bricks being used to rebuild in 1988

People visit the ancient city of Babylon near Hillah, 100 kilometers (62 miles) south of Baghdad, Iraq. Photo by Safa Daneshvar[27] See also article about the stolen bricks.[28]

"Babylon Was Never Destroyed-

"The City of Babylon [Iraq] was never destroyed according to fashion of Sodom and Gomorrah, but it has always been inhabited. When Koldewey the renowned German Archaeologist arrived there, he found the local inhabitants mining the area for bricks.

Both Isaiah and Jeremiah tell us that Babylon will never be inhabited and that the bricks will never be used ever again. Babylon currently has a population of around 400,000. The Old City has been under construction for the past 40 years. The bulk of the funding for this reconstruction comes from UNESCO. Saddam Hussein [who saw himself as the reincarnated Nebuchadnezzar] held affairs of State in one of the Grand Halls of Babylon in 1988. This destruction is something [as we discovered previously] is something that happens during **"the Day of the Lord" [Yahweh]** which is **the last** and **the final day** of this age we currently live in."[29]

A Quranic passage links the future ruler of the Babylonian Empire to the liberation of Palestine. Saddam Hussein believed he was that person. There were many prototypes of the Antichrist in Israel's past history. Gaebelein stated this:

---

[27] https://upload.wikimedia.org/wikipedia/commons/6/6c/Walls_of_Babylon_2_RB.JPG
[28] https://www.al-monitor.com/originals/2016/12/ancient-babylon-bricks-iraq.html
[29] The 33 Other Titles That Antichrist is Known By as Cited in the Hebrew Scriptures by Paul MacDonald RN RMN MA Dipl - Paul MacDonald (weebly.com)

"The King of Babylon here in this chapter is not Nebuchadnezzar, nor his grandson Belshazzar, but the final great King of Babylon. It is the little horn of Daniel 7." [30]

Some say this is a specific king-

"It seems more natural to view this proud tyrant as Sennacherib (705–681). There are interesting parallels between the description of the tyrant in Isaiah 14 and the curse against Sennacherib in 37:21–29. But wasn't Sennacherib king of Assyria rather than Babylon? He was king of both because Babylon was a vassal of Assyria from the end of the 10th century B.C.[31]"

Let's look closer:

Isaiah 14:7-11 (KJV)
[7] **The whole earth is at rest** (LB- at the end of the Tribulation), *and* is quiet: they break forth into singing.
[8] Yea, the fir trees rejoice at thee, *and* the cedars of Lebanon, *saying*, Since thou art laid down, no feller is come up against us.
[9] **Hell from beneath is moved for thee to meet** *thee* at thy coming: it stirreth up the dead for thee, *even* **all the chief ones** of the earth; it hath raised up from their thrones **all the kings** of the nations.
[10] All they shall speak and say unto thee, **Art thou also become weak as we?** art thou become like unto us?
[11] Thy pomp is brought down to the grave, *and* the noise of thy viols: the worm is spread under thee, and **the worms cover thee.**

[30] Gaebelein, A. C. (2009). The Annotated Bible: Proverbs to Ezekiel (Vol. 4, pp. 120–121). Bellingham, WA: Logos Bible Software.
[31] Martin, J. A. (1985). Isaiah. In J. F. Walvoord & R. B. Zuck (Eds.), *The Bible Knowledge Commentary: An Exposition of the Scriptures* (Vol. 1, p. 1061). Wheaton, IL: Victor Books.

What we learn about the antichrist in these verses:

1. He is called the king of Babylon, the future golden city (or city that requires tribute). This means that city will be rebuilt in the last days.
2. He is called the oppressor.
3. The golden city is ceased (comes to an abrupt end).
4. The Lord does the breaking of the staff and scepter.
5. He is called "the wicked" here corresponding with Paul in 2 Thess. 2:8.
6. He rules the nations.
7. He with his staff, struck people with unceasing blows.
8. He subdues the nations in rage with relentless persecution (HCSB).
9. He will be persecuted and will hinder no more or, no one hinders this from happening. Another interpretation in many translations like ASV- he the Antichrist persecutes and "none restrain."
10. At his defeat the whole earth will be at rest.
11. Trees will rejoice at his fall

Isaiah 14:12-15 is specifically about Satan- we will see this later. But, look at verses 16-22, which are more about the Antichrist.

Isaiah 14:16-18 (KJV)
¹⁶ They that see thee shall <u>narrowly look upon thee,</u> *and* consider thee, *saying, Is* this the man that <u>made the earth to tremble</u>, that did <u>shake kingdoms</u>;
¹⁷ *That* <u>made the world as a wilderness</u>, and <u>destroyed the cities</u> thereof; *that* <u>opened not the house</u> of his prisoners?
¹⁸ All the kings of the nations, *even* all of them, lie in glory, every one in his own house.

Isaiah 14:19-22 (KJV)
¹⁹ But thou art <u>cast out of thy grave like an abominable branch,</u> *and as* the raiment of <u>those that are slain, thrust through with a sword</u>, that go down to the stones of the pit; as a carcase trodden under feet.
²⁰ <u>Thou shalt not be joined with them in burial</u>, because thou hast <u>destroyed thy land</u>, *and* <u>slain thy people</u>: <u>the seed of evildoers</u> shall never be renowned.
²¹ Prepare <u>slaughter for his children for the iniquity of their fathers</u>; that they do not rise, nor possess the land, nor fill the face of the world with cities.
²² For I will rise up against them, saith the LORD of hosts, and <u>cut off from Babylon the name, and remnant, and son, and nephew, saith the LORD.</u>

What we learn about the antichrist in these verses:

1. Those in Hell will narrowly look (examine to understand him) on him and stare.

2. They say "Is this the man?" and mock.

3. He made the earth to tremble with fear.

4. He made nations quake.

5. He made the inhabited world as a wilderness.

6. He destroyed (to pull down in pieces) its cities.

7. He will not have a normal grave like other kings.

8. He will go down into Hell below.

9. His physical body will not be buried, but will be a carcass thrown out with those thrust though with a sword to be stepped on, and dumped into a rocky pit (Gehenna).

10. He will not be buried *because* he has destroyed (ruined and caused to decay) his land and,

11. He slaughtered (smite with deadly intent, murdered) his own people.

12. He has "children" who are those who follow him.

13. God has prepared a place of slaughter for them.

14. The Lord will destroy Babylon and its descendants forever. (Vs. 21-23).

15. His offspring will be killed so he will never leave a heritage in the earth.

Some teach from these verses that the Antichrist will die at Armageddon, be resurrected immediately, and be tried at the judgment of the nations, only to be thrown into the Lake of Fire as his final punishment right then. **Dr. Arnold Fruchtenbaum,** commenting on Isaiah 14, says:

"In fact, his body will never be buried at all (v. 20) because <u>he will be resurrected and cast alive</u> into the Lake of Fire (Rev. 19:19-21). His entire family will be destroyed so that they can not try to follow in their father's footsteps and attempt to rule the world (v. 21)." [32]

Dr. Fruchtenbaum interprets these verses to say that the Antichrist will die at Armageddon and will be resurrected immediately to then be thrown into the lake of fire. Verse 19 says he will be "cast out of his grave," and some think this to mean *resurrected*. The literal Greek word here, "*shalak,*" means "to hurl." The Holman translation reads:

Isaiah 14:19 (HCSB)
[19] **But you are <u>thrown out</u>** (LB- after being judged by Christ) **<u>without a grave</u>, like a worthless branch, <u>covered by those slain</u> with the sword and <u>dumped into a rocky pit</u> like a trampled corpse.**

Dake: "The whole thought of Isa. 14:18-20 is that ordinary kings who die in battle, sleep or lie in honor in their own tombs; but Antichrist, who will not be buried in honor, will be cast out like the common dead."[33]

Isaiah 14 describes the future king of Babylon at the coming of Christ. Physical Babylon will be rebuilt one day and destroyed during the Tribulation period (Rev 18).

---

[32] Dr. Arnold G. Fruchtenbaum. The campaign of Armageddon.
http://www.christsbondservants.org/Endtime/wys-End-Campaign%20Of%20Armageddon.pdf
[33] Finis Jennings Dake, Dake's Annotated Reference Bible: Containing the Old and New Testaments of the Authorized or King James Version Text, (Lawrenceville, GA: Dake Bible Sales, Inc., 1997), WORDsearch CROSS e-book, Under: "Chapter 14."

Verse 19 says he will be covered by those who are thrust through with a sword and be thrown into a stony pit. His spirit goes to hell below, the spirit that had possessed him goes to the lake of fire, and his physical body is piled in Gehenna and burned just outside of the city. Note: This was never the end of the last reigning Babylonian king of Babylon, Nabonidus, or his son Belshazzar. Nabonidus, the reigning king was spared by Cyrus after fleeing for his life.

How the future city of Babylon is destroyed

Jeremiah 50:26 (KJV)
26 Come against her from the utmost border, open her storehouses: cast her up as heaps, and destroy her utterly: <u>let nothing of her be left</u>.

Jeremiah 50:39 (HCSB)
39 Therefore, desert creatures will live with hyenas, and ostriches will also live in her. <u>It will never again be inhabited or lived in</u> through all generations.

Who does this?

Jeremiah 50:41-43 (HCSB)
41 Look! <u>A people comes from the north</u>. <u>A great nation</u> and <u>many kings</u> will be stirred up from the <u>remote regions</u> of the earth.
42 They grasp bow and javelin. They are cruel and show no mercy. Their voice roars like the sea, and they ride on horses, lined up like men in battle formation against you, Daughter Babylon.
43 The <u>king of Babylon</u> has heard reports about them, and <u>his hands fall helpless</u>. <u>Distress has seized him— pain, like a woman in labor.</u>

Jeremiah 51:26 (KJV)
26 And <u>they shall not take of thee a stone for a corner</u>, nor a

stone for foundations; but thou shalt be desolate for ever, saith the LORD.

Jeremiah 51:29 (KJV)
[29] And the land shall tremble and sorrow: for every purpose of the LORD shall be performed against Babylon, to make the land of Babylon a desolation <u>without an inhabitant</u>.

Isaiah 13:19-20 (KJV)
[19] And Babylon, the glory of kingdoms, the beauty of the Chaldees' excellency, shall be <u>as when God overthrew Sodom and Gomorrah.</u>
[20] <u>It shall never be inhabited</u>, neither shall it be dwelt in from generation to generation: <u>neither shall the Arabian pitch tent there</u>; neither shall the shepherds make their fold there.

Revelation 18:8-11 (KJV)
[8] Therefore shall her plagues come <u>in one day</u>, death, and mourning, and famine; and she shall be <u>utterly burned with fire</u>: for strong *is* the Lord God who judgeth her.
[9] And the kings of the earth, who have committed fornication and lived deliciously with her, shall bewail her, and lament for her, when they shall see the smoke of her burning,
[10] Standing afar off for <u>the fear of her torment</u>, saying, Alas, alas, that great city Babylon, that mighty city! for in one hour is thy judgment come.
[11] And the merchants of the earth <u>shall weep and mourn over her</u>; for no man buyeth their merchandise any more:

These four things must be true to be the final destruction of Babylon according to the Word of God:

1. Swift and sudden destruction in one day and nothing left of her- Jer. 50:26, 40; 51:8-11; Rev. 18:8. She is destroyed by fire. This "fire" is the kind that causes others to stand afar off for "fear of her torment." This

could indicate a nuclear destruction because of the radiation that follows.

2. Nobody will ever live there again- Isaiah 13:19-20; Jeremiah 51:29.

3. No Arab will ever live there again-Isaiah 13:20.

4. Not one brick will be used again- Jeremiah 51:26.

Just by reading this list, you see this event has not yet happened, therefore future Babylon will rise again and cannot be construed as New York or Rome or some other city (although there is a spiritual "mystery" Babylon in the book of Revelation 17:18 that probably is Rome and false religion, which is destroyed by the ten kings under the Antichrist after he uses her at first. This Babylon is contrasted with the destruction of the future physical Babylon, which causes the kings of the earth to lament her destruction in Revelation 18:10). These cities are certainly reminiscent of Babylon and may also be destroyed, but this city will become the headquarters once again for a mighty ruler of the earth. It will become the center of commerce for at least Europe and the Middle East. For a great article about this, read *"The Second Coming of Babylon"* article.[34]

What we learn about the Antichrist from these verses:

1. He is called the king of Babylon, she is called daughter.

2. A great country from afar and remote regions of the earth leads many other kings to battle the city.

---

[34] https://bibleprophecyaswritten.com/the-second-coming-of-babylon/

3. He is not there when she is destroyed, but hears reports.

4. His hands fall helpless to help Babylon.

5. He is greatly distressed when the city is destroyed.

Now let's consider what this chapter says about Satan.

Vs. 12-15- Satan- The spiritual, so called king

Satan is mentioned here because he will be bound in the pit the same day the antichrist is put in Hell.

Verse 12-15 are about Lucifer, the so-called "son of the morning," who has only fallen from Heaven (not the Antichrist). The spiritual king is Satan, who will be judged that day, and bound for one thousand years. While the subject has been the Antichrist, a double reference becomes about a fallen angel: Lucifer (KJV) which is Latin for "morning star," is quickly removed by the light of the true son.

Isaiah 14:12-15 (HCSB)
[12] **Shining morning star, how you have fallen from the heavens!
<u>You destroyer of nations</u>, you have been cut down
to the ground.**
[13] **You said to yourself: "I will ascend to the heavens; I will set
up my throne above the stars of God. I will sit on the mount
of the ⌊gods'⌋ assembly, in the remotest parts of the North.**
[14] **I will ascend above the highest clouds; I will make myself
like the Most High."**

¹⁵ But you will be brought down to Sheol into the deepest regions of the Pit.

Some say these verses are still about the Antichrist, but overlook the phrase "fallen from Heaven." Perhaps it could be as a double reference and may be possible.

The next *verses (16-21)* speak of a physical "man" who will be seen after the battle (see above).

Verses 22-23 are specifically about the judgment of the city of Babylon itself.

Vs. 24-26- Next, the Antichrist is possibly called the "Assyrian" and is judged

(See Micah 5:1-8. We will discuss more on this title later).

This part could be about the Assyrian king Sennacherib, and the fulfillment came in 701 B.C. when the angel of the Lord slew 185,000 Assyrian soldiers who had surrounded Jerusalem (Isaiah 37:36-37). In 689 BC, he took Babylon and destroyed it; his sons rebuilt it; and then, 8 years later, his sons killed him. Both of them fled, and his other son reigned in his stead.

> **²⁴ The LORD of hosts hath sworn, saying, Surely as I have thought, so shall it come to pass; and as I have purposed, *so* shall it stand: ²⁵ That <u>I will break the Assyrian in my land,</u> and upon <u>my mountains tread him under foot</u>: then shall his yoke depart from off them, and his burden depart from off their shoulders. ²⁶ This *is* the purpose that is purposed upon the whole earth: and this *is* the hand that is stretched out upon all the nations.**

Notice the Assyrian is broken, and his hold on them happens in Israel and her mountains, and this action breaks his hold off of the whole earth. Keep in mind that some commentators say the whole of this chapter is about Sennacherib, as the *Bible Knowledge Commentary* does.[35]

But these verses do not wholly speak of him, if at all, *for he was not destroyed in Jerusalem or in their mountains*, and he continued his hold on the world for a time later, and his children continued to rule. He was defeated by Israel prior to taking Babylon, so it is understandable that one might point to him as a fulfillment of these verses.

Verses 28-32 are a completely different prophecy that was fulfilled in history.

Other commentaries say that these beginning verses of Isaiah 14 are first about Belshazzar (wrongly stated that his father Nabonidus was the last king and Belshazzar reigned in his stead for 10 years) and then about the Assyrian Sennacherib.[36] Nabonidus was the last Babylonian king before the Medes and Persians took over. Adam Clarke, in his commentary on Daniel 5:31, says that Isaiah 13-14 and 45-47 are about the war between the Babylonians and the Medes.

It is always best to try to find the historical fulfillment of Old Testament prophecies, but they have to line up perfectly with history. If they do not, then we must look forward to a future day for its completion. These verses like those in Daniel, may have double meanings with natural kings, but are not completely fulfilled in them, and speak of the future Antichrist, the Babylonian and Assyrian king.

---

[35] Martin, J. A. (1985). Isaiah. In J. F. Walvoord & R. B. Zuck (Eds.), *The Bible Knowledge Commentary: An Exposition of the Scriptures* (Vol. 1, p. 1062). Wheaton, IL: Victor Books.
[36] Fausset, A. R. (n.d.). A Commentary, Critical, Experimental, and Practical, on the Old and New Testaments: Job–Isaiah (Vol. III, p. 611). London; Glasgow: William Collins, Sons, & Company, Limited.

Map of the Assyrian empire 900-607 BC[37]

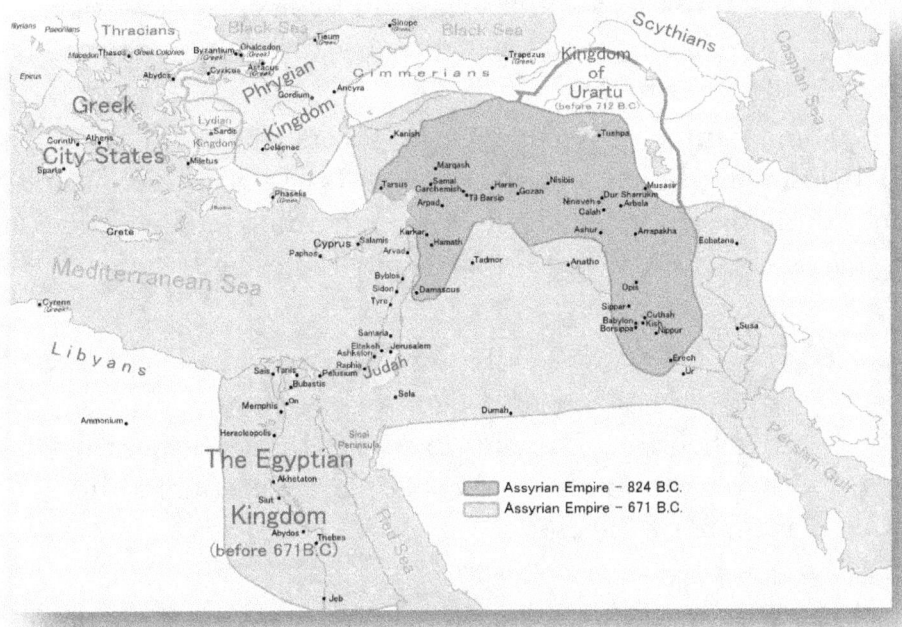

For a good history of Israel and their captivity during these days, see the article footnoted below.[38] In 614-609 B.C., the Assyrian province of Babylon (controlled by the Medes) rose up and conquered Assyria, including their capital Nineveh, in 612 B.C. Babylon thereafter was ruled by various kingdoms. Assyria today is northern Iraq, and southeastern Turkey, and possibly part of Syria. To visit Babylon today, you have to go to Iraq, 55 miles south of Baghdad. By 609 B.C. Assyria and Babylon were one, and Assyria ceased to exist as Assyria. Could we suggest here that the Antichrist appears to be from Syria or Iraq, or at least be associated with Iraq and Babylon?

---

[37] By Ningyou, Wikimedia.org, used by permission. Based on a map in 'Atlas of the Bible Lands', C S Hammond & Co (1959).
[38] https://www.conformingtojesus.com/charts-maps/en/assyrian-babylonian_captivity_map.htm

"We may say this was the current view of Christian writers on prophecy through the first ten centuries A.D."[39]

Some confuse Cyrus the Great's Persian capture of Babylon with the utter destruction of Isaiah 50, which is about the future destruction of Babylon. According to the *Cyrus Cylinder,* Cyrus the Great took the city in peace. It states:

"I took up my lordly abode in the royal palace amidst rejoicing and happiness... My vast army marched into Babylon in peace; I did not permit anyone to frighten the people ... I sought the welfare of the city ..."[40]

Keep in mind that Babylon existed long after Cyrus took it from the Babylonians.

---

[39] Arthur W. Pink, *The Antichrist,* (Swengel, PA: Bible Truth Depot, 1923), WORD*search* CROSS e-book, 97-96.

[40] "The Cyrus Cylinder," Edwin M. Yamauchi. Persia and the Bible. Grand Rapids, Michigan. Baker Book House. 1990, 1996, p. 87.

Chapter 6
The Names Daniel Used

As we carefully study the book of Daniel, we learn a great deal about the future Antichrist. Some critics have tried to discount Daniel's writings by saying they were written at a later time than Daniel lived. Notice what Jesus said:

> **Matthew 24:15 (HCSB)**
> [15] **"So when you see the abomination that causes desolation, spoken of by <u>the prophet Daniel</u>, standing in the holy place" (let the reader understand),**

Jesus foresaw people attacking the book of Daniel by discrediting his visions as *future events* and only calling them *past* historical events. He called Daniel a prophet and said his prophecies were about Israel's future. So we should not be discouraged if we see criticism of this book. Many find it hard to understand. However, Jesus authenticated this book.

"Conservative scholarship has solid reasons for interpreting the fourth kingdom as Roman as well as considering the second and third kingdoms as Medo-Persian and Grecian. As Keil has pointed out, supported by Luther, the prevailing opinion of orthodoxy has always held this position since the early church. Porphyry, the third century A.D.

pagan antagonist of Christianity who invented the idea of a pseudo-Daniel writing the book of Daniel in the second century B.C., did not find Christian support until the rise of modern higher criticism. The whole attempt, therefore, to make the book of Daniel history instead of prophecy, written in the second century and fulfilled by that date, has been considered untenable by orthodoxy. With it, the view that the fourth kingdom is Greece and not Rome has been also rejected by conservative scholars as unsupported by the book of Daniel and contradicted by the New Testament as well as historic fulfillment."[41]

Daniel had a unique view of the future of the world, as we shall see.

Daniel Chapter 2- The "subduer"-

Daniel 2:1 (KJV)
¹ And in the second year of the reign of Nebuchadnezzar Nebuchadnezzar dreamed dreams, wherewith his spirit was troubled, and his sleep brake from him.

The massive empire of Assyria was overtaken by its own city, Babylon. Babylon rose to power, conquered the world and became the Babylonian Empire. This empire invaded Israel and took the best of Israel captive to Babylon, including Daniel, as a young man. Daniel and his friends rose quickly to positions of authority as the Lord gave them favor with the king's handlers.

Read Chapter 2. The king of Babylon, Nebuchadnezzar, was troubled because he couldn't remember his dream. He

---

[41] Walvoord, J. F. (2008). *Daniel: The Key To Prophetic Revelation* (p. 146). Galaxie Software..

became furious that none of his magicians and wise men could not tell him his dream and its interpretation. They said, "No man can do this." The king threatened and then decreed to kill them all if they could not help him. Daniel was part of this group and interceded, asking the king to let him pray and ask God for this revelation. God showed Daniel the dream and its interpretation. Daniel saved all the king's wise men from the king's wrath by supernaturally knowing the king's dream and interpreting it for him. God revealed four great kingdoms in a dream of a giant statue. [42]

---

[42] Illustration by Caleb Jasper Lumingkit-© Joyful Harvest Ministries all rights reserved

In the days of these kings…God sets up His kingdom

Daniel 2:40-44 (KJV)
[40] **And the fourth kingdom shall be strong as iron: forasmuch as iron breaketh in pieces and subdueth all** *things*: **and as iron that breaketh all these, shall it break in pieces and bruise.**
[41] **And whereas thou sawest the feet and toes, part of potters' clay, and part of iron, <u>the kingdom shall be divided</u>; but there shall be in it of the strength of the iron, forasmuch as thou sawest the iron mixed with miry clay.**
[42] **And** *as* **the toes of the feet** *were* **part of iron, and part of clay,** *so* **the kingdom shall be partly strong, and partly broken.**
[43] **And whereas thou sawest iron mixed with miry clay, they shall <u>mingle themselves with the seed of men</u>: but <u>they shall not cleave one to another</u>, even as iron is not mixed with clay.**
[44] **And <u>in the days of these kings</u> shall the God of heaven <u>set up a kingdom</u>** (LB- The Messiah's kingdom is set up during the "days of these kings." Out of the fourth- Dan. 7:24. Revelation 17 teaches Daniel's fourth is also the sixth of a larger set of kingdoms- See later)**, which shall never be destroyed: and the kingdom shall not be left to other people,** *but* **it shall break in pieces and consume <u>all these kingdoms</u>, and it shall stand for ever.**

Each section of the statute represents a world ruling kingdom. Each succeeding metal is of a lower quality, but stronger. Thus, each kingdom would be more powerful than the last. In verses 40-44, Daniel explained the fourth kingdom after the previous three. The first kingdom was symbolized by the golden head, which represented the existing Babylonian kingdom that King Nebuchadnezzar ruled over. After all, it was his dream. So, God revealed to the king his kingdom and those other kingdoms that would follow after it, which would also rule the known world: the Babylonian, the Median-Persian (the breast and arms of silver), the Greek (belly and thighs of brass), and the Roman. The fourth kingdom consisted of two iron legs. This kingdom was no doubt the Roman Empire, which subdued the whole earth and was said by historians to have "stomped" their opposition for centuries. Next, it mentions the ten toes of this kingdom that were mixed with iron and clay. Daniel says they were divided and did not mix well.

We now know Daniel's fourth beast was the Roman Empire, strong as iron. It was later divided into two "legs," the Eastern and Western Empires. The ten toes are a future group that will come up out of the old Roman Empire. For centuries, these monarchs will "mingle with the seeds of men" and one day emerge on the scene as true kingdoms. They are first mentioned as future "kings" in Daniel 2:44. One person taught that there will be five kings from Europe and five kings who are Islamic, all still from the old empire. This is why they are divided and do not mix well.

The antichrist will rule through and subvert the next set of ten kings who will come up out of the fourth kingdom, a divided kingdom of iron mixed with clay. These kings out of the territory of the old Roman Empire will all exist at the same time. This is very important: According to Verse 44, *they will all exist at the same time when Jesus returns to the earth to conquer the Antichrist.* This proves that these kings are a future group.

Daniel 2:45 (HCSB)
⁴⁵ You saw a stone break off from the mountain without a hand touching it, and it crushed the iron, bronze, fired clay, silver, and gold. The great God has told the king what will happen in the future. The dream is true, and its interpretation certain."

They are the future "divided" part of the old Roman Empire. I don't necessarily like the phrase "revived Roman Empire," but we will call it the "revised Roman Empire."

In Daniel Chapter 7, God shows Daniel in a vision more details of these great kingdoms as great "beasts." In Verse 24, God shows him more about the ten toes being ten horns/kings that would arise out of the fourth beast empire and speaks of another little horn that would subdue the others.

God says the little "horn" will "subdue" three of these future kings. This Chaldean/Aramaic word (which is what this section of Daniel is written in) is "*Shepal,*" a verb which means to "humble, abase, or subdue others."

Daniel 7:24 (KJV)
²⁴ And the ten horns out of this kingdom *are* ten kings *that* shall arise: and <u>another shall rise after them</u>; and he shall be diverse from the first, and he shall subdue three kings.

Daniel mentions seven kingdoms in total

Daniel's view of 7
1. Babylonian
2. Median/Persian
3. Grecian
4. Roman
5. Ten toes king coalition
6. Antichrist-Little horn
7. Christ

Later we will see that the book of Revelation speaks of nine kingdoms total, and in Revelation the "ten king coalition" is John's seventh. We will explain this later. Finis Dake had great insight into this in his comment on these verses:

"It will be noticed in the headings of the text in Dan. 2:41 and 2:44, one kingdom is the seventh and the kingdom of God is the ninth. There is no eighth kingdom mentioned in Dan. 2, but there is in Dan. 7:23-24; Rev. 17:9-11. Daniel does not see a little toe coming out of the ten toes, plucking out three of the others by the roots; but in Dan. 7:7-8,19-24 there is a little horn coming out of the ten horns, and after them. He gets power over them by conquering three of them and by the others of the ten kings then submitting to him without further war. This is the same as Rev. 17:9-17. The ten kings give their power to the beast whose kingdom becomes the eighth kingdom. The seventh kingdom is that of the ten kingdoms being independent as separate kingdoms; the eighth is made up of the same ten kingdoms, only they are no longer independent. They continue under the beast for 42 months as subject kingdoms (Rev. 13:1-8; 17:9-17)."[43]

Ten kings will come out of the fourth kingdom

---

[43] Finis Jennings Dake, Dake's Annotated Reference Bible: Containing the Old and New Testaments of the Authorized or King James Version Text, (Lawrenceville, GA: Dake Bible Sales, Inc., 1997), WORDsearch CROSS e-book, Under: "Chapter 2."

In Daniel 7, Daniel himself now has a vision in the night, and these kingdoms are mentioned again as four great beasts.[44]

The first to represent Babylon and its king was a lion with eagle's wings, who loses his wings and is made to stand like a man. The second was a bear representing the Median/Persian Empire. He was raised on one side with three ribs in his teeth, representing three minor kingdoms that they had crushed. The third was a leopard with four bird wings and four heads. This represented the Greek Empire. The fourth was frightening and dreadful, and it was very strong, with great iron teeth. It devoured, and it crushed and trampled with its feet. It also had ten horns and another little horn. This beast was not like the others before it. This, of course, is the Roman Empire.

Daniel 7:3 (KJV)
³ And four great beasts came up from the sea, diverse one from another.

Daniel 7:23-27 (KJV)
²³ Thus he said, The fourth beast shall be <u>the fourth kingdom</u> upon earth, which shall be diverse from all kingdoms, and shall devour the whole earth, and shall tread it down, and break it in pieces.
²⁴ And the ten horns <u>out of this kingdom *are* ten kings *that* shall arise</u>: (LB- Notice "out of this fourth kingdom" ten kings will arise. So here is mentioned Daniel's fifth kingdom group and Revelation's seventh kingdom-see later) **and <u>another shall rise after them;</u>** (LB- the Antichrist's sixth kingdom. Note: we call them "kingdoms" because John numbers them so later.) **and <u>he shall be diverse from the first, and he shall subdue three kings</u>.**
²⁵ And he shall speak *great* words against the most High, and shall wear out the saints of the most High, and think to change times and laws: and they shall be given into his hand until a time and times and the dividing of time (LB- 3 ½ years that the Antichrist rules in his kingdom. So the sixth rises in the middle of the Tribulation).
²⁶ But the judgment shall sit, and they shall take away his dominion, to consume and to destroy *it* unto the end.
²⁷ And <u>the kingdom</u> (LB- the seventh and final kingdom- Rev 17:3-14, See below, in Daniel's view, Christ's kingdom is the seventh and final kingdom because Daniel did not include the first two

kingdoms of Egypt and Assyria, which is included later in the book of Revelation.) **and dominion, and the greatness of the kingdom under the whole heaven, shall be given to the people of the saints of the most High, whose kingdom *is* an everlasting kingdom, and all dominions shall serve and obey him.**

A future ten nation coalition with the Antichrist

Daniel 2:44 clearly states these kings are future because he says, "In the days of these kings shall the God of Heaven set up a kingdom." Daniel 7:24 says they will arise "out of this kingdom." They arise out of the Roman Empire and become a fifth kingdom. Some would say a revision of the old empire. I would not say a *revived* Roman Empire, as many teach today. The Roman Empire will not revive as it existed before. These ten kings will be a *revision* or a revised version of the fourth great empire. Clearly, they will be around when Jesus comes back to earth to rule supreme.

These ten are not some formation of past historical kings *after* the Roman Empire faded because Christ has not come to defeat them yet, as these verses indicate. From the demise of the old Roman Empire till now, these kings (lineages) have mixed with the seeds of men but will emerge as true monarchs-(2:43).

Here the ten toes are ten kings, who for the first half of the seven year tribulation period, or maybe some time before, will be a coalition of independent kings who will rule for a short season together. Their territory will be from the land masses that were included in the old Roman Empire. The little horn then comes up *after* the ten are in power (Dan 7:8). They will give all their force to the little horn, who will then eventually take full rule over them, by subduing three of them. Daniel 7:8 says they were "plucked up by the roots." Daniel

7:24 states the Antichrist "subdues" three of the ten kings at some point during the Tribulation. But these kings are allowed to continue until the end. "Subdue" here means to "put down," or "to humble" them.

I believe this happens sometime after the start of the seven years because the Apocalypse mentions the 10 giving their power to the beast, so when he takes full charge, he allows them to continue to be puppet kings under him. When the little horn (Antichrist) takes over fully, it is considered yet another kingdom, the sixth. Details on Chapter 7 are below. See also Rev. 13 and 17:12-17 for more details of this process. Revelation 17:14 states these 10 kings shall make war with the Lamb and be defeated.

> **Revelation 17:12-14 (KJV)**
> [12] **And the ten horns which thou sawest are ten kings, <u>which have received no kingdom as yet</u>; but receive <u>power as kings</u> one hour <u>with the beast.</u>**
> [13] **These have one mind, and <u>shall give their power</u> and strength unto the beast.**
> [14] **These shall make war with the Lamb, and <u>the Lamb shall overcome them</u>: for he is Lord of lords, and King of kings: and they that are with him *are* called, and chosen, and faithful.**

H. A. Ironside taught that these ten kings are future and not part of a past historical setting like some try to teach.

> "The commentators generally tell us that the ten-toed condition of the empire was reached in the fifth and sixth centuries, when the barbarians from the North overran the Roman empire, and it was divided into something like ten different kingdoms. A number of different lists have been made, of ten kingdoms each; but few writers agree as to the actual divisions. <u>One thing they all seem to have overlooked: the ten kingdoms are to exist</u>

at one time, not through a period of several centuries, and all are to form one confederation. There is nothing in the past history of the kingdoms of Europe that answers to this." [45]

Daniel 7- Another "Little Horn"- Came up among them

Verse one states: "**In the first year of Belshazzar king of Babylon, Daniel had a dream.**" Two visions of Daniel were seen in the reign of Belshazzar (Dan. 7 and Dan. 8). Two dreams were seen by Nebuchadnezzar, believed to be Belshazzar's grandfather on his mother's side. (Dan. 2 and Dan. 4). This vision was seen about three years before the events of Daniel 6. This chapter, which was in Aramaic, completes the whole Aramaic section of Daniel (Dan. 2:4 - Dan. 7:28).

Daniel 7:7-8 (KJV)
[7] After this I saw in the night visions, and behold a fourth beast, dreadful and terrible, and strong exceedingly; and it had great iron teeth: it devoured and brake in pieces, and stamped the residue with the feet of it: and it _was_ diverse from all the beasts that _were_ before it; and it had ten horns.
[8] I considered the horns, and, behold, there came up among them another little horn, before whom there were three of the first horns plucked up by the roots: and, behold, in this horn _were_ eyes like the eyes of man, and a mouth speaking great things.

In Chapter 2 there is no mention of the Antichrist as "another little toe" coming up from the ten already there. But in Chapter 7, Daniel's account of him here associates him with

[45] Ironside, H. A. (1953). _Lectures on Daniel the Prophet_ (2d ed., pp. 37–38). Loizeaux Bros.

the old Roman Empire and calls him the "little horn." Never was the old Roman Empire officially divided into 10 kingdoms together all at once, so this is a future group. This 10 king coalition of the Antichrist will encompass what the old Roman Empire did. This would include Europe and much of the known world at that time. These ten kings did not have kingdoms during John's day (Rev 17:12). *There will be ten kings at first, and then another will come up among them.* That makes eleven total.

This means that at first, the Antichrist is insignificant and small, like a prince or president, compared to the ten kings. Later, three of them will be plucked up by the roots and conquered by the Antichrist. In this way, this original group of ten is associated with the Antichrist (see Rev. 13). When they rule, they will be Daniel's "fifth" kingdom on the earth later in the time of the end, and will take up some of the area of the old Roman Empire. Then, after that, by the middle point of the seven years of tribulation, when the Antichrist fully takes over, he will demand that all worship him as a god. He will also rise to full power, becoming Daniel's sixth empire, still originating from the fourth beast. The ten will give all their might to him to use.

"The *"little horn"* is a secondary leader, for instance a prince, vice-president, prime minister, or governor. The term *"little horn"* is applied to Antiochus Epiphanies in Daniel 8:9. "Antiochus Epiphanies" was the son of "Antiochus the Great" the king of the Seleucid dynasty (1/4 of the Grecian empire, headquartered in Syria). Antiochus Epiphanies was initially a prince in the Seleucid dynasty until he manipulated his way onto the throne. This *"little horn"* will evidently

take away or usurp the authority of three of the
first ten kings."[46]

Please note that Daniel's listed numbers do not include the
Egyptian and Assyrian empires like the book of Revelation
does. So in John's explanation, the ten kings are the *seventh*
kingdom, and the Antichrist's kingdom becomes the *eighth*. We
will explain this in detail later.

We will see in Daniel Chapter 8 that the Antichrist appears
to come up from the old Grecian *third* kingdom model, namely
the same as Antiochus IV did: the Seleucid/Syrian quarter,
which was one of the four sections after Alexander the Great
died.

What we learn about the antichrist in these verses:

1. His kingdom begins at first as part of a fourth beast,
   diverse and very different from the others: this is
   the Roman Empire. Rome being ruled as a republic
   was a very different way of ruling.

2. It then morphs into the 10 king coalition (this is
   future). Earlier Daniel says "out of the fourth."

3. A "little horn" comes up among them (not the
   same as Daniel 8:9- Antiochus IV). This could
   mean insignificance in standing with the others, or a
   smaller country or weaker ruled position as
   compared to others, like an ambassador or vice
   president of a group.

---

[46] White., Craig C. Article- *The Antichrist is a Prince*. https://hightimetoawake.com/the-antichrist-is-a-prince/

4. It seems the little horn rips out three of the previous kingdoms by their roots (see Daniel 11:43).

5. The new king has "two eyes" (T. Constable suggests- "great intelligence") and a boastful mouth.

Daniel 7- Details of the fourth beast, "Diverse" from all the others-

The explanation to Daniel: The future revised "Roman" Empire

"In Dan. 2 Nebuchadnezzar is shown the Gentile world kingdoms from his day to the second coming of Christ. They are pictured there, from man's standpoint, as a great and beautiful metallic image. In Dan. 7 God shows Daniel the same kingdoms from God's standpoint as ferocious wild beasts (Dan. 7:17)."[47]

Daniel was given the explanation for these four beasts. The explanation spoke of the last beast with ten horns and another horn that came up among the ten. This is the Antichrist as he connects to the fourth beast, which we now know was the Roman Empire.

Daniel 7:19-27 (KJV)
[19] Then I would know the truth of <u>the fourth beast</u>, which was <u>diverse from all the others</u>, exceeding dreadful, whose teeth *were of* iron, and his nails *of* brass; *which* devoured, brake in

---

[47] Finis Jennings Dake, *Dake's Annotated Reference Bible: Containing the Old and New Testaments of the Authorized or King James Version Text*, (Lawrenceville, GA: Dake Bible Sales, Inc., 1997), WORD*search* CROSS e-book, Under: "Chapter 7".

pieces, and stamped the residue with his feet;

²⁰ And of <u>the ten horns that *were* in his head</u>, and *of* <u>the other</u> which came up, and before whom three fell; even *of* that horn that <u>had eyes, and a mouth</u> that spake very great things, <u>whose look *was* more stout than his fellows</u>.

²¹ I beheld, and <u>the same horn made war with the saints</u>, and prevailed against them;

²² <u>Until the Ancient of days came</u>, and judgment was given to the saints of the most High; and <u>the time came that the saints possessed the kingdom</u>.

²³ Thus he said, The fourth beast shall be the fourth kingdom upon earth, which shall be <u>diverse from all kingdoms</u>, and <u>shall devour the whole earth</u>, and shall tread it down, and break it in pieces.

²⁴ And the ten horns <u>out of this kingdom *are* ten kings *that* shall arise</u> (LB- The ten will have to come up out of the original Roman Empire) and <u>another</u> shall rise <u>after them; and he shall be diverse</u> from the first, and he <u>shall subdue three kings</u>.

²⁵ And he shall <u>speak *great* words against</u> the most High, and <u>shall wear out the saints</u> of the most High, and think to <u>change times and laws</u>: and they shall be given into his hand until a time and times and the dividing of time. (LB- 3 ½ years)

²⁶ But <u>the judgment shall sit</u>, and they shall take away his dominion, to consume and to destroy *it* unto the end.

²⁷ And the kingdom and dominion, and the greatness of the kingdom under the whole heaven, shall be given to the people of the saints of the most High, whose kingdom *is* an everlasting kingdom, and all dominions shall serve and obey him.

God explains more to Daniel about this vision of the fourth beast. He said the fourth beast would be different than any other kingdom before it (Rome ruled as a Republic) and will "devour the whole earth, and shall tread it down, and break it in pieces." This is what the Roman Empire did. Rome was founded around 625 BC. From then until 510 BC, this was the period of the kings. From 510 BC to 31 BC, Rome ruled as a republic where the upper-class ruled and later the public had some say. Then, roughly, the Roman Empire was founded when Augustus Caesar proclaimed himself to be the first Roman Emperor of Rome in 31 BC and centuries later came to an end with the fall of Constantinople in 1453 AD. Some say the Roman Empire, continues through the Roman Catholic Church today. It will one day, according to Daniel, consist of ten kings, or, better said, the ten kings will come from the original Roman territories. The fourth beast, according to the book of Revelation, is the sixth great empire to oppress Israel in history. It existed while Jesus walked on the earth, and Israel was under its power and control.

The coalition of ten from the "head" of the fourth beast becomes Daniel's fifth kingdom, and they rule as a group of ten kings in the future revision of the fourth kingdom. According to verses 21-22, the antichrist comes up out of this movement and subdues them, and this group of 11 will be Daniel's sixth and final "worldly" kingdom, who will rule till Jesus and the saints come to rule. This part, when the Antichrist takes full control, happens in the middle of the Tribulation. The kingdom of God under Christ is the seventh and last future kingdom that Daniel mentioned (Daniel 2:44; 7:9, 14, 18).

> "The final beast may represent Rome, with its ten horns symbolizing a later manifestation of this empire prior to the coming of God's kingdom."[48]

What we learn about the antichrist in these verses:

1. An eleventh king (the Antichrist) will rise and subdue three of the ten.

---

[48] David S. Dockery, ed., *Holman Concise Bible Commentary*, (Nashville, TN: Broadman & Holman, 2010), WORD*search* CROSS e-book, 336.

2. He has "eyes" and the ability to see and speak great things.

3. His look is *more stout* than the others.

4. He will make war with the saints and prevail against them.

5. Until or up to the time Jesus comes back to reign.

6. Out of the fourth kingdom (within the Roman Empire) will come these 10 kings (a coalition formed before the little horn appears).

7. An eleventh king will rise up after and *different* from the 10 (vs. 8, 20).

"It is clear that this "little horn" arises "after" the ten horns and not "before" them and that he does not have a thing to do with causing the rise of the ten. He does not revise the Roman Empire and is not on the scene of action until after the ten kingdoms are fully formed. These facts exclude the possibility of Stalin, the pope, or any man now prominent in world affairs from being the Antichrist of the   future." [49]

8. He will put down and humble 3 of the kings to take full control- Dan. 11:43.

9. He will speak great words against God Himself.

---

[49] Finis J. Dake, *God's Plan for Man*, (Lawrenceville, GA: Dake Publishing, Inc., 2004), WORD*search* CROSS e-book, 784."

10. He will "wear out" or mentally oppress the saints.

11. He will think to change times and laws.

> "He Will Wear Out the Holy Ones EPHREM
> THE SYRIAN: He will prevent the priests from
> performing their duties and holy service. "And
> [he] shall attempt to change the sacred seasons
> and the law," which means he shall attempt to
> delete the holy laws of God and to abolish the
> traditional festivals and Neomenias."
> Commentary on Daniel 7:25.[50]

12. The (Trib.) saints will be given into his hand for a period of 3 ½.

13. Then the court of judgment will convene- at the return of Christ.

14. Then the kingdom of all under heaven will be given to the people of the saints of the most high.

15. It will be an everlasting kingdom and all dominions shall obey and serve him- "Christ."

Daniel 8- A king of fierce countenance-

These verses explain why this vision is important to our study.

---

[50] Kenneth Stevenson and Michael Glerup, *Old Testament XIII: Ezekiel, Daniel,* (Downers Grove, IL: InterVarsity Academic, 2008), WORD*search* CROSS e-book, 245-244.

Daniel 8:19-22 (KJV)

¹⁹ And he said, Behold, I will make thee know what shall be in the <u>last end of the indignation</u>: for at the time appointed the end *shall be.*

²⁰ The ram (LB- 2ⁿᵈ beast) which thou sawest having *two* horns *are* <u>the kings of Media and Persia.</u>

²¹ And the rough goat (LB-3ʳᵈ beast) *is* the king of Grecia: and the great horn that *is* between his eyes *is* the first king (LB- Alexander the Great).

²² Now that being broken, whereas four stood up for it, <u>four kingdoms</u> shall stand up out of the nation (LB- of Greece), but not in his power.

Daniel 8:9 (KJV)

⁹ And <u>out of one of them</u> (LB- the four great divisions of the old Grecian Empire- the largest division of these was the Seleucid, in which Antiochus IV was the eighth ruler. Could this mean that the Antichrist would come from the same?) **came forth a little horn, which waxed exceeding great, toward the south** (Egypt), **and toward the east** (Iran), **and toward the pleasant** *land* (Israel).

Daniel 8:19 (KJV)

¹⁹ And he said, Behold, I will make thee know <u>what shall be in the last end of the indignation</u>: for at the time appointed the end *shall be.*

Daniel 8:23 (KJV)

²³ And in <u>the latter time</u> of their kingdom (LB- the coalition of ten kings), **when** <u>the transgressors</u> (LB- Israel is called the transgressors in 9:24) **are come to the full,** <u>a king of fierce countenance</u>, **and understanding dark sentences, shall stand up.**

A fierce and mighty Seleucid king- A vision two years later

Daniel, while in his position of authority, was in the palace in Shushan when he saw this vision. It explains yet a little more about the Antichrist. "The time of the vision was at the end of the reign of Belshazzar, which corresponds to the time of the handwriting on the wall of Daniel 5, for he only reigned a little more than two years. If Babylon had not fallen yet, then it must be understood that Daniel was on official business in Persia. Shushan was the chief city of Persia."[51]

1. **Daniel 8:1-8**- The story of the second and third kingdoms to come in Daniel's future, against the Babylonian Empire: The ram and the goat. [52]

> **Daniel 8:4 (KJV)**
> [4] **I saw <u>the ram</u> pushing westward, and northward, and southward; so that no beasts might stand before him, neither *was there any* that could deliver out of his hand; but he did according to his will, and became great.**

[51] Finis Jennings Dake, *Dake's Annotated Reference Bible: Containing the Old and New Testaments of the Authorized or King James Version Text*, (Lawrenceville, GA: Dake Bible Sales, Inc., 1997), WORD*search* CROSS e-book, Under: "Chapter 8".
[52] https://danielprojectjke.weebly.com/

a. The ram with two horns, one bigger than the other: represents the Media and Persia empires that would come after the Babylonian, with Persia being the stronger and greater. The ram was the Median/Persian Empire, which was closely connected by the relations of its rulers (Dan. 5:28).

Daniel 8:5 (KJV)
⁵ And as I was considering, behold, an <u>he goat came</u> from the west on the face of the whole earth, and touched not the ground: and the goat *had* a notable horn between his eyes.

b. The goat/large horn[53]: represents the Grecian Empire and Alexander the Great to come after the Persian.

Dake: "[**he goat come from the west**] The acknowledged symbol of Greece. Caranus, the first king going with many Greeks to seek a new habitation in Macedonia, was advised by an oracle to take goats for guides. Seeing a herd fleeing from a storm, he followed them to Edessa and there built the seat of his empire. He called the place Aegea, the goats' town and the people Aegeadae, the goats' people, names derived from *aigeos* (GSN-<G122>), goat. He chose a goat as the emblem on his standards. Aegea was the burying place of Macedonian kings. Alexander called his son by Roxana, Alexander Aegus -- Alexander   the   goat."[54]

   c. The notable horn: 336 B.C., Alexander the Great conquers all (356-323), He was broken: in 323 B.C., he died in Babylon mysteriously at age 32.

   d. Four notable ones came up in its place- 4 later divisions of the Grecian empire: Greece, Turkey, Syria, and Egypt (8:22).

Four Divisions of the Grecian Empire:

(1) Cassander took Greece, Macedon and the western parts of the empire.

---

[54] Finis Jennings Dake, *Dake's Annotated Reference Bible: Containing the Old and New Testaments of the Authorized or King James Version Text*, (Lawrenceville, GA: Dake Bible Sales, Inc., 1997), WORD*search* CROSS e-book, Under: "Chapter 8." According to Justin (7.1) citing Marsyas of Pella

(2) Lysimachus took Asia Minor, or present Turkey and Thrace, the northern part of the empire.

(3) Seleucus took all the eastern parts of the empire, including Israel, Syria and Babylon, or the modern states of Syria, Lebanon, Iraq, and Iran.

(4) Ptolemy took the Kingdom of Egypt, the southern part of the empire. Thus Alexander's empire was literally divided "toward the four winds of heaven" (Dan. 8:8).

e. A "little horn" would rise up from one of these Grecian divisions- he is Antiochus IV- a king from the Seleucus/Syrian part, reigning from 175-164 BC (V.9).

Coin depicting Antiochus IV, Greek inscription reads ΘΕΟΥ ΕΠΙΦΑΝΟΥΣ ΝΙΚΗΦΟΡΟΥ / ΒΑΣΙΛΕΩΣ ΑΝΤΙΟΧΟΥ (King Antiochus, God manifest, bearer of victory)[55]

[55] By Classical Numismatic Group, Inc. http://www.cngcoins.com, CC BY-SA 3.0, https://commons.wikimedia.org/w/index.php?curid=2155073

2. Daniel 8:9-14- Antiochus IV *and* the Antichrist

Daniel 8:9 (KJV)
⁹ **And out of one of them came forth <u>a little horn,</u> which waxed exceeding great, toward the south, and toward the east, and toward the pleasant *land*.**

The natural historic interpretation of Chapter 8 seems to be about Antiochus IV, but the interpretation given to Daniel in verses later by the person who approached him seems to be two-fold: Antiochus *and* the future Antichrist. Verse 17 refers to the "time of the end," and in Verse 19, he says the vision refers to the time of the end "at the conclusion of *the time of wrath*." This is no doubt the future 70th week of Jacob's trouble, the Tribulation period. Daniel began to worry and be sorrowful because he realized Israel would be trampled again one day. He goes into a repentant prayer for Israel. More of the explanation comes in Chapter 9 regarding that time for Israel.

C.I. Schofield: "Two "ends" are in view here: (1) historically, the end of the third, or Grecian empire of Alexander out of one of the divisions of which the little horn of **verse 9** (Antiochus) arose; (2) prophetically, the end of the times of the Gentiles **Luke 21:24**; **Rev 16:14** when the "little horn" of **Dan 7:8**, **24-26** the Beast, will arise--Daniel's *final* time of the end. (See Note for **Dan 12:4**)" [56]

Many scholars agree that this part seems to be about Antiochus IV but also has some reference to the Antichrist: both are called the "little horn."

> "This horn is quite clearly different from the little horn that came up among the 10 horns on the fourth beast in the previous vision (cf. 7:8, 11, 24-26)."- (Tom Constable's Notes on the Bible Daniel 8:9)"
>
> "History has identified this little horn as Antiochus IV (Epiphanes), the eighth king of the Seleucid dynasty. He ruled Syria from 175 to 164 B.C. (cf. 1 Macc. 1:10; 6;16), and he conducted military campaigns in all of these directions (cf. 1 Macc. 1:20). Therefore the point of reference is Syria."— (Tom Constable's Notes on the Bible Daniel 8:9)

Daniel 8:9-14 (KJV)
[9] **And out of one of them came forth <u>a little horn</u>, which waxed exceeding great, toward the south, and toward the east, and toward the pleasant *land*.**
[10] **And it waxed great, *even* to <u>the host of heaven</u>; and it cast down *some* of the host and of the stars to the ground, and stamped upon them.**
[11] **Yea, he magnified *himself* even to <u>the prince of the host</u>, and by him <u>the daily *sacrifice* was taken away</u>, and the**

Antiochus IV

---

[56] C.I. Scofield, ed., *The Holy Bible: Containing the Old and New Testaments*, WORD*search* CROSS e-book, Under: "Chapter 8."

place of his sanctuary was cast down.
[12] **And an host was given *him* against the daily *sacrifice* by reason of transgression, and it cast down the truth to the ground; and it practised, and prospered.**
[13] **Then I heard one saint speaking, and another saint said unto that certain *saint* which spake, How long *shall be* the vision *concerning* the daily *sacrifice*, and the transgression of desolation, to give both the sanctuary and the host to be trodden under foot?**
[14] **And he said unto me, Unto two thousand and three hundred days** (Heb. Literally "evening and morning" sacrifices done twice a day- 1115 days which is 3 years and almost 2 months)**; then shall the sanctuary be cleansed.**

Antiochus IV persecuted the Jewish people harshly; he plundered the temple in 169 BC and desecrated it in 167 BC by commanding that in it a pig should be sacrificed on an altar built for Zeus. After the Jews mounted a great rebellion and achieved success in 164 BC, the temple was restored in a little over 3 years.

"The Jewish authors of 1 Maccabees (in the *Apocrypha*—biblical writings not part of the accepted canon of Scripture) believed that Antiochus' actions in the Temple were the "abomination of desolation" prophesied by Daniel (1 Mac. 1:54). This act of sacrilege left the Temple defiled, requiring that the Temple be purified and rededicated to God. After God enabled the Jewish people to defeat Antiochus, they purified the Temple and decided to enact a new celebration to remember the Temple's restoration: The Feast of Dedication, as it is called in John 10:22, or Hanukkah, as it is called today."[57]

---

[57] https://www.chosenpeople.com/hanukkah-and-the-destruction-of-the-temple/

The time of the end

Daniel overheard two saints talking about this vision. It seems that each represents *a different time of fulfillment* because one of them, speaking to Daniel later, alludes to a future fulfillment, not in Daniel's time period: "The time of the end." Another way of saying: "the last days."

> **Daniel 8:17-19 (HCSB)**
> [17] So he approached where I was standing; when he came near, I was terrified and fell facedown. "Son of man," he said to me, "understand that the vision <u>refers to the time of the end</u>."
> [18] While he was speaking to me, I fell into a deep sleep, with my face [to the ground]. Then he touched me, made me stand up,
> [19] and said, "I am here to tell you <u>what will happen at the conclusion of the time of wrath, because it refers to the appointed time of the end.</u>

The person who told Daniel about this vision says it will happen at the conclusion of the time of wrath. This has to be about the final week. So, this vision has a twofold fulfillment: it is about Antiochus IV, and it is also about the future Antichrist in the last days.

> "Clearly this was future from Daniel's point in history. Yet does it refer to the time of Antiochus Epiphanes exclusively,[495] or does it refer to the end times before Jesus Christ returns,[496] or both? Most premillennial interpreters believe that it

---

[495] Driver, pp. 99, 121; Young, p. 288.
[496] G. H. Pember, *The Great Prophecies of the Centuries Concerning Israel and the Gentiles*, pp. 289-90; Clarence Larkin, *The Book of Daniel*, p. 165; S. P. Tregelles, *Remarks on the Prophetic Visions in the Book of Daniel*, pp. 82-83.

refers to both in some sense, either as a double fulfillment[497] or as a type and antitype." [498] [58]

The Antichrist- an insolent king- HCSB

Daniel 8:23-25 (HCSB)
[23] **Near the end of <u>their kingdoms </u>(LB- the four divisions), when <u>the rebels have reached the full measure</u> of their sin, <u>an insolent king</u>, <u>skilled in intrigue</u>, will come to the throne.**
[24] **His power will be great, but <u>it will not be his own</u>. He will cause terrible destruction and succeed in whatever he does. <u>He will destroy the powerful</u> along with the holy people.**
[25] **He will cause <u>deceit to prosper</u> through <u>his cunning</u> and by <u>his influence</u>, and in his own mind he will make himself great. He will destroy many <u>in a time of peace</u>; he will even stand against <u>the Prince of princes.</u> (Rev. 1:5) <u>Yet he will be shattered—not by human hands</u>.**

Antiochus IV did not fulfill all of these verses. "Near the end of *their kingdoms*" refers to *our* future. There were four divisions after Alexander the Great. These kingdoms today are Greece, Turkey, Syria/Babylon, and Egypt. Antiochus was defeated by human hands. He is a type of the Antichrist. It happens "when the rebels have reached the full measure of their sin." So these verses speak of the *type* Antiochus IV and the antitype, the Antichrist who will be destroyed by Christ Jesus and "not human hands." The

---

[497] Louis T. Talbot, *The Prophecies of Daniel*, p. 143; William Kelly, *Lectures on the Book of Daniel*, p. 132; Nathaniel West, *Daniel's Great Prophecy*, p. 103; Seiss, p. 221; Pentecost, *"Daniel,"* pp. 1359; idem, *Prophecy for Today*, pp. 82-83; idem, *Things to Come*, pp. 332-34; *The New Scofield ...*, p. 911; Campbell, p. 97.
[498] Walvoord, *Daniel ...*, pp. 196-200; Archer, *"Daniel,"* pp. 104-105.
[58] Constable, T. (2003). *Tom Constable's Expository Notes on the Bible* (Da 8:19). Galaxie Software.

KJV reads: "a king of fierce countenance," or a king of "strong or vehement presence or face."

What we learn about the Antichrist from these verses:

1. Near the end of their kingdoms, when their rebellious *expansion* has reached full measure, (Greece, Turkey, Syria/Babylon, and Egypt) *an insolent king* will come to the throne. These kingdoms exist today. Could this rebellion refer to Islam? Antiochus IV came through and ruled the Syrian quarter, which covered Iraq, Syria, and Palestine.

   While Finis Dake believed that the first part of Chapter 8 was referring to Alexander the Great and the four Greek divisions in the vision, he states in his Annotated Bible notes that the little horn only refers to the Antichrist.

   "In the latter time of their kingdom" reveals the time of the coming of Antichrist and the complete fulfillment of the prophecy. These kingdoms will not cease to exist before the little horn or the Antichrist comes from one of them (Dan. 8:23; note, Dan. 8:9; note, Dan. 7:24; 9:26-27; 11:36-45). Since they are all still in existence, and since the Antichrist has not yet come, his coming from one of them must be future."[59]

---

[59] Finis Jennings Dake, <u>Dake's Annotated Reference Bible</u>: Containing the Old and New Testaments of the Authorized or King James Version Text, (Lawrenceville, GA: Dake Bible Sales, Inc., 1997), WORDsearch CROSS e-book, Under: "Chapter 8."

Dake taught that he would come from one of the four breakdowns of the Grecian Empire that later became the Roman. Seleucus took all the eastern parts of the Grecian empire, including Israel, Syria and Babylon, or the modern states of Syria, Lebanon, Iraq, and Iran. Antiochus IV ruled the Seleucid Empire from 175 to 164 BC.[60] Rome later ruled all of this, except the farthest eastern part.

2. An insolent king in presence- fierce, mighty, strong and harsh.

3. He will be skilled in dark trickery, craftiness, puzzles and dark sayings- perhaps sciences.

4. His strength will be awesome bone breaking power, but it is not from his own power.

5. He succeeds in terrible corruption and destruction. AMP- "He shall corrupt and destroy astonishingly."

6. He will prosper in whatever he does.

7. He will destroy powerful nations and also the holy people Israel.

8. He will cause deceit to prosper by his knowledge and way of influence.

9. He will make himself great in his mind.

10. He will destroy many in a time that is peaceful.

11. He will stand against the Prince of princes (Jesus).

---

[60] Ibid

12. He will be shattered not by human hands.

It is possible that this vision is pointing to the fact that the Antichrist would arise from the Syrian/Babylonian quarter of what was then previously ruled by the Grecian Empire.

Daniel 9- The coming prince- A Covenant maker with many, sacrifice stopper-

All three visions of Daniel 7-9 were seen by Daniel before the events of Daniel 6, of him being thrown into the Lion's den. Now we move forward again for more about the fourth beast. At first, these verses in Daniel 9 speak of the Roman prince Titus (the siege of Jerusalem- 67-70 A.D.), from Daniel's future fourth kingdom to come, but all this prophecy was not completely fulfilled in him. Titus was a prince of Rome, and his father had quickly been made the Emperor, so Titus was tasked with dealing with Israel. Although some today try to twist these verses, Titus never made a "covenant" with anybody for seven days or seven years. So the "he" referred to in Verse 27 is a future "he." Jesus, hundreds of years later, speaks of this particular verse and says that its fulfillment is the "time of the end." Notice both Jesus and the Antichrist are called "prince" and "king" in Daniel.

Daniel 9:25-27 (HCSB)
²⁵ Know and understand this: From the issuing of the decree to restore and rebuild Jerusalem until Messiah <u>the Prince</u> will be <u>seven weeks and 62 weeks</u> (LB- 483 yrs.). It will be rebuilt with a plaza and a moat, but in difficult times.

²⁶ After those 62 weeks the Messiah will be cut off (33AD) and will have nothing. The <u>people</u> of the coming prince (LB- the coming prince is the future Antichrist, but his "people" here are the

111

Roman people) **will destroy the city and the sanctuary** (LB-70 AD). **The end will come with a flood, and until the end there will be war; desolations are decreed.** (LB- Israel was no longer a nation in 136 BC after 3 wars)

[27] **He** (LB- the coming prince) **will make a firm covenant with many for one week** (LB- the final week), **but in the middle of the week he will put a stop to sacrifice and offering. And the abomination of desolation will be on a wing of the temple until the decreed destruction is poured out on the desolator."** (LB- Verse 27 has never been fulfilled).

Daniel's Prophetic Weeks

Chart by Larry Booth

The Command To Restore   **70 Weeks- 490 years to finish the transgression**

1948- Jews return to Israel

7 Weeks	62 Weeks	Church Age	The Final Week
(49 Years)	(434 Years)	Pause in Daniel's	(3 ½ Years- 3 ½ Years) Daniel 9:27
Daniel 9:25	Daniel 9:25	timeline	The Tribulation

Israel ceases After 3 wars- 136 AD

Treaty- Abomination- 1260 Days of Desolation

The Decree of Artaxerxes Nehemiah Ch. 2

The Messiah cut off Daniel 9:26

The Catching away 1 Thess. 4:16-17 Romans 11:25

Jesus Returns Rev. 19:11-21

This must be about the Antichrist: Antiochus *nor* Titus did these last things. Jesus is called the Messiah Prince here during His first visit. But He will return as King. The people of the coming prince who came and destroyed the second temple, were Titus and the Romans in 70 AD. The "he" referred to here is the future Antichrist (the use of "prince" may be in the context), for Titus was a prince, but he never made a covenant for seven years nor did he accomplish the abomination in the temple. If anything, his goal was to preserve it. Preterists (those who try to say all was fulfilled in the past) try to say all this happened in 70 AD with Titus and do away with all the last future events to come. The Antichrist will surely fulfill the last part.

Verse 27 states that in the middle of the last week of seven years, the Antichrist will go into the Jewish Temple and desecrate it. This is the abomination that Jesus also spoke of as happening in the future. Of course, this means that the Temple will be rebuilt one day. I am told that they are ready to do this in Israel today.

What we learn about the Antichrist in these verses:

1. The "he," the "prince that shall come" here may have a possible connection to the Roman Empire or Titus himself (with the union of 10- The revised Roman Empire).

2. 69 weeks finished *before* Jesus died. There now is a great gap of time since then. This time marks the church age. Titus came 35 years later, not immediately or even 7 years later. The "end" for the nation of Israel came another 66 years later. Even now, the last seven years have *not been* fulfilled.

3. A covenant will be agreed upon with many for seven years, the last "week" (7 years) of Daniel. He will come at first with a false peace while nations submit to him. Rev. 6:1-2.

4. In the middle of the 7 years, he will put a stop to sacrifice and offering. After Titus and 70 AD, John, in the book of Revelation at 95AD, was still prophesying about a future "beast" the Antichrist. So this last person in Daniel was not referring to Titus.

5. He will cause the abomination that makes desolate in the temple until he is destroyed.

6. What Antiochus IV Epiphanes did in 168 B.C. (before Christ) was an abomination, but Jesus said Daniel's prophecy is a future event (Matthew 24:14-16).

7. What Titus did in 70 A.D. (35 years after Jesus), was not the "abomination of desolation." He did not fulfill this literal last week of Daniel. The Antichrist will do this.

These verses are not a past-tense historical fact fulfilled by Antiochus or Titus. Did Antiochus IV ever make a "covenant" with Israel for seven years? No. However, wicked Jews during that time tried to do so with their neighboring countries. But the "prince" did not.

1 Maccabees 1:10-12 (KJVApocrypha)

[10] And there came out of them a wicked root Antiochus surnamed Epiphanes, son of Antiochus the king, who had been an <u>hostage at Rome,</u> and he reigned in the hundred and thirty and seventh year of the kingdom of the Greeks. [11] In those days went there out of Israel <u>wicked men, who persuaded many, saying, Let us go and make a covenant with the heathen that are round about us:</u> for since we departed from them we have had much sorrow. [12] So this device pleased them well.

This *does not* fulfill Verse 37, remember even Jesus made this clear by stating that Daniel's prophecy was in *His* future around the date 33 A.D.

Matthew 24:14-16 (KJV)
¹⁴ **And this gospel of the kingdom shall be preached in all the world for a witness unto all nations; and then shall <u>the end come.</u>**
¹⁵ **When ye therefore <u>shall see the abomination of desolation,</u> spoken of by Daniel the prophet, stand in the holy place, (whoso readeth, let him understand:)**
¹⁶ **Then let <u>them which be in Judaea</u> flee into the mountains:**

Jesus said this event was in the future of his time, not the past. Some say that the Roman Titus, who was still in the future of Jesus, fulfilled these verses. But Titus did not fulfill this prediction, for he never made a covenant with Israel. But the future Antichrist will. The Antichrist with the ten nations will one day make a covenant with many, including Israel. This will happen at the beginning of the Tribulation period. This 10 king revised Roman Empire is called the *seventh* kingdom in the book of Revelation.

Daniel 11- The "King of the North"- Selfish and self-exalting- More about him in Daniel 11

Remember, this is a future prophecy given to Daniel that was fulfilled beyond Daniel's lifetime, about the future of the world. **Daniel 11:2-35** is about the Grecian Empire (800 BC-146 BC) which would come after the Persian Empire (559 BC-331 BC), when Daniel lived (Approximately 620-538 BC), and includes Alexander the Great (356-323 BC) and what occurred after him with great details.

This first part foretells and includes the Grecian Empire being split into four sections at Alexander's death and how one part (the Seleucid) became the dominant one. Years later, it was ruled by a man we know by our history books as

Antiochus IV (he reigned 175-164 BC), and we remember what horrible things he did. Daniel was told all of this hundreds of years before it happened.

The last part: **Daniel 11:36-45** is about the future Antichrist stemming from this empire. More details will come about this later, but let's look at this chapter first in context. Verse 35 begins the "time of the end," as we will see later.

Daniel 11:35 (HCSB)
[35] Some of the wise will fall so that they may be refined, purified, and cleansed until <u>the time of the end</u>, for it will still come at the appointed time.

> ### Bust of Alexander the Great
> Curtesy British Museum

First, we see mentioned again in Daniel 11 the third empire spoken of before to Daniel, and some details of what would come including its leader, Alexander the Great.

Daniel 11:3 (HCSB)
[3] Then <u>a warrior king will arise</u>; he will rule a vast realm and do whatever he wants.

At the beginning of Chapter 11, the third empire (Grecian) is mentioned again to Daniel and is brought back up. Remember all of this part is future events for Daniel, who received this around 539 BC. The future Greek Emperor, Alexander the Great, is spoken of as *the warrior king*, and then, after he died unexpectedly in Babylon and his sons died, the four separate smaller divisions followed. The period from Alexander to the conquest of these four kingdoms by the Romans (336-100 B.C.) is called the Hellenistic or Alexandrian Age.

Each of Alexander's generals took one piece.

Antipater	Macedon-Greece
Lysimachus	Thrace-Asia Minor
Seleucus	Asia
Ptolemy	Egypt, Cyrenaica, and Palestine

The Greek *Seleucid* Empire becomes the greatest of these four separated smaller divisions after the split. The following verses tell the saga of that empire and the Egyptian/Ptolemaic. **Verses 4-20** tell the detailed history of the kings of the North (Seleucid) and the kings of the South (Egyptian- Ptolemy) up to Antiochus IV. See Tom Constable's Commentary for a great historical breakdown of these verses. Eventually Palestine belonged to the Seleucid Empire.

Next, Daniel 11, **verses 21-34**, foretells the coming of the *eighth* Seleucid ruler Antiochus IV, called Epiphanes.

Daniel 11:21 (KJV)
[21] **And in his estate shall stand up a vile person, to whom they shall not give the honour of the kingdom: but he shall come in peaceably, and obtain the kingdom by flatteries.**

A prophecy of future events for Daniel of a "little horn" who would devastate Israel and the Temple worship- Antiochus IV, some 400 years later. It would take three years after his death to restore the Temple and rededicate the altar, which is still celebrated today as *Hanukah*.

Bust of Antiochus IV-

This next verse is about Antiochus IV (215-164 BC) and happened on December 6th 168 BC. Keep in mind that this is NOT the same desolation as Daniel 9:27 depicts.

Daniel 11:31 (KJV)
[31] **And <u>arms shall stand on his part</u>, and <u>they shall pollute</u> the sanctuary of strength, and shall take away the daily *sacrifice*, and <u>they shall place</u> the abomination that maketh desolate.**

Antiochus is a "type" of the future Antichrist. So some of these verses here loosely apply to the future Antichrist. This man, because of many circumstances, rose to be the king of this empire. He was very eccentric and was considered a bit demented. Antiochus IV did rage against the Jews just like the future antichrist will do, but not as badly.

"However, Antiochus also tried to interact with common people, by appearing in the public bath houses and applying for municipal offices, and his often eccentric behavior and capricious actions led some of his contemporaries to call him *Epimanes* ("The Mad One"), a word play on his title *Epiphanes*."[61] Epiphanes means "god manifest."

According to 2 Maccabees, this strange thing happened in the skies above Jerusalem for 40 days. There will be a future war in the heavenlies just after the Rapture of the Church and just before the future Antichrist takes over, as found in Revelation 12. But these events were said to have happened during the time of turmoil over Jerusalem with Antiochus IV. We look at the historical book of Maccabees for this history.

2 Maccabees 5:1-4 (KJV Apocrypha)
1 About the same time Antiochus prepared his second voyage into Egypt:
2 And then it happened, that through all the city, for the space almost of forty days, there were seen <u>horsemen running in the air, in cloth of gold, and armed with lances, like a band of</u>

---

[61] https://military-history.fandom.com/wiki/Antiochus_IV_Epiphanes

soldiers,
<u>soldiers,</u>
³ And troops of horsemen in array, encountering
and running one against another, with shaking of
shields, and multitude of pikes, and drawing of
swords, and casting of darts, and glittering of
golden ornaments, and harness of all sorts.
⁴ Wherefore every man prayed that that
apparition might turn to good.

Jewish history speaks of the horrible things that
Antiochus did: partially because of a supposed uprising by
the Jewish leader Jason, who thought that Antiochus was
dead because of a rumor, Antiochus rushed to Israel and
took vengeance on Israel. They had not revolted. But
Antiochus believed that they had.

"When these happenings were reported to the
king, he thought that Judea was in revolt. <u>Raging
like a wild animal</u>, he set out from Egypt (***LB***- *his
second attempt to finish conquering Egypt, then foiled by
Rome*) and <u>took Jerusalem by storm</u>. He ordered
his soldiers to cut down without mercy those
whom they met and to slay those who took refuge
in their houses. There was a massacre of young
and old, a killing of women and children, a
slaughter of virgins and infants. In the space of
three days, <u>eighty thousand were lost, forty
thousand meeting a violent death, and the same
number being sold into slavery</u>."-- *2 Maccabees
5:11–14*

"Antiochus decided to side with the <u>Hellenized
Jews</u> in order to consolidate his empire and to
strengthen his hold over the region. He outlawed
<u>Jewish religious rites and traditions</u> kept by

observant Jews and ordered the worship of <u>Zeus</u> as the supreme god (2 Maccabees 6:1–12). This was anathema to the Jews and they refused, <u>so Antiochus sent an army</u> to enforce his decree. The city of Jerusalem was destroyed because of the resistance, many were slaughtered, and Antiochus established a military Greek <u>citadel</u> called the <u>Acra</u>."[62]

2 Maccabees 6:1-2 (KJVApocrypha)

[1] Not long after <u>this the king sent an old man of Athens</u> to compel the Jews to depart from the laws of their fathers, and not to live after the laws of God:
[2] And to pollute also the temple in Jerusalem, and to call it <u>the temple of Jupiter Olympius</u>; and that in Garizim, of Jupiter the Defender of strangers, as they did desire that dwelt in the place.

Tom Constable's Notes on the Bible-

"11:31 Antiochus ordered his general, Apollonius, and a contingent of 22,000 soldiers into Jerusalem on what he claimed was a peaceful mission. However when they were inside the city, they attacked the Jews on a sabbath, when the Jews were reluctant to exert themselves. Apollonius killed many Jews, took many Jewish women and children captive as slaves, plundered the temple, and burned the city. Antiochus' objective was to exterminate Judaism and to Hellenize the Jews. Consequently he forbade them to follow the Mosaic Law and did away with

---

the Jewish sacrifices, festivals, and circumcision (1 Macc. 1:44-54). He even burned copies of their law. As a culminating measure, he installed <u>an image of Zeus, his Greek god</u>, in the temple <u>and erected an altar to Zeus</u> on the altar of burnt offerings (cf. 2 Macc. 6:2).

Then he sacrificed a pig, an unclean animal to the Jews, on it. This happened on December 16, 168 B.C. The Jews referred to this act as "the abomination that caused desolation" (cf. 12:11) since it polluted their altar and made sacrifices to Yahweh on it impossible (cf. 8:23-25). Antiochus further ordered his Jewish subjects to celebrate his subsequent birthdays by offering a pig to Zeus on this altar."[63]

Bible History.com-

"Antiochus IV (175-164 BC), was the 8th ruler of the Seleucid empire. He gave himself the surname "Epiphanes" which means "the visible god" (that he and Jupiter were identical). He acted as though he really were Jupiter and <u>the people called him "Epimanes" meaning "the madman."</u> He was violently bitter against the Jews, and was determined to exterminate them and their religion. <u>He devastated Jerusalem in 168 BC, defiled the Temple, offered a pig on its altar</u>, erected an altar to Jupiter, prohibited Temple worship, forbade circumcision on pain of death, sold thousands of Jewish families into slavery,

---

[63] [63]Constable, T. (2003). *Tom Constable's Expository Notes on the Bible* (Dan. 11:31). Galaxie Software.

destroyed all copies of Scripture that could be found, and slaughtered everyone discovered in possession of such copies, and resorted to every conceivable torture to force Jews to renounce their religion. This led to the Maccabaean revolt, one of the most heroic feats in history. The Antiochus bust discovery is important in the study of Biblical archaeology, it reveals an image of the man who was mentioned in the Book of Daniel."[64]

Daniel 11:32 (KJV)
[32] And such as do wickedly against the covenant shall <u>he corrupt by flatteries</u>: but the people that do know their God shall be strong, and do *exploits*.

Greek and Roman:

He corrupted those in Israel with "flatteries." Read more about Antiochus in these verses. Remember, he was Syrian (Greek) and raised Roman as a boy, so he had both cultures. Likewise, the Antichrist will possibly be too, because it seems Antiochus is a "type" or shadow of the Antichrist.

Finally, Daniel's account of the Antichrist comes later in **Daniel 11:35-45.** Keep in mind that these later verses were not fulfilled by Antiochus IV.

"A few scholars, liberal and conservative, believe that Antiochus Epiphanes fulfilled some of these predictions, especially those

---

[64] https://www.bible-history.com/archaeology/greece/2-antiochus-iv-bust-bb.html

in verses 36-39. However, I am not aware of anyone who believes that he fulfilled them all literally."— Tom Constable's Notes on the Bible

Daniel 11:35 (HCSB)
³⁵ Some of the wise will fall so that they may be refined, purified, and cleansed <u>until the time of the end</u>, for it will still come <u>at the appointed time</u>.

Several times in history, the Jewish Temple has been defiled. Keep in mind that General Pompey entered Jerusalem in 63 BC and entered the Holy of Holies also defiling it. Titus destroyed it in AD 70. Finally, in the year 132, the emperor Hadrian, installed two statutes to Jupiter Capitolinus and himself, on the very spot where the temple of God before stood, and banished the remnant of Jews from Jerusalem and its neighborhood. These still do not fulfill the future prophecies of the temple's abomination by the Antichrist.

Warren Baker- The Complete Word Study Old Testament:

"11:36 There is a gap here in the prophetic revelation, as in Chapter eight, which moves from the type (Antiochus IV) to the antitype (the Antichrist). The shift is made obvious by the fact that Antiochus was one of the "kings of the North" (a Seleucid), while the Antichrist is attacked by the kings of the North and the South (Dan. 11:40). Furthermore, his voicing of blasphemies against God is also a characteristic of the Antichrist (Dan. 11:36, cf. 7:8, 20, 25). Finally, Daniel 12:1 (which continues the narrative from chap. 11) identifies <u>the time of his activity as the</u>

<u>"time of distress" known as the Great Tribulation</u> (cf. Isa. 26:20; Jer. 30:7; Matt. 24:21; Mark 13:19)."[65]

While the previous verses describe a type of the antichrist by using a historic figure as an example, the next verses are *actually* about the Antichrist. Warren Baker gives three reasons:

a. Antiochus IV was the king of the North, but the Antichrist at some time will be attacked by the kings of the North and South.
b. The statements here of how this person speaks against God Himself, does not sound like Antiochus IV.
c. Daniel 12:1 says clearly this time period is the very last days.

Verse 35 is clearly the transition to the end times in this chapter and to the Antichrist. This king shall do according to his will:

Now let's look onward to the future- The time of the end:

The selfish King

Verse 36 puts these verses further into the future, to the time of indignation and tribulation when Israel would be refined all the way till the end. Because Chapter 11 finalizes

---

[65] Warren Baker, ed., *The Complete Word Study Old Testament*, (Chattanooga, TN: AMG, 1994), WORD*search* CROSS e-book, Under: "Chapter 11."

with Antiochus IV and ends with the Antichrist, we must understand that these two must have some connection. This is probably the *area* where they both rule, and the similarities of their *personalities* in how they attack God's people.

Daniel 11:35-45 (KJV)
[35] And *some* of them of understanding shall fall, to try them, and to purge, and to make *them* white, *even* to the time of the end: because *it is* yet for a time appointed.
[36] And the king shall do according to his will; and he shall exalt himself, and magnify himself above every god, and shall speak marvellous things against the God of gods, and shall prosper till the indignation be accomplished: for that that is determined shall be done.
[37] Neither shall he regard the God of his fathers, nor the desire of women, nor regard any god: for he shall magnify himself above all.
[38] But in his estate shall he honour the God of forces: and a god whom his fathers knew not shall he honour with gold, and silver, and with precious stones, and pleasant things.
[39] Thus shall he do in the most strong holds with a strange god, whom he shall acknowledge *and* increase with glory: and he shall cause them to rule over many, and shall divide the land for gain.
[40] And at the time of the end shall the king of the south push at him: and the king of the north shall come against him like a whirlwind, with chariots, and with horsemen, and with many ships; and he shall enter into the countries, and shall overflow and pass over.
[41] He shall enter also into the glorious land, and many *countries* shall be overthrown: but these shall escape out of his hand, *even* Edom, and Moab, and the chief of the children of Ammon. (LB- Mostly Jordan today and part Arabia. The Greek and Roman Empires did rule Jordan.)
[42] He shall stretch forth his hand also upon the countries: and the land of Egypt shall not escape.
[43] But he shall have power over the treasures of gold and of silver, and over all the precious things of Egypt: and the Libyans and the Ethiopians *shall be* at his steps.

> **⁴⁴ But <u>tidings out of the east and out of the north shall trouble him</u>: therefore he shall go forth with great <u>fury to destroy</u>, and utterly to make away many.**
> **⁴⁵ And <u>he shall plant the tabernacles of his palace between the seas in the glorious holy mountain</u>; yet he shall come to his end, and none shall help him.**

The king of the south here is Egypt, and the king of the north is the Antichrist, and he rules from Iraq, Syria, or Turkey. Or, perhaps, all three.

Dake: "Notes For Verse 45

> **a [he shall plant the tabernacles of his palace between the seas in the glorious holy mountain]** The Antichrist, or king of the north (Syria), will make his capital the Jewish temple in Jerusalem between the Dead Sea and the Mediterranean Sea in the glorious holy mountain, Mount Moriah; yet he shall come to an end at Armageddon (Dan. 7:11,26-27; 8:25; 9:27; 2Th. 2:8; Rev. 19:19-21).

> **b [his end]** His end will be the lake of fire (Dan. 7:11; Isa. 11:4; Rev. 19:20; 20:10).

> **c [none shall help him]** His army will be destroyed except a sixth part (Ezek. 39:2). His supernatural backers (Satan, angels, and demons) will be cast into the bottomless pit (Rev. 20:1-3; Isa. 24:21-22), and he will be left alone to die as all men must do (Rev. 19:20)."[66]

What we learn about the last Syrian king (the king of the North) from these verses:

---

[66] Finis Jennings Dake, Dake's Annotated Reference Bible: Containing the Old and New Testaments of the Authorized or King James Version Text, (Lawrenceville, GA: Dake Bible Sales, Inc., 1997), WORDsearch CROSS e-book, Under: "Chapter 11."

1. The time of the end, an appointed time, is coming. But also it relates to this period of time.

2. God's people will also fall, be tried, and purified all the way up to the time of the end (70th week of years).

3. It appears by association that the Antichrist will be another Seleucid/Syrian (or possibly a Grecian- from the original territories of the old ¼ Grecian Empire- a king who rules over this same area of Iraq or Babylon). First, we connect him to the Roman union of 10 nations. Now specifically, we see a connection with Antiochus' Seleucid Empire.

   Biblehistory.com: "At the height of its power after the conquest of the entire Persian Empire, the empire encompassed millions of square miles spanning three continents: Asia, Africa and Europe. At its greatest extent, the Greek empire included the entire ruins of the Persian Empire: modern territories of Iran, Turkey, parts of Central Asia, Pakistan, Thrace and Macedonia, much of the Black Sea coastal regions, Afghanistan, Iraq, northern Saudi Arabia, Jordan, Israel, Lebanon, Syria, and all significant population centers of ancient Egypt as far west as Libya."[67]

   Map from Wikimedia[68]

---

[67] https://www.b -empire.html
[68] https://upload.wikimedia.org/wikipedia/commons/7/7d/Seleucid_Empire_323_-_60_%28BC%29.GIF

The Seleucid Empire (323-60 BC) was one division of the Greek Empire that became the countries of eastern Turkey, Syria, Iraq, Iran, Jordan, and Israel. The rulers were Greek.

4. This king (the Antichrist) will do according to his will-whatever he wants to do- The opposite of that was the Seleucid king Antiochus IV, who was turned back from Egypt by Rome. The Roman Ambassador Popillias drew a circle in the sand around him and made him decide before he left the circle. He was forced to do something he obviously didn't want to do. So these verses are not about Antiochus IV.

5. Vs. 37- "He shall exalt himself and magnify himself above every god"- While Antiochus did stop official worship in Israel, he did not necessarily do this

verse. He acted like he was Zeus/Jupiter in the flesh thus, the second name "Epiphanes," which meant "manifest god." However, he honored other gods.

According to Encyclopedia Britannica online, Antiochus erected a statue in the Temple of Zeus Olympios, and "sacrifices were to be made at the feet of an idol in the image of the king."[69] Zeus was the god figure of his fathers, and by all accounts, Antiochus IV was trying to establish Greek culture in his territories, which included Israel. He forced this in other places too.

2 Maccabees 5:16 (KJV Apocrypha)

[16] And taking the holy vessels with polluted hands, and with profane hands pulling down the things that were dedicated by other kings to the augmentation and glory and honour of the place, he gave them away.

2 Maccabees 6:1-2 (KJV Apocrypha)

[1] Not long after this the king sent an old man of Athens to compel the Jews to depart from the laws of their fathers, and not to live after the laws of God:
[2] And to pollute also the temple in Jerusalem, and to call it the temple of Jupiter Olympius; and that in Garizim, of Jupiter the Defender of strangers, as they did desire that dwelt in the place.

---

[69] https://www.britannica.com/biography/Antiochus-IV-Epiphanes

According to 2 Maccabees, Antiochus, in his anger, came and killed many. He desecrated the Temple first, and then later gave governors instruction to wipe out Judaism. The Sabbath massacre happened later under a smaller garrison who pretended to come in peace. They called the Temple, the "temple of Jupiter" after the Roman god. Zeus and Jupiter were essentially the same god figure but one was Grecian and the other Roman.

Also according to a popular preterist site, these verses were about Titus in AD 70.[70] However, Titus did not fulfill these verses either. These verses describe neither Antiochus nor Titus but a future king- the Antichrist.

6. He will say outrages things against the God of gods.

7. He will prosper until the indignation (Tribulation) be fulfilled (70th week of years).

8. Neither will he regard or "understand" the "gods" or "god" of his fathers or ancestors (Greek or Roman, Christian, Islam, Hindu?). "This king will abandon the religion in his past, whatever that religion may be."- Constable

9. He will not desire the delight of women, or the god that women desire after- (this according to Dake's comments and the HCSB). NRSV reads: "to the one (LB- god) beloved by women." If connected to the previous statement then these versions would be correct. However, in the Hebrew it simply says: "or a woman's pleasant desire, or passion." Some

---

teach that this means he will be gay or homosexual, while this may possibly be true, we know he will have offspring according to Isaiah 14:21.

10. He will not regard or understand any god including God Himself because he magnifies himself above all of them.

Key | 11. Instead, in his "office or stand," he will glorify or *honor* the "god of forces or fortresses" (towers-possibly Ashtoreth) *with* gold, silver, precious stones, and riches. Because of the previous statements, this "god" would not be necessarily a god of his fathers. Maybe this means he will put his wealth into military might. See the article below for another plausible explanation.

> "I believe the intent of the verse is meant to convey that this god was **"THE"** god worshipped time and time again, not "a" god, which would, perhaps, infer one of many. "The god of fortresses," as used, an idol (#433, #410); the Israelites knew of her well, as did most of the pagan world. The following are some excerpts from an article by Mr. Stearman (Prophecy In The News), to whom I owe a debt of gratitude.
>
> "Ishtar, Goddess of the Tower, the goddess, or "Mother of Harlots," as she is called in Revelation 17:5, is found throughout Scripture. She is the Canaanite Ashtoreth, the "Queen of Heaven" in Jeremiah 7:18, and the Diana of the Ephesians" of Acts 19:28. Though her identity changes, her purpose never does. She is the great "virgin queen" who gives birth to an immortal redeemer. In short, she is Satan's counterfeit of the Bible's redemption story.
>
> The Babylonian Semiramis, under the name of Astarte, was known as "the tower goddess." Alexander Hislop, writing in "The Two Babylons," notes, "Now, no name

Babylon's
Queen

132

could more exactly picture forth the character of Semiramis, as the queen of Babylon, than the name of "Asht-tart," for that just means 'The woman that made towers.' Thus, in the Hebrew, this is the meaning of the goddess Ashtoreth.

Elsewhere, commenting on the Greek (where "tart" becomes "turis") he adds, "Turis is just the Greek form of Turit, the final t, according to the genius of the Greek language, being converted into s. Ash-turit, then, which is obviously the same as the Hebrew 'Ashtoreth,' is just 'The woman that made the 'encompassing wall'.'"

She was the ancient goddess of "towers" or "surrounding fortifications." Mr. Hislop cites instances from ancient Greek history in which citizens appealed to the goddess to protect their city when it was under threat. It is especially interesting that ancient statuettes of the goddess were cast with the figure of a tower upon their heads. They were tower goddesses or goddesses of the fortress, to whom was attributed the power to protect a city or an empire.
In the Greek, she was known as Artemis, but in reality, was none other than Ashtoreth or Astarte. As recorded in Acts Chapter 19, Paul threatened the livelihood of the guild of silversmiths. They cast souvenir goddesses from silver to be purchased by the faithful who made pilgrimages to her temple. More than that, she was their protector goddess. Paul's gospel preaching threatened to overturn their worship...and their business.

Of great interest is that the ancient goddess from the land of Shinar was considered to be the chief protector (defender) of the empire. The Roman Diana, was considered just as powerful an image as any of her predecessors.
But in the centuries following the death, burial and resurrection of the Lord Jesus Christ, she faded into obscurity, and was considered as good as dead. But today, with the massive New Age resurgence of pagan

superstition, she is springing back to life. Millions are once again calling for the protection of the goddess. It is most interesting then, to observe what may be an obscure reference to the tower-goddess in Daniel 11:38.

This is the well-known prophecy of the antichrist- the willful king who rises out of the memory of Antiochus IV Epiphanes, the infamous model of the antichrist. Daniel's prophecy points to the antichrist's worship: "But in his estate, shall he honour the God of forces: and a god whom his fathers knew not shall he honour with gold, and silver, and with precious stones, and pleasant things."
Here, the antichrist, is shown offering gifts to an image called the "God of forces." Using the original Hebrew text, some Jewish expositors translate this verse, "But he will honor the god of the fortress in his place; and a god whom his ancestors knew not, he will honor with gold, silver, precious stones, and desirable things."

The word "fortress" is from maozim, meaning "fortresses." The same word is used in verse 39: "Thus shall he do in the most strong holds with a strange god, whom he shall acknowledge and increase with glory: and he shall cause them to rule over many, and shall divide the land for gain."
In the Hebrew, this sentence literally begins, "He will develop strong fortresses with a strange god..." Again the word Maozim is used. This is the standard word for "fortress."

Even the Jewish Temple was referred to as a fortress. In Daniel 11:31, we find the phrase, "the sanctuary of strength," that used the same Hebrew word (maoz, in the singular) to imply that the Temple is an impregnable stronghold.

The point is clear. The antichrist's god will be the god of the fortress. Throughout history, the leading example of the fortress god is none other than

Ishtar/Ashtoreth/Astarte, also known in certain contemporary circles as "Ashtar."[71]

Ashtoreth, or Asherah, was the mother goddess, the goddess of towers or protection, war, and increase in Scripture. Some say the fertility goddess. Many cultures call her by different names. In many instances, she is the wife of another head false deity like Baal.

In addition, she is also known by the following names: • Astarte -- the mother and creator of mankind • Dido and Tanith -- African goddess of fertility • Diana -- Prostitute goddess of Ephesus • Aphrodite -- Goddess of the Greeks • Venus -- Goddess of love • Rhea -- Olympian mother of the gods • Isi -- Goddess of fertility • Egyptian Isis -- Goddess of fertility – Freemason linkage • Shing Mao -- Mother of China • Irene -- Goddess of peace • Holy mother of God -- • Madonna -- Arts • Queen of Heaven • Moon goddess.

See an important article in the Jewish Encyclopedia for her many names-[72]

Judges 10:6 (KJV)
[6] And the children of Israel did evil again in the sight of the LORD, and served Baalim, and Ashtaroth, and the gods of Syria, and the gods of Zidon, and the gods of Moab, and the gods of the children of Ammon, and the gods of the Philistines, and forsook the LORD, and served not him.

It seems this old Semitic "mother" goddess was worshiped by many different names in many countries.

---

[71] Article: "The True God Of Catholicism: The God Of Fortresses"
http://www.deceptioninthechurch.com/3-5.htm
[72] https://www.jewishencyclopedia.com/articles/2005-ashtoreth

This form of worship was linked to fertility, fortune, and all kinds of sexual immorality, including prostitution and child sacrifice. In Babylon, it is said that every woman had to offer herself at least once in her temple. According to 1 Kings 11:5, she was one of the gods that Solomon went after. She became the goddess of love and war.

So, in Daniel, this reference could mean that the Antichrist would promote the glorification of a false god, which previously in Biblical times was worshiped, or he would promote what that *god* represented, which is: fortune, force, and protection by supernatural might, sexual immorality in many forms, and child sacrifice.

This "goddess" pops up everywhere, from all the way back to Babel to the present day. I believe she is the common denominator that existed in all of the major world kingdoms in one form or another. Some also go further to say that this entity is the controlling demon and is worshipped by the *harlot* that the Antichrist will join forces with in the Apocalypse- the false one world religion that worships this goddess. They also believe this "harlot" includes a future form of the Roman Catholic Church (whom they believe to be the manifested worship of Ashtoreth- Mary herself in a Christian form).

While in Jerusalem at their *Israeli Museum,* I looked for this idol and found a version of her as the Greek goddess "Tyche" and Roman Fortuna. From the Hellenistic to the Byzantine periods, she was considered the patroness of cities and responsible for their prosperity.

Photo by Larry Booth curtesy Jerusalem Israeli Museum

This stone medallion carving of her was strangely found hanging in a church and was said to be a gift of Flavius, son of Theodorus, in 645. Why wasn't there outrage for this to be in a church?

Brought forward into the book of Revelation, as we will see, this could mean that the Antichrist will use the "one world" religious group that is driven by the worship of Ashtoreth for at least for the first 3 ½ years of the Tribulation period. This could be the foreign god that is mentioned in Daniel that the Antichrist's forsakes his original faith for.

He uses what is powerful and controlling in other nations at that time to gain rule over many. To me, this suggests that the Antichrist originates from an Islamic background

137

but uses false Christianity and other religions to gain control of most of the world. Yes, even after the Rapture of the Church, there will still exist a form of Christianity on earth and the Antichrist will use this to his advantage.

Interesting enough, the Pope announces a One World Religion Headquarters which opened February 16th 2023.

"The announcement of the Abrahamic Family House, on the Saadiyat Island in Abu Dhabi, follows a visit by Pope Francis to the UAE in February, the first by a pope to the Arabian Peninsula. During the trip, the pope signed a joint declaration with the grand imam of al-Azhar, Dr. Ahmed el-Tayeb, that called for religious tolerance and dialogue. An interfaith council to oversee projects advancing tolerance was formed as a result of the declaration, and named the

Higher Committee of Human Fraternity. The Abrahamic Family House is its first initiative."[73]

"With the adoption this week (Sept 14-15th 2022) by the 7th World Religions Congress of the Human Fraternity document created by Pope Francis and Mohamed bin Zayed, Chrislam is now the official One World Religion.

It's official, Chrislam has now been codified and ratified, with the approval at the **7th Congress of Leaders of World and Traditional Religions**, of the Human Fraternity document **created by Pope Francis** of the Vatican, and financed and promoted by **Mohamed bin Zayed** of the UAE. Question – Guess who they forgot to invite to the festivities? Answer – Jesus Christ, His Name appears nowhere and is *never* mentioned. I

---

wonder who the 'honored guest" is then? Hmm."[74]

The concern here would be that the religions of the world have already begun to unite as one to be controlled by the Antichrist in the future.

12. He will do this in the strongest fortresses with a foreign god.

Key

Daniel 11:39 (HCSB)
[39] **He will deal with the strongest fortresses with ⌊the help of⌋ a foreign god. He will greatly honor those who acknowledge him, making them rulers over many and distributing land as a reward.**

One person interpreted this passage this way: "He will develop strong fortresses with a strange god." This may well be the correct translation, but no translation reads this way. The word "deal" and in the KJV "thus shall he do" in the Hebrew is the word *asa,* which has various meanings, many of which include: "made," "wrought," "execute," "prepare," and "perform." The main interpretation should be "to do" or "make." This verse sounds like he will create fortified cities and appoint rulers over them.

This "foreign" god, here, could quite possibly still be *Ashteroth*, who will be used to coerce other cities/countries into falling in line. The Antichrist will reward with land those who follow his command.

---

[74] by Geoffrey Grider-https://www.thethirdheaventraveler.com/2022/09/chrislam-confirmed-led-by-pope-francis.html. Photo also same source.

Some commentaries try to say the last few verses are still about Antiochus IV by mentioning a few things that he did, but still acknowledge that he did not fulfill verses 40-45 at all. If this is even partially true, then these verses are about another person who would fulfill them entirely. These verses must be about the Antichrist. Mancer:

"Antiochus had coins struck describing himself as THEOS EPIPHANES ("God Manifest") (11:36), and set aside the traditional gods, including Apollo and Tammuz (or Adonis, the darling god of women) (11:37), and set up a temple to Jupiter Capitolinus in Antioch (11:38), and acknowledged him as his guardian (11:39). 11:40-45 have given rise to various interpretations. They do not describe what actually happened towards the end of Antiochus' life. There are three main lines of interpretation:

1. Antiochus is a type of Antichrist, and in these verses we jump to an attack on the Holy Land before the final coming of Christ." [75]

I do not believe these verses are about Antiochus IV. Mancer refers to Antiochus erecting a temple to Jupiter Optimus Maximus, also known as the Temple of Jupiter Capitolinus. He also had erected a statue to Zeus, the Greek head god, in Jerusalem. Some say he believed he was the incarnate

---

[75] Martin Manser, *Open Your Bible Commentary: The Old Testament Page by Page, The*, (Bath, UK: Creative 4, 2013), WORD*search* CROSS e-book, 923.

Jupiter/Zeus. Jupiter wasn't ever called the "god of fortresses." Mancer goes on to say that the 2nd line of popular interpretation is that of a *later* history of the end of Syria against Rome, and the third would be that this is a summary of Antiochus' entire life. Neither of these two suggestions hold out for fulfilling these verses. If anything, his history proves that Antiochus did honor the gods of his fathers, unlike what the Antichrist will do.

13. He will honor those who know him and help him, with authority over peoples and gifts of land for a price.

The final campaigns before Armageddon (vs. 40-45)

14. At the time of the end- Egypt (the king of the south) will push against him (the Antichrist is the king of the north-Syrian like Antiochus IV-Syria, Iraq, and Iran) and the Antichrist will come down like a whirlwind with chariots and horsemen and ships and defeat him (v. 40).

One person believes the eighth kingdom is a "Revival of the Grecian Empire:"

"The above quotation refers to the little horn or Antichrist coming out of the 10 horns of Revised Rome, and after them to get power over them in the first half (3 1/2 years) of Daniel's 70th week. He subdues 3 of them (Dan. 7:23, 24). The others submit to him without further struggle (Rev. 17:12-

17). <u>He comes from Syria, one of the 4 divisions of the Grecian Empire</u> (Dan. 8:9, 23; 11:36-45) and overthrows the other 3 divisions -- Greece, Turkey, and Egypt. <u>He thus revives the old Grecian Empire</u>, which is symbolized by a leopard (Dan. 7:6; Rev. 13:1-2). The other 7 kingdoms of the old Roman Empire submit to him, making him their leader in a war with the north and east (Dan. 11:44; Rev. 17:12-17)."[76]

Joel 3:6 (KJV)
6 The children also of Judah and the children of Jerusalem have <u>ye sold unto the Grecians</u>, that ye might remove them far from their border.

15. He will invade countries and sweep through them like a flood (v. 40).

16. He will invade Israel and many will fall- at the 3 ½ year mark he will desecrate Israel and the Temple. Then and later just before Armageddon will he come to attack Jerusalem.

17. Edom, Moab and the prominent ones of Ammon will escape his powerful hand. Modern Jordan and parts of Arabia today (v. 41).

18. He will extend his authority over nations, including Egypt (v. 42).

19. He will control the hidden treasures of Egypt: Silver, gold and all the riches

---

[76] Finis Jennings Dake, *Dake's Annotated Reference Bible: Containing the Old and New Testaments of the Authorized or King James Version Text*, (Lawrenceville, GA: Dake Bible Sales, Inc., 1997), WORD*search* CROSS e-book, Under: "Chapter 11:40"

20. Libya and Ethiopia will submit to him (v. 43). Three subdued in Dan. 7:24?

21. Reports from the east and the north will terrify him and he will go out with great fury to destroy (v. 44).

22. He will move his headquarters to between the Dead Sea and Mount Moriah. This is probably referring to when he comes against Jerusalem the second time, at the very end and rifles Jerusalem (Zech. 14:2). Further proof of the latter would be the next reference that it is there where he will come to an end: in Jerusalem (v. 45).

23. He will meet his end there with no one to help him.

This sculpture was just erected outside the UN building in New York NY USA. In a tweet the UN commented on Nov. 9th 2021:

"A guardian for international peace and security sits on the Visitor's Plaza outside #UN Headquarters. The guardian is a fusion of jaguar and eagle and donated by the Government of Oaxaca, Mexico@MexOnu. It is created by artists Jacobo and Maria Angeles. UN Photo/Manuel Elías"[77]

This is a real statue erected outside the U.N. headquarters in New York City! This secular depiction is very similar to the one in Rev. 13, except that the one in Revelation is represented with seven heads. Does this mean that secretly the U.N. recognizes the kingdom of the beast? Sometimes the truth is right in front of our eyes. Daniel 7:6 says the *leopard* represents the third empire, the Grecian. In the last days, the seventh and eighth empires will include the leopard, lion, bear, and aspects of the dragon. It looks like the artist came close. Perhaps this represents the eighth beast kingdom in its final state. Of all place, this was installed at the United Nations building in New York!

So, this last vision in Daniel 11 once again indicates that the Antichrist originates from the same area that Antiochus IV ruled over. This must mean Iraq or Syria. If this were in our day, it would mean that the Antichrist would come from an Islamic background and probably fulfill the general idea of who they are looking for to arise and put down the rest of the world. This is where Saddam Hussein tried a few years ago to rise up and rebuild the city of Babylon. He spent millions to rebuild Babylon in Iraq, hoping to be the image of Nebuchadnezzar. Stopped in his tracks by the United States and her allies, he was hung to death in his own country. Keep an eye on Iraq for a relatively unknown person to arise there.

It is clear in Daniel that the ten nation coalition has to arrive on the scene first, before the escalation of the

---

[77] https://twitter.com/UN_Photo/status/1458178013082816513

Antichrist. Saddam Hussein could have been a candidate for the Antichrist, but he had it backwards. The future Antichrist will allow them to rise first and then take control.

Chapter 7
Names John Used of Him in the Book of Revelation

Revelation 13- The eighth kingdom. Illustration by Caleb Jasper Lumingkit-©

"No other book in the Bible is so strongly
supported as to its divine inspiration."[78]

John, while exiled on the island of Patmos in AD 95,
wrote what he saw. He was given great visions of the future of
the world. These visions give great details of many things
involved in the last days leading up to and beyond the return
of Jesus Christ on the Day of the Lord. Much like Daniel, we

---

[78] J. B. Smith, *A Revelation of Jesus Christ*, p. 9.

learn so much about the Antichrist here. We also learn much about the kingdom of the beast.

The beast with a blasphemous "mouth"- More about him in Revelation 13

Revelation 13:1-8 (KJV)
[1] And I stood upon the sand of the sea, and saw <u>a beast</u> rise up <u>out of the sea</u>, having <u>seven heads</u> (LB- past kingdoms) **and ten horns** (LB- ten kings), **and upon <u>his horns ten crowns</u>** (LB- now living ruling monarchs), **and upon his heads the name of blasphemy.**
[2] And <u>the beast</u> (LB-the antichrist empire) **which I saw <u>was like unto a leopard</u>, and his feet were as *the feet* of a bear, and <u>his mouth</u> as the mouth of a lion: and <u>the dragon gave him his power</u>, and his seat, and great authority.**
[3] And I saw <u>one of his heads</u> (LB- one of his world kingdoms, not "horn") **as it were wounded to death; and <u>his deadly wound was healed</u>: <u>and all the world wondered</u> after the beast.**
[4] And they worshipped the dragon which gave power unto the beast: and they worshipped <u>the beast</u>, saying, Who *is* like unto the beast? <u>who is able to make war with him</u>?

Here the "beast" is an *antichrist* system of political and religious power, a kingdom that has seven kingdoms in its powerful history and ten kings who give their strength to the Antichrist. But the beast later is also a powerful man- the Antichrist. The dragon mentioned in Chapter 12 is Satan, and his seven kingdom heads have crowns and ten horns that are not crowned. This is a picture before the Antichrist's kingdom blossoms. Here in Chapter 13, we have a group of seven, and a group of ten. The seven heads are seven past kingdoms not crowned because the Antichrist never ruled any of those kingdoms. The ten horns are ten kings over their own territories, who will eventually submit to the Antichrist.

In Revelation 12, we see a different representative picture of Satan's kingdom.

Revelation 12:3 (KJV)
³ **And there appeared another wonder in heaven; and behold a great red dragon, having seven heads and ten horns, and <u>seven crowns</u> upon his heads.**

Why the difference in description? Dake states in his Bible commentary on Rev. 12:3, describing the dragon,

> **"b [having seven heads]** Symbols of the 7 world empires that precede the kingdom of Antichrist, which is the 8th...
>
> **c [ten horns, and seven crowns upon his heads]** <u>His 10 horns are not crowned</u>, while those on the beast are (Rev. 13:1), symbolizing his power over the 10 kingdoms will be given to the beast. His 7 heads are crowned (Rev. 12:3), symbolizing his rule over the 7 kingdoms preceding the Antichrist kingdom. <u>The 7 heads on the beast are not crowned</u> (Rev. 13:1), <u>meaning that the Antichrist has not ruled the 7 kingdoms preceding his</u>, the 8th kingdom (Rev. 17:8-11)." [79]

So the dragon in Rev 12 represents Satan's *first seven world empires* that have come against Israel. The beast of Revelation 13 is the Antichrist's kingdom and himself, in coalition with the ten kings. The difference is that the Antichrist has not ruled over the last seven world empires, but Satan has. This is why their heads are pictured as being crowned with Satan's kingdom, and not the beast's. Now notice that the ten kings are given to be kings, and had no physical kingdom *during John's day*, but will later in time have great power with the Antichrist because of him. This is why they will have crowns with the figure of the beast in the future.

---

[79] Finis Jennings Dake, *Dake's Annotated Reference Bible: Containing the Old and New Testaments of the Authorized or King James Version Text*, (Lawrenceville, GA: Dake Bible Sales, Inc., 1997), WORD*search* CROSS e-book, Under: "Chapter 12".

Revelation 13:1-4 is about <u>the 7th beast empire</u> developing into the eighth

What we learn from Rev. 13:1-4 about the Antichrist and his kingdom:

1. A beast or antichrist world system will come that incorporates 10 horns (kings) with seven heads (kingdoms), and all of the territories they covered. The seventh kingdom (one of the heads) will be greater than all the six before it, but it will cover the same areas and include a time of peace with Israel. (See explanation below in Rev. 17). The ten-king coalition at the beginning of the Tribulation is the seventh kingdom. But this picture really is of the antichrist's eighth kingdom, which is the final one that morphs from the sixth and seventh. This happens after the Tribulation is in full force.

   After reading Daniel, we understand Daniel's visions began with the Babylonian kingdom because that was the kingdom in rule when he lived. So God revealed and Daniel wrote of the four kingdoms: Babylonian, Median/Persian, Grecian, and Roman. All of these kingdoms appeared as predicted and all before Christ appeared on the earth. Daniel also mentioned three others: the future coalition of ten kings, the Antichrist's kingdom, and Christ's kingdom to come. All these make seven.

   Now, in the Apocalypse, we wrap everything up, but in the Apocalypse, John pictures the seven kingdoms before the Antichrist's kingdom comes. His personal kingdom is the eighth, and the Lord's is the ninth.

Daniel 2, 7, 8 and Revelation 13, 17

Daniel's View of 7 kingdoms	John's view of 9 kingdoms
	1. Egyptian
	2. Assyrian
1. **Babylonian-** Golden head/Lion with eagle wings	3. **Babylonian**
2. **Median/Persian-** Chest and arms of silver /Bear raised up on one side with three ribs in his mouth/ Ram with two sized horns	4. **Median/Persian**
3. **Grecian-** Bronze belly and thighs/leopard with four wings and four heads/ Goat with big horn	5. **Grecian**
4. **Roman-** Two iron legs/Nondescript beast with iron teeth, different than the others	6. **Roman**
5. **Ten toes/ten horns-** iron mixed with clay/10 horns-kings comes from the fourth	7. **Ten horns/king group revised Roman**
6. **Little horn-** rises up among the 10 horns	8. **Antichrist revived Grecian/ Babylonian/Assyrian?-** Seven heads, ten horns, like a leopard with bear feet and mouth of a lion
7. **Christ's kingdom**	9. **Christ's kingdom**
	Chart by Larry Booth

The Nine kingdoms that ruled and will rule Israel

One- Egyptian

Two- Assyrian

Three- Babylonian- Daniel's first beast

Four- Median/Persian- Daniel's second

Five- Grecian- Daniel's third

Six- Roman- Daniel's fourth (who was ruling during Jesus
   and John's day)

Seven- Future 10 kings revised Roman

Eight- A future revised Babylonian/Assyrian/Grecian?-
   The kingdom of the Antichrist, whose fifth head is
   brought back to life and joined with the seventh
   (revised Roman kingdom).

Nine- Christ Jesus the Messiah will rule forever.

Including Christ's kingdom, Daniel had only mentioned seven in total. Therefore, we understand that there are two more previous kingdoms that Daniel did not include that existed before the Babylonian: namely, the Egyptian and the Assyrian empires. So this would make nine total. See the chart to match the two prophets' visions together.

Daniel 2 recap

Daniel only described the last four beasts in Chapters 2, 7, and 8, and it was very clear that the fourth one (Roman) would advance through the ages (continue in various forms) and become the last empire that would fight against the Messiah and be defeated on the last day.

2. Daniel's fourth kingdom, the Roman, with the iron legs, was the sixth kingdom in history to have ruled over Israel. It will later morph into the seventh and eighth kingdoms.

In Daniel 2 and 7, the fourth kingdom in *Daniel's* visions is said to change over time and become this last kingdom before Christ's kingdom comes. In Daniel 7, this fourth beast (Roman) has iron teeth and brass nails. This proves that this is not altogether the same beast as in Revelation 13, pictured earlier. The future Antichrist beast in Revelation 13 has changed and become even worse. In Revelation 13, what is pictured would be Daniel's fifth and sixth kingdoms, represented by the *ten-king* coalition and the Antichrist's kingdom. If God had pictured it as a beast for Daniel, this is what it would have looked like. What he did picture was the ten toes at the end of those iron legs, and he described the insolent king.

This is the same as Revelation's seventh and eighth kingdoms, with the 10 crowned kings. This is why in Revelation 13:1-4 there are seven world kingdoms represented, and ten kings.

This is Daniel's explanation of the last part of the fourth kingdom (Revelation's sixth kingdom) that he saw, which again was the Roman kingdom: Both passages are great keys to seeing the other three kingdoms.

Daniel 2:42-44 (HCSB)
[42] and that the toes of the feet were <u>partly iron and partly fired clay</u>—part of the kingdom will be strong, and part will be brittle.
[43] You saw the iron mixed with clay—the peoples will mix with one another but will not hold together, just as iron does not mix with fired clay.
[44] "<u>In the days of those kings, the God of heaven will set up a kingdom</u> that will never be destroyed, and this kingdom will not be left to another people. It will crush all these kingdoms and bring them to an end, but will itself endure forever.

Keys

Daniel 7:24 (KJV)
²⁴ **And the ten horns <u>out of this kingdom</u> *are* ten kings *that* shall arise: <u>and another</u> shall rise after them; and he shall be diverse from the first, and he shall subdue three kings.**

Daniel's Vision of Four Beasts
Daniel 7:4-7

Daniel 7:4	Daniel 7:5	Daniel 7:6	Daniel 7:7
Babylonian Empire	Medo-Persian Empire	Empire of Greece	Roman Empire

Daniel 7 Recap

Perry Stone, in his book *The Eighth Kingdom*, stated that the seventh kingdom of ten kings will be a mixture of iron and clay in the end. He explains that it will consist of parts European and parts Islamic. What we need to understand is that Christ will come and conquer *during the time* of these kings. Of course, this will be at the time that the Antichrist controls and rules them.

3. Daniel 7:44 proves that this kingdom will go into the last day and is marked by the union of the 10

kings. This is when those in the world will know that they have entered this future seventh kingdom. *Ten kings from the original Roman Empire will be united as one.* As the seventh kingdom and union of 10 kings, according to Daniel, the iron and clay do not mix and will not work well together. This union, from its beginning, spans up to the first half of the Tribulation period.

4. In Revelation 13, the last kingdom is pictured like a leopard, with the feet of a bear and a mouth like a lion. See the illustration above. This might allude to a mixture of the strengths of the Roman, Babylonian, Persian, and Grecian empires. His terrible speech links him with Daniel's third kingdom and Antiochus IV. The body of the leopard says this system of the seventh is similar to but different from all the rest. Perhaps a mixture of them.

5. His kingdom is swift, strong, loud, and is likened to a leopard. (Dan. 7:6; the Greek Empire- Dan. 8; The Seleucid quarter).

6. Another horn/king (the Antichrist, the 11th horn) must specifically, at first, rule over three of the other nations- his and three more of the ten he conquers. HE IS THE "MOUTH" OF THIS BEAST.

7. All are united under one "name of blasphemy."

8. His power, reign, and authority come from the dragon himself (Satan).

9. One of the heads was wounded to death. Remember, that these represent kingdoms, not a person. The horns represent people. The angel explains this to John later in Chapter 17.

10. His deadly wound is healed, and all the world marvels (the Babylonian, Assyrian or Greek Empire revived?). This relates specifically to the Antichrist area of rule, which should include all the areas that Greece had ruled in Europe and the Middle East at the time of Antiochus IV.

11. This miracle marks the very beginning of the eighth kingdom when the Antichrist makes his move.

12. This creates or merges into the *eighth* kingdom, the one the Antichrist fully controls in his possessed state. Technically, this is what is pictured in Chapter 13.

13. This causes them to worship Satan and the beast.

14. Saying, "Who is like this beast?"

15. Saying, "Who is able to make war with him?" This would include all nations.

The seventh and eighth kingdoms

G.H. Pember: "All things seem to be prepared for the fulfilment of the solemn prediction in the twelfth Chapter of the Apocalypse, when Michael, leading the van of the host which will come with Christ to take the kingdom, shall drive the rebel High Ones down to earth. And in the following Chapter we see the consequences of that marvellous event: <u>the peoples of Satan's last refuge, of the only remaining portion of his once vast dominions, must be organised for the final struggle.</u> And so, out of the troubled sea of anarchy and perplexity of nations, there arises, in greater majesty and power than it ever before possessed, the resuscitated empire of Rome under the immediate direction and government of the Wicked One."[80]

Let's be clear. The Antichrist will make his rise inside of a group that will look like the old Roman Empire (Daniel 7:24- the seventh kingdom-the revised "Roman"). This group could form very quickly in today's world conditions. There will be ten nations that comprise this group. He will be an *eleventh* person who Daniel calls a king. For sure, he is just a "little horn," or ruler, that will rise up and take over three other territories inside of the seventh kingdom (Dan. 7:8, 20). At some point just before or at the middle point of the Tribulation, his kingdom will expand, causing the others to fully submit to him. Then, they will morph into the eighth and final kingdom. Daniel 7 describes this event.

Revelation 13:4-10 is specifically about a man (the Antichrist) the last 3 ½ years

[4] **And they worshipped the dragon which gave power unto <u>the beast</u>: and they worshipped <u>the beast</u>, saying, Who *is* like unto the beast? <u>who is able to make war with him</u>?**

---

[80] Pember M. A., G. H.. Earth's Earliest Ages and Their Connection with Modern Spiritualism and Theosophy . 1866. Kindle Edition.

⁵ And <u>there was given unto him a mouth</u> speaking great things and blasphemies; and <u>power was given unto him to continue forty *and* two months.</u>
⁶ And he opened his mouth in blasphemy against God, to blaspheme <u>his name</u>, and <u>his tabernacle</u>, and <u>them that dwell in heaven.</u>
⁷ And <u>it was given unto him</u> to make <u>war with the saints</u>, and <u>to overcome them</u>: and power was given him over <u>all kindreds, and tongues, and nations.</u>
⁸ And all that dwell upon the earth shall worship him, whose names are not written in the book of life of the Lamb slain from the foundation of the world.

In this section, we see an individual, not his kingdom. This is clearly the last half of the seven-year period, the last 42 months. This is when the Antichrist rises above all the rest and claims himself to be God. This is when he unleashes his anger against the people of God, Jews, and newly converted Christians alike.

What we learn about the Antichrist from these verses:

1. People will worship the dragon (Satan) and the beast system.

2. "Who is able to make war with *him?*" implies no nation dares to.

3. Now (after 42 months), the beast is given a "mouth"- who is the Antichrist. Now he has the ability to speak powerfully and hypnotically of blasphemous things.

4. Power is given to him by the 10 kings, and then he rises as all powerful with his kingdom the eighth, and to continue 42 months.

5. He speaks against God, His name, His tabernacle, and those raptured and already in heaven.

6. He is given the motivation demonically to "war" against the saints (Israel and the Tribulation saints).

7. To "overcome" the saints.

8. The *legal right to rule* was given to him over all offshoot tribes, peoples, those with different languages, and nationalities (races).

9. *All that dwell on the earth* whose names are not in the book of life, shall worship him.

Will the Antichrist die and then be resurrected?

Revelation 13:3
³ **And I saw <u>one of his heads</u>** (LB. one of his world kingdoms, not "horns.") **as it were wounded to death; and <u>his deadly wound was healed</u>: <u>and all the world wondered</u> after the beast.**

The false prophet rises up out of the earth. He is another of the same kind (Gr. *allo therion*, "one of the same kind"). He performs miracles and has powers in the presence of the Antichrist. He creates an "image" of this fallen beast kingdom (some would say the Antichrist himself) and makes it come alive. Notice that the "image" will come to life, speak, and kill those who do not worship it.

Revelation 13:11-15 (KJV)
¹¹ **And I beheld <u>another beast</u> coming up out of the earth; …**

¹³ And <u>he doeth great wonders,</u> so that <u>he maketh fire come down from heaven on the earth</u> in the sight of men,
¹⁴ And <u>deceiveth them that dwell on the earth</u> by *the means of* those miracles which he had power to do <u>in the sight of the beast</u>; saying to them that dwell on the earth, that they should <u>make an image</u> to the beast, which <u>had the wound by a sword, and did live</u>.
¹⁵ And he had power to give life unto <u>the image</u> of the beast, that <u>the image</u> of the beast should both speak, and cause that as many as would not worship the image of the beast should be killed.

The false prophet tells the worshippers to make an image of the "beast" that had the "wounded head." The "beast" that is described as having been "wounded by a sword" and "his deadly wound was healed" is referring to the beast who had one of its heads die and, in context, is a *kingdom* and not a man.

So, this "image" of the beast that the false prophet brings to life is quite something different. The word "image," which is the Greek word "*eikon*," means "statue or similar representation." If this is an image or statue of the past *kingdom* that comes back to life, then this image could very well be a beast like image like the one that Daniel saw, representing this revived kingdom and not a man. Verse 2 describes this image. This brings to mind the image outside the U.N. building in New York City.

Verse 14 says of the kingdom: He "had the wound by a sword and did live." Could this have a double reference to the *man* Antichrist? Possibly, but not necessarily. Tom Constable and many others seem to think it does.

"The reference to the first beast's fatal wound being healed highlights another counterfeit impersonation, this one of Christ who rose from the dead. Believers worship Christ because He rose from the dead (cf. Acts 17:30–31), and unbelievers will worship the beast because he will have done a similar thing (cf. v. 14). Here some type of personal revivification seems to be in view, <u>not just the revitalization of a nation</u> (cf. v. 3)." [81]

So, if there is a double reference here to the Antichrist being wounded also, it will be a wound that occurs during the Tribulation. He then miraculously "revives" from this wound with a sword. But if this is only speaking of a "kingdom," which is more likely, then there will be one of the great previous empires before John the revelator that was destroyed, and it will spring forth revived as the eighth and final kingdom. The world will marvel at this.

This is not likely to be a *resurrected* Antichrist. One could look at it this way: having a deadly wound does not necessarily mean he is fully "dead." At best, some think it could be a revival of the same *spirit* that possessed many men throughout history, called "the spirit of the Antichrist." Nero was the fifth Roman Emperor and ruled for fourteen years. He was so evil toward Christians that some in history took these verses to mean that he would one day rise again to be the final Antichrist. Keep in mind that he committed suicide long before the Book of Revelation was written in AD 95 and he was not wounded by a sword. Early on, some have tried to teach using this 13th Chapter and Revelation 17:9-11, that the Antichrist will be a resurrected Nero from Hell, back from the first century. This was taught as early as AD 304 by Victorinus and on into the 400s. This is reincarnation, which is unscriptural.

I do believe this: Antiochus IV and Nero were both possessed by the *spirit* of the Antichrist, and the future man will be too. I do not believe God would allow Antiochus nor

---

[81] Constable, T. (2003). *Tom Constable's Expository Notes on the Bible* (Re 13:12). Galaxie Software.

Nero to exist again in any form. Even if it were possible for someone to "clone" Nero from regathered DNA, it would not be the same Nero in his upbringing and environment. It would not include his memories or mindset.

However, I am not against the idea that this Antichrist *spirit* is possibly now on earth and will be allowed to somehow possess the *man* who is the Antichrist. Note: If *that* spirit was *in the world* during John's day, according to him, after Nero had died, as he says in 1 John 4:3 (AD 85-95), why would it be in Hell today, as some teachers claim? This would not be Nero's *human* spirit, as some have taught either. See Revelation 17:8, which states, "He shall ascend out of the bottomless pit." In Chapter 17, the angel explains the mystery of the harlot to John and about this "beast" that had the wound. This "beast" *spirit* comes up out of the bottomless pit to revive one of its previous heads (kingdoms or mountains), and essentially restores itself as the eighth and final kingdom (see also Rev. 11:7). Now this is *another* spirit altogether and not the demonic spirit of the Antichrist, which is apparently bound up at this time. It is the principality that previously governed that kingdom on earth. While this could be figurative speech, much like the picture of Satan in Chapter 12, it also might be taken literally as the ancient spirit principality that governed the previously dead kingdom. It will be released to return and "revive" this "beast" of a kingdom. Every major kingdom the Devil used against Israel had a demonic angelic principality controlling it (see Dan. 10:13, 20; Eph. 6:12).

> "Why would intelligent and biblically knowledgeable scholars accept a theory that an emperor who had passed away more than three hundred years earlier could return from the grave to become the Antichrist? It appears to have been a misunderstanding in the interpretation of passages from the book of Revelation. As stated

earlier, John saw this beast with a wound to one of its heads, and the deadly wound was suddenly healed. Since Nero was the first persecutor, it was assumed he would return and be the last."[82]

He partners with the Harlot- Revelation 17 and the harlot (False religious system)

Revelation 17:1-2 (KJV)
[1] **And there came one of the seven angels which had the seven vials, and talked with me, saying unto me, Come hither; I will shew unto thee the judgment of <u>the great whore</u> that <u>sitteth upon many waters</u>:**
[2] **With whom <u>the kings of the earth</u> have committed fornication, and <u>the inhabitants of the earth have been made drunk</u> with the wine of her fornication.**

The first vision in this chapter is of a *religious* system pictured as a woman (not a king, but with many she has fornicated). She is first seen as having ruled over *many peoples all over the world,* including nations and tongues, and is also *a city* that reigns over the kings of the earth. She is both a religious system and a city.

> **Dake:** "The angelic explanation of the great whore proves her to be a religious system reigning over kings spiritually. The Greek reads, "And the woman whom thou sawest is the city the great, which has a kingdom over the kings of the earth" (Rev. 17:18). She has a kingdom within the kingdoms and over them. She is to be a religious system inside the old Roman Empire territory; <u>one that has headquarters in a great city;</u> and one

---

[82] Stone, Perry. <u>The Eighth Kingdom</u> (2015). Frontline. Charisma Media Charisma House Book Group Lake Mary FL. P. 109

that has a religious kingdom or reign over the kings of the earth."[83]

Revelation 17:15 (KJV)
[15] And he saith unto me, <u>The waters</u> which thou sawest, where <u>the whore</u> sitteth, <u>are</u> peoples, and multitudes, and nations, and tongues.

> Key

Revelation 17:18 (KJV)
[18] And <u>the woman</u> which thou sawest is <u>that great city</u>, which reigneth over the kings of the earth.

Revelation 17:6 (KJV)
[6] And I saw the woman drunken with the blood of the saints, and with the blood of the martyrs of Jesus: and when I saw her, I wondered with great admiration.

This harlot is two-fold: one is a religious system, and the other is a city called "Mystery Babylon." A physical city, probably the city of Rome at the time of John, no doubt comes to mind. Notice that it is "*that*" great city, one that existed in John's day. Now, 2000 years later, there is no other city but Rome, which absolutely describes a religion *and* a city that existed in John's day. The city where the Roman Catholic Church sits today. Some try to infer New York, America, or Mecca here. If the Lord tarries, what other city might become this? Her official name is *Mystery Babylon*. What other city could represent both? Understand, I came from a Catholic background and love Catholics. I am not against true Catholic Christian believers in Christ. They have no part in this. This evidence seems hard to overlook.

Keep in mind, I believe there will be a future physical city called Babylon that will be erected near the original site and that will become the headquarters for the Antichrist. That city

---

[83] Finis Jennings Dake, Dake's Annotated Reference Bible: Containing the Old and New Testaments of the Authorized or King James Version Text, (Lawrenceville, GA: Dake Bible Sales, Inc., 1997), WORDsearch CROSS e-book, Under: "Chapter 17."

is destroyed by a northern army and by God very quickly, not by the ten kings. However, this particular city, "Mystery Babylon," as she is called, will be destroyed by the ten kings during the Tribulation period.

Key   Two Babylons- A tale of two cities

So there are two Babylon cities mentioned in Revelation that will be destroyed. One is called "mystery" Babylon, which when John sees it by the Spirit he marvels at it because it seems Christianity has succeeded in Rome in his future. She is the harlot and a great city, according to verse 18. She will be burned by the *ten-nation coalition* because they hate her. The second is another physical city called Babylon, which is the capital city of the Antichrist. It will be destroyed by a great nation and many kings from the North near the end of the Tribulation, according to Jeremiah 50:41-43 (P. 71). See also, my study "Prophetic Days of the Lord," lesson 8, for details about this.

> **Revelation 17:5 (KJV)**
> **5 And upon her forehead was a name written, MYSTERY, BABYLON THE GREAT, THE MOTHER OF HARLOTS AND ABOMINATIONS OF THE EARTH.**

This harlot is a spiritual Babylon and rides the red beast, the 10-kinged coalition comprising the *revised* Roman Empire. Most people think of Rome and Catholicism here because verse six states she is drunk with the blood of the saints and martyrs of Jesus. This one is destroyed to make way for the Antichrist claiming his godhood at some point during the Tribulation by the ten kings. False religion coupled with Islam, or perhaps universal Islam as we might perceive it in our time today, will replace true Christianity after the Rapture of the Church. See the article about the one world religion proposal and agreement called "Chrislam Abrahamic Family House" to build its temples in 2022.[84] The pope leads Muslims, Jews, and Christians into one faith.

Photo from article[85]

Then, according to verses 16-17, the 10 kings, as they rule in the seventh kingdom for a short time, destroy her (the city) and give over their kingdoms to the Antichrist, forming the eighth and last kingdom. I believe that their joined kingdom is ruled from a physical Babylon, and later in the last part of the Tribulation, it will also be destroyed by God and foreign forces. All of this destruction of the Harlot city *"mystery Babylon,"* occurs before or around the middle point of the Tribulation.

> **Revelation 17:16-17 (KJV)**
> **16 And the ten horns which thou sawest upon the beast, these shall hate <u>the whore,</u>** (LB.- Why would they hate their real Capital city of Babylon or Mecca?) **and shall make her desolate and naked, and shall eat her flesh, and <u>burn her</u>**

[84] https://believersportal.com/one-world-religion-headquarters-to-open-2022/
[85] https://www.nowtheendbegins.com/chrislam-pope-francis-issues-order-create-global-committee-implement-decree-human-fraternity-world-peace-signed-united-arab-emirates-february/

with fire.
[17] **For God hath put in their hearts to fulfil his will, and to agree, and give their kingdom unto the beast, until the words of God shall be fulfilled.**

Here, the ten nations destroy this system and the city by burning it. Islam has vowed to do this to Rome for centuries. At this point, they will give over their seventh "kingdom" and submit to the beast. This cannot be Jerusalem because she will continue to exits forever. However, these two "Babylons" will not according to the Word of God.

The second vision is after verse 1-2 in Revelation 17:3-17 and is of the same harlot riding the "beast" world system (V. 18 is proof that it's the same woman).

Revelation 17:3-14 (KJV)
[3] **So he carried me away in the spirit into the wilderness: and I saw a woman** (LB- religious system) **sit upon a scarlet coloured beast,** (LB- world political system) **full of names of blasphemy, having seven heads and ten horns.**
[4] **And the woman was arrayed in purple and scarlet colour, and decked with gold and precious stones and pearls, having a golden cup in her hand full of abominations and filthiness of her fornication:**
[5] **And upon her forehead *was* a name written, MYSTERY, BABYLON THE GREAT, THE MOTHER OF HARLOTS AND ABOMINATIONS OF THE EARTH.**
[6] **And I saw the woman drunken with the blood of the saints, and with the blood of the martyrs of Jesus:** (LB- only one religious system could claim over 200 million dead souls in the past, and countless martyrs in the future.) **and when I saw her, I wondered with great admiration.** (LB- at a city that is steeped in what seems to be religiousness)
[7] **And the angel said unto me, Wherefore didst thou marvel? I will tell thee the mystery of the woman, and of the beast that carrieth her, which hath the seven heads and ten horns.**
[8] **The beast that thou sawest was, and is not;** (LB- In John's day- a previous world kingdom- The Grecian Empire where Antiochus came

from) **and shall ascend <u>out of the bottomless pit,</u> and go into perdition: and they that dwell on the earth shall wonder, whose names were not written in the book of life from the foundation of the world, when they behold the beast that was, and is not, and <u>yet is.</u>**
⁹ **And here** *is* **the mind which hath wisdom. The <u>seven heads</u> are <u>seven mountains,</u> on which the woman sitteth.** (LB- Possibly alluding to physical Rome, or seven kingdoms where this religious system has operated in the earth which makes more sense here).

D.A. Carson & Beale Commentary:

"Mountains" are symbolic for kingdoms in the OT and Judaism (e.g., Isa. 2:2; Jer. 51:25; Ezek. 35:3; Dan. 2:35, 45; Zech. 4:7; *1 Enoch* 52; *Targum Isaiah* 41:15 (see commentary on Rev. 8:8–9 above; for the interchangeableness of "kings" and "kingdoms," see Dan. 7:17, 23).[86]

These seven kingdoms are no doubt the seven great kingdoms that have persecuted the Jews from Egypt on. In every one of these kingdoms, there has been a form of worship that has been present throughout and continues even today. It is interesting to note that the cult of "Mystery Babylon" existed in and before John's day and is still associated today with Rome.

"7 Her name, "MYSTERY BABYLON," indicates that she is not literal Babylon. The word "mystery" identifies her with the religious rites and mysteries of ancient Babylon. According to Hislop's "The Two Babylons" (which quotes 260 sources), the ancient Babylonian cult, <u>started by Nimrod and his queen, Semiramis,</u> spread among all nations. The objects of

---

[86] Beale, G. K., & McDonough, S. M. (2007). Revelation. In *Commentary on the New Testament use of the Old Testament* (p. 1138). Grand Rapids, MI; Nottingham, UK: Baker Academic; Apollos.

worship were the Supreme Father, the Incarnate Female, or Queen of Heaven, and her Son. The cult claimed the highest wisdom and the most divine secrets. Besides confession to priests there were many mysterious rites. Julius Caesar became head of the Roman branch of the Babylonian Cult in 63 B.C. Other emperors held the office until 376 A.D. when the emperor Gratian, for Christian reasons, refused it because he saw that Babylonianism was idolatrous. Demasus, bishop of the Christian church at Rome, was elected to the headship in 378 A.D. and from here on Babylonianism and organized Christianity became one. The rites of Babylon were soon introduced into the Christian church. Heathen temples were restored, beautified, and their rituals encouraged. Worship and veneration of images, saints, relics, private confessions, penances, scourgings, pilgrimages, sign of the cross, Christmas, Lady Day, Easter, Lent, and other pagan rites and festivals, little by little, became a part of Christian worship.[87]

8. The name, "MOTHER OF HARLOTS," identifies the whore as a religious system (Rev. 17:5). The harlots refer to many branches which have sprung from her and have become as apostate as the great whore herself. She is a symbol of apostate religions being linked together after the rapture of the church to dominate the 10 kings of the Revised Roman Empire until Antichrist comes to full power over the 10 kingdoms by the middle of Daniel's 70th week (Rev. 17:1,3,9-17).

---

[87] Finis Jennings Dake, *Dake's Annotated Reference Bible: Containing the Old and New Testaments of the Authorized or King James Version Text*, (Lawrenceville, GA: Dake Bible Sales, Inc., 1997), WORD*search* CROSS e-book, Under: "Chapter 17".

9. The name, "MOTHER OF ABOMINATIONS OF THE EARTH," identifies her to be a religious system fostering and tolerating all the abominations that go with idolatry and spiritual fornication. The word abominations is used many times of idolatry and whoredoms associated with pagan worship (Dt. 18:9-12; 29:17-18; 32:16-17; 1Ki. 14:24; 2Ki. 16:3-4; 21:2-11; Ezek. 16:22-58; etc.). The great whore of the future tribulation will be the mother of abominations in God's sight because she will exceed all others in wickedness.

10. Her drunkenness -- being drunken with blood of the martyrs of Jesus -- proves beyond doubt that she is a religious institution. Only religion has killed the martyrs of Jesus in all ages. Governments have carried out the dictates of leaders in religion, doing the actual killing of saints because of religion. Although this prophecy speaks of the future drunkenness of mystical Babylon after the rapture of the church, who among us does not know of the martyrdom of 200 million people in the past because they would not conform to organized religion?

Five classes that have martyred saints:

(1) Jews (Acts 7:51-60; 8:1; 9:1). Their religious prejudice caused many to be put to death.

(2) Pagans of the old Roman Empire. History records the martyrdom of many Christians by pagan emperors because of religious differences.

(3) Muslims killed Christians in all their conquests.

(4) Greek Catholics have also persecuted and martyred Christians.

(5) Roman Catholics have been guilty of martyrdoms in many centuries and many lands. <u>Martyrdom of saints will again be revived in the old Roman Empire territory</u> between the rapture and the second coming. <u>In the first 3 1/2 years of Daniel's 70th week, the great whore will murder the saints of Jesus</u> (Rev. 17:6). In the middle of the week when Antichrist comes to power over the 10 kingdoms the great whore will be destroyed and martyrdom of Christians will be carried on by the beast and the 10 kings until the second coming (Rev. 13:1-18; 14:9-11; 17:9-17; Rev. 19:11 -- Rev. 20:6)."[88]

Many clearly believe the Roman Catholic Church is the harlot of Revelation. The harlot is definitely a world religion that will persecute the Tribulation saints. Could this harlot be Islam in the end? Or does she represent all false religions united as one? We shall see. To be clear, I don't believe that the Pope will be the antichrist, but a one world religious leader like the Pope could be used by him and he could become the false prophet.

Seven "mountain" kingdoms explained in more detail

Revelation 13:3
[3] **And I saw <u>one of his heads</u>** (LB. one of his world kingdoms, not "horn") **as it were wounded to death; and <u>his deadly wound was healed</u>: <u>and all the world wondered</u> after the beast.**

---

[88] Finis Jennings Dake, Dake's Annotated Reference Bible: Containing the Old and New Testaments of the Authorized or King James Version Text, (Lawrenceville, GA: Dake Bible Sales, Inc., 1997), WORDsearch CROSS e-book, Under: "Chapter 17:18."

Revelation 17:7-14 (KJV)
⁷ And the angel said unto me, Wherefore didst thou marvel? I will tell thee the mystery <u>of the woman</u>, and <u>of the beast</u> that carrieth her, which hath the seven heads and ten horns.

⁸ The beast (LB- A demonic prince of Satan over the kingdom of the Antichrist which includes seven mountains, is not likely the Antichrist himself as some teach for this would mean that the Antichrist would be allowed to resurrect from Hell itself) **that thou sawest was, and is not; and <u>shall ascend out of the bottomless, pit,</u>** (LB- This principality was over one of the previous five kingdoms and revives it to be the eighth) **and go into perdition: and they that dwell on the earth shall wonder, whose names were not written in the book of life from the foundation of the world, when they behold the beast that was, and is not, and yet is.**

⁹ And here *is* the mind which hath wisdom. <u>The seven heads are seven mountains</u>, on which the woman sitteth. (LB- The woman is positioned atop these seven "mountain kingdoms." This may infer or allude to the demonic princes that ruled over and through these seven kingdoms.)

¹⁰ And <u>there are seven kings</u> (LB- 7 demonic kings or kingdoms who oppressed and co-existed with Israel from her beginning to the 8th kingdom) **five are fallen,** (⁸⁹ LB- Egypt, Assyria, Babylon, Medo-Persia, and Greece) **and one is** (LB- the Roman Empire ruled in Johns day) **, *and* the other is not yet come** (LB-the "revised," not "revived," Roman Empire with ten kings)**; and when he cometh, he** (LB- the seventh) **must continue <u>a short space</u>.**

Barnes: "It would be contrary to the whole spirit of this passage, and to what is demanded by the

---

⁸⁹ **Are fallen (ἔπεσαν)** Lit., *fell.* Constantly used in the Septuagint of the violent fall or overthrow of kings or kingdoms. See Ezekiel 29:5; 30:6; Isaiah 21:9; Jeremiah 50:15; 51:8.Marvin R. Vincent, *Word Studies in the New Testament*, (New York: Scribners, 1887), WORD*search* CROSS e-book, Under: "Revelation 17:10".

proper meaning of the word, to insist that the word should denote literally *kings*, and that it could not be applied to emperors, or to dictators, or to dynasties."

Tom Constable's Notes on the Bible, Rev. 13:3: "If the beast's heads represent nations (v. 1), verse 3 seems to be saying that one of the nations under Satan's authority perished, but then it revived. The apparent resurrection of this nation will be so amazing to the world that many people will give their allegiance and their worship to Antichrist (cf. vv. 8, 12; 14:9, 11; 20:4). In so doing they will also submit to Satan who is behind him. Antichrist's ability to revive this nation will make him appear invincible."

Key: The eighth is of the seven

11 And <u>the beast</u> (LB- world Empire) **that was, and is not** (LB- likely the revived Babylonian/Syrian, and probably the Seleucid quarter specifically, from which Antiochus IV was from), **even <u>he is the eighth</u>, and is of the seven, and goeth into perdition.** (LB- This is the eighth kingdom that the Antichrist will finally rule and will be defeated by Christ).

12 And the ten horns which thou sawest are <u>ten kings</u>, which have received no kingdom as yet; (LB- During John's day) **but <u>receive power as kings one hour with the beast</u>** (LB- Satan's kingdom/Antichrist during the Tribulation).

The key to understanding this passage is this: the Antichrist is a "horn" here and not a "head." His "kingdom" is a beast with many "heads." According to Daniel 7:20, 27 he is an eleventh horn to arise and subdue the others. He is not a "head" here, for they represent something else. They are kingdoms and not kings. Otherwise there would be a group of eleven and a group of seven more kings. This makes no sense.

Dake: "No kingdom in John's day, but will receive kingdoms when the 10 are formed inside the Roman Empire territory in the last days. The kings will rule for 3 1/2 years independent and along side of the Antichrist and then give their power to him the last 3 1/2 years of this age (Rev. 17:10-17; 13:5.)"[90]

¹³ These have one mind, and <u>shall give their power</u> and strength unto <u>the beast.</u>
¹⁴ <u>These shall make war with the Lamb,</u> and the Lamb shall overcome them: for he is Lord of lords, and King of kings: and they that are with him *are* called, and chosen, and faithful.

Dake: "Here 5 of the 7 kingdoms "are fallen (Egypt, Assyria, Babylon, Medo-Persia, and Greece), and one is (the 6th, the old Roman Empire), and the other is not yet come (the 7th, made up of the 10 kingdoms that are yet to be formed inside the Roman Empire, Dan. 7:23-24); <u>and when he (the 7th, or the Revised Roman Empire) cometh, he must continue a short space"</u> (3 1/2 years, Rev. 12:12,14). The beast "that was (had existed on earth before John's day), and is not (on earth in John's day), even he is the 8th (8th kingdom, succeeding the 7 preceding kingdoms), and is of the 7 (of one of the 7, the 5th or Greece, that had fallen before John's day and becomes the 8th after the 6th and 7th

---

⁹⁰ Finis Jennings Dake, Dake's Annotated Reference Bible: Containing the Old and New Testaments of the Authorized or King James Version Text, (Lawrenceville, GA: Dake Bible Sales, Inc., 1997), WORDsearch CROSS e-book, Under: "Chapter 17:12."

kingdoms), and goeth into perdition" (Rev. 17:9-11)."[91]

Whatever we may learn about the spirit beast out of the abyss, we have to conclude that he is one of the ruling demons from the first of five kingdoms.

Dake taught that it will be a revived *Grecian* Empire that the Antichrist finally rules as the eighth kingdom. Remember, in Chapter 13, John saw a group of seven and a group of ten. If they were all kings alike, this would have been a group of seventeen on the beast. The beast is altogether the ruling prince over the Babylonian or Greek Empire (Dan. 10:20) that has been bound and will be released during the Tribulation period.

> "We conclude, therefore, that the beast of the abyss is this satanic prince of Grecia who will inspire the Antichrist and use him in the formation of the eighth kingdom, which will be a revival of the kingdom he controlled before he was defeated in the heavenlies and cast into the abyss." [92]

What empire will be revived if not the Grecian? Could the Egyptian, Assyrian, Babylonian, or Persian?

Because Verse 11 states that "the beast that was and is not is of the seven and goes down into perdition," we must conclude that this revived beast was not of the Romans, and has to be either Egyptian, Assyrian, Babylonian, Persian, or

[91] Finis Jennings Dake, Dake's Annotated Reference Bible: Containing the Old and New Testaments of the Authorized or King James Version Text, (Lawrenceville, GA: Dake Bible Sales, Inc., 1997), WORDsearch CROSS e-book, Under: "Chapter 17."
[92] Dake, F. J. (n.d.). *Revelation Expounded: Eternal Mysteries Simplified* (p. 279).

Greek. We do know, according to Daniel 7:19-22, that the Antichrist will come up among the ten kings that represent the revised Roman Empire, but all of these other empires were almost entirely in the lands that Rome conquered. The world will wonder at the revival of one of these kingdoms. It would only happen because the demonic prince that ruled that kingdom was released from the pit. He will take control over the Antichrist through demonic possession and reestablish through him his kingdom's rule.

Greece as a nation still exists today, and this may not cause the world to wonder if they made a move to rule by themselves. I am open to the possibility of an Assyrian or Babylonian revival, especially because the Antichrist is called "the Assyrian, and "the King of Babylon" in certain passages, as we will see. This beast is said to have the parts of many of these past empire kingdoms, but primarily the body of a leopard, which represents the Greeks in Daniel (see Daniel 7:6- the leopard with four wings and four heads). So we cannot rule out a revival of the Grecian.

There seems to be a closeness with Greece in the "last days" with the Antichrist. In Joel 3:6 and Zech. 9:13, we have two definite prophecies of the Grecian Empire in the last days under the Antichrist concerning the time of the deliverance of Israel from other nations at the second coming of Christ. These passages require some cooperation with the Antichrist and Greece.

> **Joel 3:6 (KJV)**
> ⁶ **The children also of Judah and the children of Jerusalem have ye sold unto the Grecians, that ye might remove them far from their border.**
>
> **Zechariah 9:13-14 (HCSB)**
> ¹³ **For I will bend Judah ⌊as My bow⌋; I will fill that bow with Ephraim. I will rouse your sons, Zion, against your**

sons, Greece. I will make you like a warrior's sword.
14 Then the LORD will appear over them, and His arrow
will fly like lightning. The Lord GOD will sound
the trumpet and advance with the southern storms.

So much of Daniel's visions in Chapters seven, eight, and eleven are about the Grecian Empire and its four divisions, especially the Syrian/Iraqi, from which Antiochus IV was to appear and rule. We know that he represents a "type" of the Antichrist. So as a whole, I'm inclined to believe that the Antichrist will rule from Shinar, the land of Babylon, which is now Iraq. Even today, Greece and Iraq have a certain familiarity because of their days in the Grecian Empire together.

What we learn from Rev. 17:

1. There is a woman who is called a harlot who rides the beast system for a time.

2. She comes out of a large group of nations and peoples- V.15

3. She is "drunken" with the blood of saints and Christian martyrs (historically before *and* during the Tribulation).

4. John marvels at her (possibly because she *appears* to be Christian and is spectacular like Rome and the Vatican are even today, (or perhaps a whole different religion that he had never seen before like Islam) and the angel asked "why are you admiring her?"

5. The "beast" here has seven heads and ten horns (seven kingdoms and ten kings).

6. It will arise out of the bottomless pit and go into destruction and ruin.

7. This beast (worldly kingdom of the Antichrist) was, and is not, and yet is, and the world will marvel at its return.

8. The woman is seated not only on the beast, but also sits on seven "mounts," which could mean hills or the seven kingdoms that are mentioned next. This could mean she has had influence over the last *seven* kingdoms.

9. The seven heads are seven kings/mountains (mountains/kingdoms: demonic principality/king ruled- "kingdoms"). Five are fallen, one is now in John's day in operation (the sixth- was the old Roman), and the seventh is not yet here (the revised Roman).

Daniel 2, 7, 8 and Revelation 13, 17

Daniels view of 7	John's view of 9
Egyptian	1. Egyptian
Assyrian	2. Assyrian
1. Babylonian	3. Babylonian
2. Median/Persian	4. Median/Persian
3. Grecian	5. Grecian
4. Roman	6. Roman
5. Ten toes/horns-Kings	7. Ten kings revised Roman
6. Little horn defeated by Christ	8. Antichrist revived Babylonian/Assyrian/Grecian?
7. Kingdom of Christ	9. Kingdom of Christ

Chart by Larry Booth

10. When the seventh comes, it only last a short time-
Revised Roman Empire

11. The eighth kingdom that rises is most likely one of
the first five kingdoms revived (or one of the seven
total kingdoms, if the phrase "was and is not" is
referring to the statement of the seventh kingdom
lasting a short time before ending, and then
morphing into the eighth).

12. Daniel's prophecies pinpoint the sixth and revised
seventh (what he called the *fourth* beast) kingdom to
be *Roman*, by stating "of the people of the prince"
in Daniel 9:27. The prince to come, spoken of
there, was the Roman Titus, who would destroy the
temple in AD 70. Then Daniel describes the future
Antichrist by saying "he" would stop the sacrifices
in the middle of the week of seven years left to
come for Israel. This connects the Antichrist to the
future revised *Roman* Empire.

13. Daniel also pinpoints his *third* kingdom in his vision
(the fifth worldly kingdom) around a future "type"
of Antiochus IV., who was of the Grecian Empire.
He described him in detail but ended up speaking
about the Antichrist, and revealing things about him
that Antiochus did not fulfill. (Dan. 11:36-45). *This
kingdom was likened to a leopard and would produce a
future oppressor of Israel who would be destroyed by the
Messiah Himself.* Daniel 7:6 correlated with
Revelation 13:2 gives us a clue as to why we believe
the eighth and final kingdom will be
Grecian/Babylonian. *They both are likened to a leopard.*
So the Antichrist would be out of the Roman
(Middle East/and Europe), but specifically ruling

over the same Greek area like Antiochus did, which was the Syrian/Babylonian and part of Europe. It was called the Seleucid (312-63 BC).

14. The ten horns are ten kings on the Roman beast who *during John's day had no real kingdoms.*

15. They all agree and will give their strength and authority to the "beast," the Antichrist's eighth kingdom.

16. They will war with Jesus, and He will overcome them.

17. That kingdom will destroy the harlot in the future. Rev. 17:15-18

18. The woman separate from the beast not only sits on the beast, but is on, or over multitudes of people, and nations, and languages.

19. The ten kings eventually hate the harlot and *destroy her* by stripping her, eating her "flesh," and finally by burning her.

20. God originates this judgment to fulfill what He wants to happen. Even in the fact of them giving their kingdom (the seventh) to the beast. This fulfills more than one word from God.

21. The woman is THAT great city, (one that existed in John's day- probably Rome, this could not be Mecca or New York, for they had not existed yet) which reigns over kings of the earth.

The "Beast" partners with the false prophet

The word "beast" in the Apocalypse represents four things: a supernatural angel out of the Abyss (Rev. 9:11; 17:7); the Antichrist- a mortal man (Rev. 19:19); the false prophet (Rev. 13:11); and a kingdom (Rev. 17:7-8).

The false prophet is another dark figure represented in the Apocalypse that partners with the Antichrist, a dynamic duo of sorts but with a sinister end. He seems to be a religious figure who performs demonic miracles in the presence of the Antichrist.

Revelation 19:19 (KJV)
[19] **And I saw <u>the beast</u>, and the kings of the earth, and their armies, gathered together to make war against him that sat on the horse, and against his army.**

Revelation 19:20 (HCSB)
[20] **But <u>the beast</u> was taken prisoner, and <u>along with him the false prophet</u>, who <u>had performed the signs in his presence</u>** (KJV- "wrought miracles"). **He deceived those who accepted the mark of the beast and those who worshiped his image with these signs. <u>Both of them were thrown alive</u> into the lake of fire that burns with sulfur.**

H.A. Ironside:

> "The Beast is seen marshalling his hosts, and with him his blasphemous ally and satellite, the false prophet—that is, the Antichrist...

> Two men, be it noted, are taken alive. They are the two arch-conspirators who have bulked so largely in this book—the Beast and the false prophet, the civil and religious leaders of the last

league of nations, which will be Satan-inspired in its origin, and Satan-directed until its doom."[93]

The false prophet does miraculous signs in the presence of the Antichrist for others to see and believe. He is also responsible for deceiving those who take the mark of the beast and those who worship his image. He is called "another beast," which could imply another demonic possession by a high ranking demon.

> "13:12 The second beast will exercise all the authority of the first beast by acting as his prophet (19:20; 20:10; cf. Exod. 7:1). Compare the ministries of Moses and Aaron (Exod. 4:16; 7:9), and the Lord and Elijah (1 Kings 17:1). The false prophet will be Antichrist's effective agent in directing the persecution of believers. He will lead earth-dwellers to worship the first beast— evidently as the leader of a worldwide religious movement that involves a form of emperor-divinity worship or personality cult. This will be a satanic counterfeit of the Holy Spirit's ministry of leading people to worship Christ." [94]

Revelation 13:11-17 (KJV)
[11] And I beheld <u>another beast</u> coming up out of the earth; and he had two horns like a lamb, and he spake as a dragon.
[12] And <u>he exerciseth all the power of the first beast before him</u>, and <u>causeth the earth</u> and them which dwell therein <u>to worship the first beast</u>, whose <u>deadly wound was healed</u>.
[13] And <u>he doeth great wonders</u>, so that <u>he maketh fire come down from heaven on the earth</u> in the sight of men,
[14] And <u>deceiveth them that dwell on the earth</u> by *the means of*

---

[93] Ironside, H. A. (1920). <u>Lectures on the Book of Revelation</u> (pp. 329–330). Neptune, N. J.: Loizeaux Brothers.
[94] Constable, T. (2003). *Tom Constable's Expository Notes on the Bible* (Re 13:12). Galaxie Software.

those miracles which he had power to do <u>in the sight of the beast</u>; saying to them that dwell on the earth, that they should <u>make an image</u> to the beast, which <u>had the wound by a sword, and did live</u>.

[15] And he had <u>power to give life</u> unto <u>the image of the beast</u>, that <u>the image</u> of the beast should both speak, and <u>cause that as many</u> as would not worship the image of the beast <u>should be killed</u>.

[16] And <u>he causeth all</u>, both small and great, rich and poor, free and bond, <u>to receive a mark</u> in their right hand, or in their foreheads:

[17] And that no man might buy or sell, save he that had <u>the mark</u>, or <u>the name</u> of the beast, or <u>the number</u> of his name.

Let's summarize:

Here, the False Prophets role becomes clear:

1. He comes out of the earth (or peoples, he is a man possessed by a demon).

2. Two horns like a lamb. He appears to be peaceful like a lamb.

3. Speaks as a dragon or with authority

4. He stands in place of, and with the same authority as the Antichrist.

5. The kingdom/Antichrist has a deadly wound that is miraculously healed.

6. He does great wonders.

7. He causes fire to come down from the sky to the earth in plain sight.

8.   Doing miracles in front of the Antichrist, he deceives those on earth.

9.   During the time of the kingdom's/Antichrist's wound being healed, he deceives men to make an image of the Antichrist.

10. He brings to life this image that people are worshiping.

11. This image speaks and murders those who do not worship him.

12. He causes all to receive a mark in their right hand or forehead.

13. No one is allowed to buy or sell unless he has the mark, or the name of the Antichrist, or the number of his name on them.

14. He is not only possessed by devils, but directs demon spirits in other men, as ambassadors to other countries to work miracles.

15. The false prophet is used to gather men to Armageddon.

16. On the day of the Lord they both will be taken alive and cast into Hell. KJV- the Lake of Fire.

Revelation 16:13-14 (KJV)
[13] And I saw <u>three unclean spirits</u> like frogs *come* out of the mouth of the dragon, and <u>out of the mouth of</u> the beast, and out of the mouth of <u>the false prophet.</u>
[14] For they are the <u>spirits of devils, working miracles,</u> *which* <u>go forth unto the kings of the earth and of the whole world,</u> to gather them to the battle of that great day of God Almighty.

Revelation 20:10 (KJV)
[10] **And the devil that deceived them was cast into the lake of fire and brimstone, where the beast and <u>the false prophet</u> *are*, and shall be tormented day and night for ever and ever.**

Chapter 8
The Antichrist's Identity
Related to Locations

The Northerner

Joel 1:6 (KJV)
⁶ For <u>a nation is come up upon my land</u>, strong, and without number, whose teeth *are* the teeth of a lion, and he hath the cheek teeth of a great lion.

No doubt this "nation" in the Day of the Lord is the Antichrist.

Joel 1:15 (KJV)
¹⁵ Alas for the day! for <u>the day of the LORD *is* at hand</u>, and as a destruction from the Almighty shall it come.

Joel 1:19-20 (KJV)
¹⁹ O LORD, to thee will I cry: for <u>the fire hath devoured</u> the pastures of the wilderness, and <u>the flame hath burned</u> all the trees of the field.
²⁰ The beasts of the field cry also unto thee: for <u>the rivers of waters are dried up</u>, and <u>the fire hath devoured the pastures</u> of the wilderness.

Here we see the desolation of the land of Israel by the time the Lord returns, but a great event precedes it: the national repentance of the remnant of Israel (Isaiah 26:16). When the Tribulation is nearing its end, they will openly repent of their sins and call on the true Messiah to return, which He does (Joel 1:13-14; 2:11-18).

> **Joel 2:12-13 (KJV)**
> [12] **Therefore also now, saith the LORD, turn ye *even* to me with all your heart, and with fasting, and with weeping, and with mourning:**
> [13] **And rend your heart, and not your garments, and <u>turn unto the LORD</u> your God: for <u>he *is* gracious and merciful</u>, slow to anger, and of great kindness, and repenteth him of the evil.**

> **Joel 2:16 (KJV)**
> [16] **Gather the people, sanctify the congregation, assemble the elders, gather the children, and those that suck the breasts: let <u>the bridegroom go forth of his chamber, and the bride out of her closet.</u>**

The call will be made, and the remnant of Israel will repent (Psalm 102:16-17). After the Lord sees the true repentance of His people, He returns to bring vengeance upon the enemies of God (Duet. 32:36,40). The bridegroom (Christ) comes out, along with the bride (the church). The Lord swiftly moves to save the remnant of Israel. Verse 18 is one of the most amazing verses in the Bible:

> **Joel 2:18 (HCSB)**
> [18] **Then the LORD became jealous for His land <u>and spared His people.</u>**

There is still a time of tribulation to come for Israel. It is a future period of seven years that concludes Daniel's seventy weeks. Will Israel repent? Joel says that she will, and that the Lord will spare His people. He still cares about Israel and his land. Those who believe the Church replaced Israel hold that she didn't, nor will she ever repent, and that they should get what's coming to them. Some translators translate this as a conditional statement. "If" they repent, "then" God will spare His people. Joel tells the story before it ever happens. God knows, that one day they will repent and that His response will be to spare them. Prophecy sees the future in advance.

> "It is unclear whether he meant that the Lord had responded or would respond. The problem is the Hebrew perfect verbs, which can be rendered in English with either past for future verbs. Several English translations (NASB, NIV, AV) interpreted the Lord's response as being conditioned on the people's repentance and translated the verbs in the future tense. It is equally possible that Joel meant that God had already responded positively because the people had repented, which the prophet did not record."[95]

In Deuteronomy 30:1-3, Moses predicted that Israel would in the future fall away and that the Lord would restore them and bless them to a better position than before.

Zechariah 12:10 (KJV)
[10] **And I will pour upon the house of David, and upon the inhabitants of Jerusalem, the spirit of grace and of supplications: and they shall look upon me whom they have pierced, and <u>they shall mourn for him</u>, as one mourneth for *his* only *son*, and shall be in bitterness for him, as one that is in bitterness for *his* firstborn.**

Joel 2:11 (KJV)
[11] **And the LORD shall utter his voice before <u>his army</u>: for his camp *is* very great: for *he is* strong that executeth his word: for the day of the LORD *is* great and very terrible; and who can abide it?**

---

[95] Constable, T. (2003). *Tom Constable's Expository Notes on the Bible* (Joel 2:18). Galaxie Software.

In Joel 2:1-11, we see the description of the army of the Lord. Many try to say that this is an army of locusts, but consider that they are the angels and saints who follow Christ when He returns from heaven as the "clouds" of heaven to save Israel and Jerusalem. God promises to restore Israel quickly.

Joel 2:23 (KJV)
²³ Be glad then, ye children of Zion, and rejoice in the LORD your God: for he hath given you the former rain moderately, and he will cause to come down for you the rain, the former rain, and the latter rain in the first *month*.

But before this, he will deal with the Antichrist.

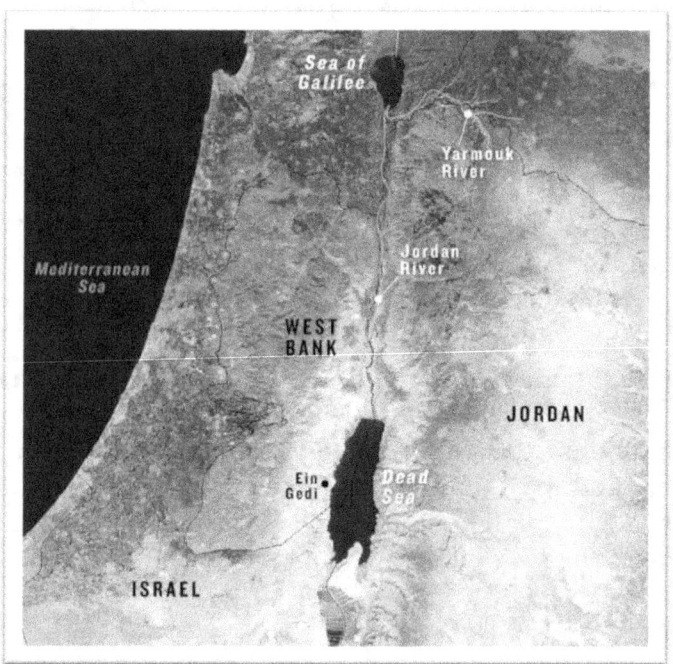

Joel 2:20 (HCSB)
²⁰ I will drive <u>the northerner far from you</u> and banish him to a dry and desolate land, his front ranks into the Dead Sea, and <u>his rear guard</u> into the Mediterranean Sea. His stench

will rise; yes, his rotten smell will rise, for <u>he has done catastrophic things</u>.

"The prophet now revealed that this invader would come from the North. Both Assyria and Babylon, as well as all other eastern invaders, entered Israel from the north because of the impassability of the Arabian Desert to Israel's east." — **Tom Constable's** Notes on the Bible Comments on Verse 20.

Bible Knowledge Commentary-

"Consequently prophecies pertaining to his own generation are merged here with those that await future realization. <u>This is common in Old Testament prophecies</u> (e.g., Isa. 9:6–7; 61:1–2; Zech. 9:9–10)." [96]

Leadership Ministries Worldwide Commentary-

"Note that the northern army is not identified by Scripture. Thus it is applicable to all the armies that have invaded or will invade Israel from the North. This would include the Assyrians, Babylonians, Romans and, in particular, the massive army of the end times that will launch the final battle against the LORD and His people, <u>the battle known as Armageddon</u>." [97]

"Some of their divisions would be driven into a desert land, others into the eastern sea (Dead Sea),

[96] Chisholm, R. B., Jr. (1985). Joel. In J. F. Walvoord & R. B. Zuck (Eds.), *The Bible Knowledge Commentary: An Exposition of the Scriptures* (Vol. 1, p. 1419). Victor Books.
[97] Leadership Ministries Worldwide. (2008). Joel–Nahum (p. 29). Leadership Ministries Worldwide.

and still others into the western sea (Mediterranean Sea)." [98]

What we learn from Joel about the Antichrist:

1. He attacks Israel like others, from the North, thus he is called the "northerner."

2. The Antichrist is attacking at the same time the remnant is repenting.

3. The "army" of the Lord lays everything waste.

4. The Antichrist has factions all over, attacking from different sides.

5. He is defeated on all sides (the North, the wastelands, the Dead Sea, and the Mediterranean Sea.).

The Assyrian

In many places, the Antichrist is referred to by the name of the "Assyrian." Ancient Assyria encompassed portions of four modern-day countries in northern Mesopotamia: eastern Syria, south-eastern Turkey, Iran, and northern Iraq. At times, it included Saudi Arabia, Jordan, and Egypt.

---

[98] IBID

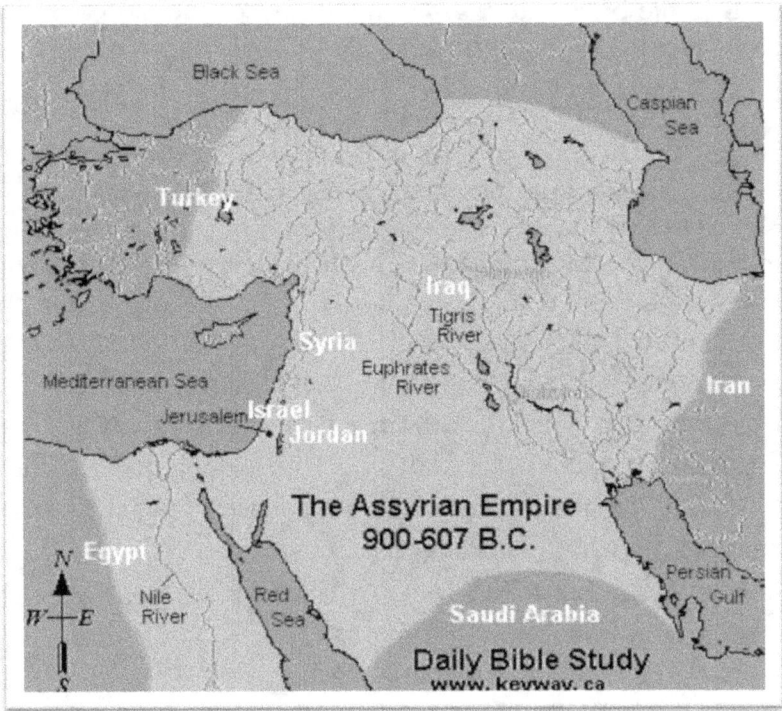

The Assyrian Empire collapsed in 612 BCE. So obviously, when a prophecy that has not been fulfilled about an evil man called "Assyrian" occurs in the Word of God, especially around passages concerning the Day of the Lord, we see the possibility that it may be speaking of the Antichrist. This is also a strong indication that the Antichrist will come from this same territory.

>   **F. Dake:** "[the Assyrian] "The Assyrian" is often a title of Antichrist (Isa. 10:24; 14:25; Mic. 5:5-6)."[99]

Isaiah 10:32 (KJV)
[32] **As yet shall he** (LB- the Assyrian) **remain at Nob that day: he**

---

[99] Finis Jennings Dake, Dake's Annotated Reference Bible: Containing the Old and New Testaments of the Authorized or King James Version Text, (Lawrenceville, GA: Dake Bible Sales, Inc., 1997), WORDsearch CROSS e-book, Under: "Isaiah 30:31."

shall shake his hand *against* the mount of the daughter of Zion, the hill of Jerusalem.

Isaiah 27:13 (KJV)
¹³ And it shall come to pass in that day, *that* the great trumpet shall be blown, and they shall come which were ready to perish in the land of Assyria, and <u>the outcasts in the land of Egypt,</u> and shall worship the LORD in the holy mount at Jerusalem.

Isaiah states that Israel will find refuge in Egypt during this troubled time. When I was in Egypt and Jordan recently, I did a quick study and found that some of the Jews during the tribulation would flee to Egypt and Jordan and find some refuge. While most of Jordan will resist the control of the Antichrist, Egypt will eventually fall under his command. I have a greater love and respect for my friends in those countries who share the faith of Jesus.

Isaiah 30:31 (KJV)
³¹ For <u>through the voice of the LORD</u> shall <u>the Assyrian</u> be beaten down, *which* smote with a rod.

These next few passages, coupled with what we have learned about the remnant of Israel repenting, are very important to identifying the Antichrist as the "Assyrian."

Isaiah 10:21-27 (KJV)
²¹ <u>The remnant shall return,</u> *even* the remnant of Jacob, unto the mighty God.
²² For though thy people Israel be as the sand of the sea, *yet* a remnant of them shall return: <u>the consumption decreed</u> shall overflow with righteousness.
²³ For the Lord GOD of hosts shall make a consumption, even determined, in the midst of all the land.
²⁴ Therefore thus saith the Lord GOD of hosts, O my people that dwellest in Zion, <u>be not afraid of the Assyrian: he shall smite thee with a rod,</u> and shall lift up <u>his staff against thee,</u> after the manner of Egypt.
²⁵ For yet <u>a very little while,</u> and <u>the indignation</u> shall cease,

and mine anger in their destruction.

²⁶ And the LORD of hosts shall <u>stir up a scourge for him</u> according to the slaughter of Midian at the rock of Oreb: and *as* his rod *was* upon the sea, so shall he lift it up <u>after the manner of Egypt.</u>

²⁷ And <u>it shall come to pass in that day,</u> *that* his burden shall be taken away from off thy shoulder, and his yoke from off thy neck, and <u>the yoke shall be destroyed because of the anointing</u> (LB- the Messiah).

Isaiah 14:25 (KJV)

²⁵ That I will break <u>the Assyrian in my land,</u> and upon <u>my mountains</u> tread him under foot: then shall his yoke depart from off them, and his burden depart from off their shoulders.

Micah 5:5-6 (KJV)

⁵ And this *man* shall be the peace, <u>when the Assyrian shall come</u> into our land: and when he shall tread in our palaces, then shall <u>we raise against him seven shepherds, and eight principal men.</u>

⁶ And they shall waste the land of Assyria with the sword, and the land of Nimrod in the entrances thereof: thus shall he deliver *us* from the Assyrian, when he cometh into our land, and when he treadeth within our borders.

In Isaiah 10, God tells the Jewish remnant in Israel not to be afraid of the Antichrist. Yes, he will smite you and lift up his staff against you, but the anointed one will break his oppression off of you. He will do this to him while he is still in the mountains of Israel.

The Antichrist will push one last time to destroy Jerusalem, but this time, Christ will stop him. Micah had already spoken of Christ doing this and setting up His kingdom in Chapter 4. These verses in Chapter 5 have never been fulfilled in history.

Dake: "Notes for Verse 5:

"a [the Assyrian] Antichrist is called "the Assyrian," for <u>he will come from the territory Assyria ruled over in ancient times.</u> For this same reason he can be called "the king of Babylon" (Isa. 14), the Syrian (Dan. 11:35-45), the Roman "prince that shall come" (Dan. 9:26-27), and the Grecian (Zech. 9:13). <u>He will come from the territory ruled by Assyria, Babylon, Greece, Syria, and Rome.</u> In the days of Micah and Isaiah the Assyrians had the great empire of Bible lands, so the future Antichrist could rightly be termed "the Assyrian." The fact of a latter-day fulfillment of Mic. 5:3-15 confirms that whoever the Assyrian will be, he will fulfill these Scriptures in the day that:…" [100]

Nahum 1:11-15 (KJV)

[11] **There is *one* come out of thee** (LB-out of Nineveh/Assyria, today near Mosul Iraq- Sennacherib was the Assyrian king in view here, but he did not fulfill all of these verses, this is the Antichrist) **that imagineth evil against the LORD, <u>a wicked counsellor.</u>**
[12] **Thus saith the LORD; Though *they be* quiet, and likewise many, yet thus shall they be cut down, when he shall pass through. <u>Though I have afflicted thee, I will afflict thee no more.</u>**
[13] **For now will <u>I break his yoke from off thee</u>, and will burst thy bonds in sunder.**
[14] **And the LORD hath given a commandment concerning thee, *that* no more of thy name be sown: out of the house of thy gods will I cut off the graven image and the molten image: I will make thy grave; for thou art vile.**
[15] **Behold upon the mountains <u>the feet of him</u> that bringeth good tidings, that publisheth peace! O Judah, keep thy solemn feasts, perform thy vows: for <u>the wicked shall no more pass through</u> thee; <u>he is utterly cut off.</u>**

---

[100] Finis Jennings Dake, Dake's Annotated Reference Bible: Containing the Old and New Testaments of the Authorized or King James Version Text, (Lawrenceville, GA: Dake Bible Sales, Inc., 1997), WORDsearch CROSS e-book, Under: "Chapter 5."

Wicked Counselor and the "Wicked"
"I will break his yoke from off thee"

Nineveh, the capital city of Assyria, which had repented from Jonah's preaching, had repented of their repentance, and their future destruction is prophesied by Nahum. in his commentary, C.I. Scofield, likens Nineveh to a *type* of future apostate Christendom, stating

> "Nineveh stands in Scripture as the representative of apostate *religious* Gentiledom, as Babylon represents the confusion into which the Gentile *political* world-system has fallen Dan 2:41-43 (See Note for Isa 13:1) Under the preaching of Jonah, B.C. 862, the city and king had turned to God (Elohim), Jnh 3:3-10 But in the time of Nahum, more than a century later, the city had wholly apostatized from God. It is this which distinguishes Nineveh from all the other ancient Gentile cities, and which makes her the suited symbol of the present religious Gentile world-system in the last day."[101]

This prophecy of the looming destruction of Nineveh is laid out in the next few chapters; however, in Chapter 1, it seems that there is a far more expansive prophetic language involved. For instance Verses 2-4, describe God's future wrath in detail, and in Verse 5, he speaks about Christ's return, **"The mountains quake at him, and the hills melt, and the earth is burned *at his presence* (italics mine), yea, the world, and all that dwell therein."** Also, in Verse 15, there is a clearly millennial view of Christ and His saints, stating, **"Behold**

---

[101] C.I. Scofield, ed., *The Holy Bible: Containing the Old and New Testaments*, WORD*search* CROSS e-book, Under: "Chapter 1".

upon the mountains the feet of him that bringeth good tidings, that publisheth peace! ..." (See also Isaiah 52:7). So, it makes sense to me that Sennacherib, who invaded Judah in the days of Hezekiah (2 Ki. 18:13- 2 Ki. 19:37; Isa. 36:1- Isa. 37:38), is a past example of a future Antichrist. Remember, as stated before in Chapter 5, that this king did not die in the mountains of Israel as predicted in Isaiah 14:25.

Here in Nahum 1, the Antichrist is from Assyria, and he is called the "wicked counselor" and "the wicked." In Verse 12, the promise is given to Israel, "I will afflict thee no more," and this can only be true for Israel ultimately at the time of the end of the Tribulation period when Christ comes back. This title is also used by Paul of the Antichrist later in the New Testament in 2 Thess. 2:8.

"In the first Chapter of Nahum "one who plots evil against the LORD, A wicked counselor," (Verse 11) comes forth from Nineveh, (Nahum 2:8 and 3:7) the ancient capital of Assyria. In the next to the last verse of the prophecy, this "wicked counselor" is expressly called the "king of Assyria." (Nahum 3:18) The Lord declares that He will make "an utter end" of this invasion, adding that "affliction will not rise up a second time." (Nahum 1:9) He then tells His people that "though I have afflicted you, I will afflict you no more." (Verse 12) The Divine history and many prophecies clearly show that Judah's affliction did not end at the destruction of Sennacherib. The Assyrian invasion was only the beginning of her great and long affliction, which has not yet ended. Indeed, their greatest affliction is still future."[102]

---

[102] Morris, James C. . Keys to Bible Prophecy (p. 67). Dispensational Publishing House, Inc.. Kindle Edition.

Many times and places in the Word of God, we see double references to the king of Assyria and the Antichrist, much like in Daniel with Antiochus IV. The Assyrian seems to be one of the most commonly used names for the Antichrist and puts him in the Middle Eastern territories.

What we learn from these verses:

1. He, the Assyrian/Antichrist, will set up his headquarters for battle in Nob. Nob was about ten miles north of Jerusalem, and that is where the high priest resided.

2. His anger is directed at Jerusalem.

3. The voice of the Lord will defeat him one day.

4. He will smite (to strike quickly) Israel with a rod (the rod was used for protection and also used as an instrument for either remedial or penal punishment.),[103] like Pharaoh did in Egypt.

5. He will lift up his staff, (*natah* (: נטה, 5186), "to stretch forth, spread out, stretch down, turn aside." This verb also occurs in Arabic, late Aramaic, and postbiblical Hebrew. The Bible attests to it in all periods and about 215 times.[104]) against them like it was in Egypt. This could mean he exercises authority over them improperly, like Pharaoh did in Egypt.

---

[103] Waltke, B. K. (1999). 2314 שבט. R. L. Harris, G. L. Archer Jr., & B. K. Waltke (Eds.), *Theological Wordbook of the Old Testament* (electronic ed., p. 897). Chicago: Moody Press.
[104] Vine, W. E., Unger, M. F., & White, W., Jr. (1996). *Vine's Complete Expository Dictionary of Old and New Testament Words* (Vol. 1, p. 248). Nashville, TN: T. Nelson.

6. He would only oppress them for "a little while." Or, see the HCSB translation below. A little while until God's judgment comes.

> When "*:mě'aṭ* is joined with the word *'ôd* to form the expression *'ôd mě'aṭ* "a little while." It occurs seven times, six of these indicating the cessation of God's patience with the wicked and the beginning of judgment: Ps 37:10; Isa 10:25; 29:17; Jer 51:33; Hag 2:6." [105]

Isaiah 10:25 (HCSB)
[25] In just a little while My wrath will be spent and My anger will turn to their destruction."

7. This will mark the end of the age and God's anger toward Israel. Isaiah 10:22-23.u

> "The Hebrew: for "consumption" is *killayown* (HSN-<H3631>), pining; destruction; failing. Translated consumption here and failing (Dt. 28:65). It is from kalah, to end, cease, finish; perish; consume; destroy; accomplish; fail. The consumption decreed refers to the end of the age and the completion of all God's dealings with Israel in sin and rebellion, the culmination of all things that bring to end the times of the Gentiles and restore Israel in

[105] Hamilton, V. P. (1999). 1228 מְעַט. R. L. Harris, G. L. Archer Jr., & B. K. Waltke (Eds.), *Theological Wordbook of the Old Testament* (electronic ed., p. 519). Chicago: Moody Press.

eternal, overflowing righteousness"[106]

8. The Lord will "stir up," in Hebrew, "wake up," a whip (scourge) against him *like he did* against Median when Gideon called for help in Judges 7:25 and the tribe of Ephraim came out to fight, and *took the two princes* and killed them.

9. The Lord will raise up his staff like he did in Egypt, with plagues and disasters.

10. The burden and yoke of bondage shall be destroyed by the anointing-Messiah means "Anointed One."

11. The Assyrian will be broken on the mountains of Israel, and the Lord will tread him under foot.

12. Again, his burden and yoke will be broken.

13. When he comes to tread in Israel's palaces (these verses have never happened in history), Israel will raise up seven shepherds (Leaders) and eight principle men. There will be plenty of leaders to help with the transition.

14. These leaders will destroy what is left of "Nimrod" or Assyria, where the Antichrist hails from.

Much like the association with the revised Roman Empire, the antichrist is also likened to the threat to Israel of the Assyrian Empire from before. These verses above have never

---

[106] Finis Jennings Dake, *Dake's Annotated Reference Bible: Containing the Old and New Testaments of the Authorized or King James Version Text*, (Lawrenceville, GA: Dake Bible Sales, Inc., 1997), WORD*search* CROSS e-book, Under: Isaiah "Chapter 10:25."

been fulfilled by the old Assyrian Empire. This Assyrian is the Antichrist, who has some association with modern-day Iraq. *It seems each past major kingdom had an antichrist type who oppressed Israel.* When mentioned in Scripture, the past historical figure doesn't seem to completely fulfill all of the prophecies, and it allows a double reference to the future Antichrist. The Biblical Assyrian kingdom of northern Mesopotamia became the center of one of the great empires of the ancient Middle East. It was mainly located in what is now northern Iraq and southeastern Turkey.

"He" the Roman?

Daniel 9:26-27 (KJV)
²⁶ And after threescore and two weeks shall Messiah be cut off, but not for himself: and <u>the people of the prince that shall come shall destroy the city and the sanctuary</u>; and the end thereof *shall be* with a flood, and unto the end of the war desolations are determined. (LB- Gap of time here called the church age).
²⁷ <u>And he</u> shall confirm the covenant with many for one week: and in the midst of the week <u>he</u> shall cause the sacrifice and the oblation to cease, and <u>for the overspreading of abominations</u> he shall make *it* desolate, even until the consummation, and that determined shall be poured upon the desolate.

While the Roman Titus of 70 A.D. fulfilled Verse 26, he never fulfilled Verse 27. Even the best misguided historicists cannot twist the true facts as much as they do to say that this event has already taken place, along with their mistaken preterist's notions. Preterists are those who believe most of what we call "future" events have already been fulfilled in some past event. Some have even said that Jesus has already come back.

Verse 27 is about a *future* man who wants to rule the world. Because he is so close to the mention of Daniel's future, "the prince that shall come," who we know was the Roman prince Titus who *did* destroy the city and the sanctuary, most infer a Roman connection for the Antichrist. However, the Bible just says "he" here and suggests any possible time *after* the last phrase. Therefore, "he" may not necessarily be a Roman person, but from the *territory* that was called "Roman." Some teach that "he" may possibly be another "prince" that would come, although in other places the Antichrist is called a king. We know this verse is speaking of the Antichrist because of Paul's teaching in 2 Thess. 2, which confirms Daniel's prophecy about him.

1. He is mentioned with Rome and assumed to be somehow connected, but not necessarily so.

2. He will establish a covenant with many nations for seven years.

3. He will desecrate the Jewish temple.

4. He is associated with the Harlot of Rome.

Revelation 17- The red beast system that the harlot rides during the Tribulation period as it relates to Rome.

Revelation 17:3-14 (KJV)
³ So he carried me away in the spirit into the wilderness: and I saw a woman sit upon <u>a scarlet coloured beast, full of names of blasphemy, having seven heads and ten horns.</u>
⁴ And the woman was arrayed in purple and scarlet colour, and decked with gold and precious stones and pearls, having a golden cup in her hand full of abominations and filthiness of her fornication:
⁵ And upon her forehead *was* a name written, MYSTERY, BABYLON THE GREAT, THE MOTHER OF HARLOTS

AND ABOMINATIONS OF THE EARTH.

[6] And I saw <u>the woman drunken with the blood of the saints,</u> and with <u>the blood of the martyrs of Jesus</u>: and when I saw her, I wondered with great admiration.

[9] And here *is* the mind which hath wisdom. <u>The seven heads are seven mountains,</u> on which the woman sitteth.

[10] And <u>there are seven kings</u>: five are fallen, and <u>one is,</u> *and* the other is not yet come; and when he cometh, he must continue <u>a short space.</u>

[11] And <u>the beast that was, and is not, even he is the eighth, and is of the seven,</u> and goeth into perdition.

[12] And the ten horns which thou sawest are ten kings, which have received no kingdom as yet; but receive power as kings one hour with the beast.

[13] These have one mind, and shall give their power and strength unto the beast.

[14] These shall make war with the Lamb, and the Lamb shall overcome them: for he is Lord of lords, and King of kings: and they that are with him *are* called, and chosen, and faithful.

The "beast" has seven heads, which are seven mountains (hills) according to verse nine. We have already discussed this beast in detail before, but now, its color is red from the slaughter of men during the Tribulation. Generally, we believe that the seven represent the seven kingdoms that will exist up

Rome's seven hills

to the middle of the Tribulation period. But notice on the map that the Italian city of Rome sits on seven hills.

> "There is more than one interpretation for this text. Literally speaking, Rome is known as the city of seven hills. The Vatican sits on one side of the Tiber River, facing the seven hills."[107]

I only leave this suggestion in because I do believe the future harlot of false religion will be connected to the city of Rome.

Revelation 17:18 (KJV)
[18] And the woman which thou sawest is <u>that great city</u>, which reigneth over the kings of the earth.

In ancient times, hills were sacred high places used to worship and offer sacrifices to deities. "That great city," had to be a city that existed in John's day. These seven hills may be a clue that Rome will be involved in the last day. Maybe a false religion will make its headquarters there. Some folks have said it already has for centuries and that it is the Roman Catholic Church. I believe that there are true Christians in the Catholic faith and they do not represent this *false* religion. The "harlot sits on seven hills" (v. 9 AMP). I believe that this theory may be too easy, although possible. The woman is a *city* where saints and martyrs of Jesus have died (v. 6). This city is a place that kings and nations of the earth have committed fornication with (v. 2). She as a city is called "mysterious Babylon" (v. 5). Meaning this Babylonian idolatrous religion has reigned through the seven demonic kingdoms, even until now. Today, she has even hidden herself in the form of false Christianity

---

[107] Professor Walter J. Veith, Phd. https://amazingdiscoveries.org/S-deception_end-time_Babylon_Revelation_hills_Rome

itself. Now that form seeks to partner with other world religions to become a unified world religion.

Another possibility could exist in our time: Islam in control of Rome in the future. Islam wants to conquer Rome, prompted by an old prophecy that they would take Rome and convert the rest of the western world. Below is a citation from the Israeli National News:

"In the propaganda videos of the Islamic State there are many prophecies about the fall and the conquest of Rome. There is a long Islamic tradition aiming at Rome, "Romiyyah", aiming to make it the fourth holiest city of Islam (after Mecca, Medina and Jerusalem) and the base from which Islam will conquer the Western world. Rome is the greatest magnet of the mystical Islamic universe.

Roger Garaudy, the French intellectual who converted to Islam, in 1986 launched his challenge, boasting: "I'll bring Islam to Rome." The foundation of this prophecy is the thirtieth Sura of the Koran, called ar Rum, "Romans." The fall of Rome is based on the myth of the Emperor Heraclius and a letter that he would have written to Muhammad, recognizing him as "the messenger of God."

Ahmad ibn Hanbal, the founder of the Islamic Hanbali school (now in power in Saudi Arabia) reported among the "hadith," the sayings of Muhammad, that the Prophet of Islam predicted that "the city of Heraclius (Constantinople) would fall first, then Rome."

In 2003, Osama Bin Laden made a speech on "The new Rome" and three years later, in the footsteps of Pope

Benedict's Islamic speech at Regensburg University, Al Qaeda proclaimed: "Servants of the Cross, expect defeat, the Muslims will conquer Rome as they conquered Constantinople." [108]

While this may be part of this interpretation to involve Rome here, there is more, as I taught before concerning the seven "mountains" in Verse 10-11. Seven mountains are definitely seven kings/kingdoms, and then later an eighth. The interpretation in Verse 9 calls these heads mountains or kings, and in Verse 12 there are another literal ten kings mentioned. It is not hard to see that the seven are speaking of kingdoms and not "kings" only. Many teach as I do: the sixth kingdom is the Roman Empire. All are related to the history of Israel. They list them as such:

"1. The Egyptian Empire 2. The Assyrian Empire 3. The Babylonian Empire 4. The Medo-Persian Empire 5. The Greek Empire 6. The Roman Empire 7. The Empire of Antichrist I (The little horn between the 10 horns) 8. The Empire of Antichrist II (The little horn – became larger than its associates)." [109] -From Nils Ibstedt- "Seven World Empires."

A son of revived Greece?

Zechariah 9:13-14 (KJV)
[13] When I have bent Judah for me, filled the bow with Ephraim, and raised up thy sons, O Zion, against thy sons, O Greece, and made thee as the sword of a mighty man.

---

[108] Read entire Article by Giulio Meotti, 10/03/15 Israel National News
http://www.israelnationalnews.com/Articles/Article.aspx/16609
[109] Seven World Empires.pdf Chapter index. www.nils-ibstedt.com. See also Nils Ibstedt - Wikipedia, the free encyclopedia

¹⁴ And <u>the LORD shall be seen over them</u>, and his arrow shall go forth as the lightning: and <u>the Lord GOD shall blow the trumpet</u>, and shall go with whirlwind

Dake: "Notes for Verse 13

"a [Judah for me, filled the bow with Ephraim] Both Judah and Ephraim are spoken of as being a bow in the hands of God, and as a sword in the hands of a mighty man to help God in the battle of Armageddon against <u>Antichrist who, with his armies surrounding Jerusalem, will have taken the city at the very moment Christ comes to earth to deliver Israel</u> (Zech. 14:1-5,14-15). If both Judah and Ephraim will be used by God in that day, then both will be gathered back to Palestine by this time to fulfill this passage; therefore, not only Judah, but also Ephraim will be gathered from all nations in sufficient numbers to fight in this battle for their own existence.

b [raised up thy sons, O Zion, against thy sons, O Greece, and made thee as the sword of a mighty man] This is one of a number of scriptures predicting the revival of the Grecian Empire under Antichrist to fight against Israel in the last days. See <u>Seven-Headed, Ten-Horned Beast</u>, and <u>Eight Mountain Kingdoms and Israel</u>. When we read here of the sons of Zion being raised up against the sons of Greece we are to understand it as a reference to the battle of Armageddon when warriors of the Revived Grecian Empire of Dan. 8 and Dan. 11 will be fighting against the sons of Zion (Israelites) at the second coming of Christ (Zech. 9:13). <u>In this battle the Lord will literally be seen over the sons</u>

of Zion (Zech. 9:14; 14:1-5; Isa. 63:1-6; Joel 2:11; 2Th. 1:7-10; Jude 1:14-15; Rev. 11:15; 19:11-21). The arrow of the Lord that will "go forth as the lightning" must refer to the flaming fire with which Christ and His angels will come. The blowing of a trumpet by God will be literally true in that day (Isa. 27:13; Joel 2:1,15; Mt. 24:31). The Lord of Hosts will defend His people (Zech. 9:15) and save them (Zech. 9:16). [110]

Antiochus IV ruled the Eastern Greek Empire that divided after Alexander the Great died (called the **Seleucid Empire**, a <u>Hellenistic</u> state ruled by the Seleucid dynasty that existed from 312 BC to 63 BC). It became the greatest of the four divisions of the divided Grecian Empire, and Antiochus IV was from Macedonia but ruled the area that is now the Middle East today. He was a *"type,"* representing the future Antichrist, who will revive this Grecian/Babylonian area as his own and rule from Babylon in the future. Perhaps this suggests to some a Grecian heritage for the Antichrist, but I see a more probable Iraqi or Syrian heritage. Notice that Joel states that Israel's remnant will be sold there during the last half of the Tribulation.

Joel 3:6 (KJV)
6 The children also of Judah and the children of Jerusalem have <u>ye sold unto the Grecians</u>, that ye might remove them far from their border.

The king of Sheshach (Babylon)

Jeremiah 25:26-29 (HCSB)
26 all the kings of the north, both near and far from one

---

[110] Finis Jennings Dake, Dake's Annotated Reference Bible: Containing the Old and New Testaments of the Authorized or King James Version Text, (Lawrenceville, GA: Dake Bible Sales, Inc., 1997), WORDsearch CROSS e-book, Under: "Chapter 9."

another; that is, <u>all the kingdoms of the world</u> which are on the face of the earth. <u>Finally, the king of Sheshach</u> (LB- Babylon) <u>will drink after them.</u>
²⁷ "Then you are to say to them: This is what the LORD of Hosts, the God of Israel, says: Drink, get drunk, and vomit. Fall down and <u>never get up again,</u> as a result of the sword I am sending among you.
²⁸ If they refuse to take the cup from you and drink, you are to say to them: This is what the LORD of Hosts says: You must drink!
²⁹ For <u>I am already bringing disaster on the city that bears My name, so how could you possibly go unpunished?</u> You will not go unpunished, for I am summoning <u>a sword against all the inhabitants</u> of the earth"—[this is] the declaration of the LORD of Hosts.

It is clear that Jeremiah 25 is about the final day when Christ comes back. God commands Jeremiah to make all these nations drink from God's cup of fury, but he mentions one king separately: the king of Babylon. This is the Antichrist. The title "king of Babylon" is obviously also used in Isaiah 14 of the Antichrist. Remember, Babylon was originally part of and controlled by Assyria until they rebelled and conquered it. One day, disaster is forecast for the future of Jerusalem at the hands of this king.

Isaiah 14:3-7 (KJV)
³ And it shall come to pass <u>in the day that the LORD</u> shall give thee rest from thy sorrow, and from thy fear, and from the hard bondage wherein thou wast made to serve,
⁴ That thou shalt take up this proverb against <u>the king of Babylon,</u> and say, How hath the oppressor ceased! the golden city ceased!
⁵ The LORD hath broken the staff of the wicked, *and* the sceptre of the rulers. (LB.-Perhaps the false prophet and the Antichrist?)
⁶ He who smote the people in wrath with a continual stroke, <u>he that ruled the nations in anger,</u> is persecuted, *and* none hindereth.

7 **The whole earth is at rest, *and* is quiet: they break forth into singing.**

Isaiah 14:9-11 (KJV)
9 **Hell from beneath is moved for thee to meet *thee* at thy coming: it stirreth up the dead for thee, *even* all the chief ones of the earth; it hath raised up from their thrones all the kings of the nations.**
10 **All they shall speak and say unto thee, Art thou also become weak as we? art thou become like unto us?**
11 **Thy pomp is brought down to the grave, *and* the noise of thy viols: the worm is spread under thee, and the worms cover thee.**

We spoke of this chapter before in detail. Babylon today, if it were rebuilt, would be in the country of Iraq, about 52 miles southwest of the Iraqi capital, Baghdad. Most of these nations that surround Israel are under the religious control of Islam, including Iraq. If the Antichrist possibly comes from Iraq, he would most likely be a Muslim who champions the Islamic faith at first. He would partner with the false Christian leader(s) and the newly chosen Jewish messiah. In this way, he would champion world religions and Middle Eastern peace. For years, prophecy teachers have been teaching that the Antichrist would be the false Jewish messiah, but the Jews would never choose a Muslim as their Messiah.

The prince of Tyrus- (Tyre, Lebanon) A "type" of the Antichrist

Ancient Tyre

Ezekiel 28:2-10 (KJV)

[2] Son of man, say unto <u>the prince of Tyrus</u>, Thus saith the Lord GOD; Because thine heart *is* lifted up, and thou hast said, <u>I *am* a God</u>, I sit *in* <u>the seat of God</u>, in the midst of the seas; yet thou *art* a man, and not God, though <u>thou set thine heart</u> as the heart of God:

[3] Behold, thou *art* wiser than Daniel; there is no secret <u>that they can hide</u> from thee:

[4] With <u>thy wisdom</u> and with thine understanding <u>thou hast gotten thee riches</u>, and hast gotten gold and silver into thy treasures:

[5] By thy great wisdom *and* by thy traffick hast <u>thou increased</u> thy riches, and <u>thine heart is lifted up because of thy riches</u>:

[6] Therefore thus saith the Lord GOD; <u>Because</u> thou hast set thine heart as the heart of God;

[7] Behold, therefore <u>I will bring strangers upon thee</u>, the terrible of the nations: and <u>they shall draw their swords</u> against the beauty of thy wisdom, and they shall defile thy brightness.

[8] <u>They shall bring thee down to the pit</u>, and thou shalt die the deaths of *them that are* slain in the midst of the seas.

[9] Wilt thou yet say before him that slayeth thee, I *am* God? but thou *shalt be* a man, and no God, in the hand of him that

slayeth thee.

10 Thou shalt die the deaths of the uncircumcised <u>by the hand of strangers:</u> for I have spoken *it,* **saith the Lord GOD.**

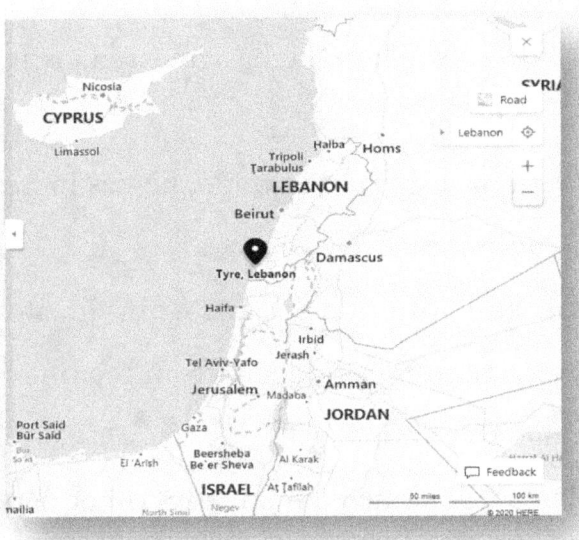

Tyre was an ancient Phoenician city in what is now Lebanon. It still exists today, directly north of Jerusalem. It is one of the oldest continuously inhabited cities in the world. Ezekiel's prophecy here about the prince or ruler of Tyrus was about the physical man, who was either a type of the future Antichrist or he himself. This man was possessed or directly controlled by Satan himself (who is the spiritual *king* of Tyrus), based on what seems to be in the next few verses (see below). This was a real person, just like Antiochus IV, who was called Ethbaal II or Ithobalus II (590-573) according to Josephus. He either represented the future Antichrist as a *type,* or the Antichrist is considered to be *like* him. Why Arthur Pink did not list him as one of his past types of the Antichrist is unknown.

What we learn about the Antichrist from the *type,* **the Prince of Tyre:**

1. He says I am God; I sit in the seat of God.

2. He fixes it in his heart that he is God.

3. With his wisdom, he has amassed great personal wealth.

4. With his expertise in trade, he has increased his wealth immensely.

5. He is full of pride because of his great wealth.

6. God will bring strangers from the outside who will wage war against you.

7. They will be fierce men from other nations.

8. They will destroy your bright splendor (city?).

9. He will die at a stranger's hands.

10. You will die the death of the uncircumcised.

11. You will go down into the "pit" like someone drowning in the sea.

Arthur Pink wrote *The Antichrist* in 1923 and listed 10 "types" of the Antichrist in Scripture in Chapter 15:

1. Cain- Gen 4:5
2. Lamach- Gen. 4:24
3. Nimrod- Gen. 10,11
4. Chedorlaomer- king of Elam (pre-Persia) Gen. 14

"Colossians Rawlinson searched for his name on the tablets of ancient Assyria, and there he found that his official title was, "Ravager of the west!"

214

Thus was he a true type of the coming one who shall wade through a sea of blood to his coveted position as Emperor of the world."[111]

5. Pharaoh- Exodus 1, an Assyrian who did not know Joseph and what he did for Egypt.

Isaiah 52:4 (KJV)
⁴ For thus saith the Lord GOD, My people went down aforetime into Egypt to sojourn there; and <u>the Assyrian oppressed them</u> without cause.

Acts 7:18 (KJV)
¹⁸ Till another king arose, which knew not Joseph.

6. Abimelech- Judges 9- Son of Gideon king over Israel
7. Saul- 1 Sam. 9-10 king of Israel
8. Goliath- 1 Sam 17 A giant who worked with the Philistines
9. Absalom- 2 Sam. 13-18 David's son born of Maacah daughter the king of Geshur (2 Sam. 3:2)
10. Herod- Matt. 2

History has a few more, and maybe we should only look at kings or rulers who oppressed Israel in the six previous kingdoms and were failed attempts.

1. King of Elam Chedorlaomer - Gen. 14
2. Egyptian/Assyrian Hyksos Pharaoh-Ex. 1:8, Acts 7:18, Isaiah 52:4[112]

---

[111] Arthur W. Pink, *The Antichrist*, (Swengel, PA: Bible Truth Depot, 1923), WORD*search* CROSS e-book, 224.

[112] https://www.knowingthebible.net/topical-studies/the-pharaohs-of-the-exodus "Assuming the traditional date of the exodus this "new king" most likely was a Hyksos ruler. The Hyksos were a blend of Semitic people from the northern part of the Mesopotamia and took over the Egyptian throne from 1720 to 1570 BC. As foreigners they would have had no knowledge of Joseph. This

3. Assyrian king Sennacherib
4. Babylonian king Nebuchadnezzar
5. Persian king Cyrus the great
6. Greek ruler Antiochus IV
7. Roman Emperor Nero, or Prince Titus (who attacked Jerusalem)
8. Muslim Mohammed/Islam
9. The Popes/Hitler-Germany/ Europe
10. The Antichrist who will come up among the 10 who are crowned in Dan. 7:7-8; Rev. 13, 17.

> **Dake: "[the prince of Tyrus]** According to Josephus, he was Ithobalus II. He had such pride that he even claimed to be God and exalted his heart as the heart of God (Ezek. 28:2,6,9), making a suitable picture of the coming Antichrist who will likewise exalt himself and claim to be God (2Th. 2:4). Satan ruled the king of Tyre, as proved by the association of Lucifer with him in Ezek. 28:11-19. Satan will also rule through Antichrist (2Th. 2:8-12; Rev. 13:1-8)."[113]

After his words against the RULER/PRINCE, Ezekiel describes the true KING of Tyrus, who is no doubt Satan himself. Ezekiel's prophecy mentions the RULER/PRINCE who most certainly was a man, and the KING who *controlled* the prince, who was the Devil. This relationship will also be the case with the Antichrist. We don't know what role Lebanon has in this, except that this was a spiritual seat of Satan in the earliest ages.

---

possibility is supported by Isa. 52:4, which refers to the pharaoh that oppressed the Israelites as being an Assyrian, a people group from the northern part of the Mesopotamia."
[113] Finis Jennings Dake, *Dake's Annotated Reference Bible: Containing the Old and New Testaments of the Authorized or King James Version Text*, (Lawrenceville, GA: Dake Bible Sales, Inc., 1997), WORD*search* CROSS e-book, Under: Ezekiel "Chapter 28."

Ezekiel 28:12-13 (KJV)
[12] Son of man, take up a lamentation upon <u>the king of Tyrus</u>, and say unto him, Thus saith the Lord GOD; Thou sealest up the sum, full of wisdom, and perfect in beauty.
[13] <u>Thou hast been in Eden</u> the garden of God; every precious stone *was* thy covering, the sardius, topaz, and the diamond, the beryl, the onyx, and the jasper, the sapphire, the emerald, and the carbuncle, and gold: the workmanship of thy tabrets and of thy pipes was prepared in thee in the day that thou wast created.

A cruel ruler, strong and fierce king over Egypt during the last days

Isaiah 19:4 (KJV)
[4] And the Egyptians will I give over into the hand of <u>a cruel lord; and a fierce king</u> shall rule over them, saith the Lord, the LORD of hosts.

Daniel 11:42 (KJV)
[42] He shall stretch forth his hand also upon the countries: and the land of Egypt shall not escape.

Egypt will not escape the hand of this cruel and fierce king of the future. Isaiah 19:2 declares that this will be preceded by a civil war and great confusion.

The chief head or leader of the Earth

Psalm 110:5-6 (KJV)
[5] The Lord at thy right hand shall strike through kings (Gk.-plural) in the day of his wrath.
[6] He shall judge among the heathen, he shall fill *the places* with the dead bodies; he shall wound the heads (Gk. Singular "head") over many countries (Heb. actually *earth*).

217

"The further statement "He shall execute the heads of many countries" could also be translated "He shall strike through the head over a wide land." This could be a reference to the doom of the Man of Sin, "whom the Lord will consume with the breath of His mouth and destroy with the brightness of His coming" (2 Thess. 2:8)."[114]

Notice in Revelation 16 that there are still kings during the last day. There are still countries with rulers, even though the Antichrist is ruling. Revelation 16:13 proves that spirits come out of Satan, the Antichrist, and the false prophet to deceive and prepare these kings to come to battle.

Revelation 16:13-14 (KJV)
[13] And I saw three unclean spirits like frogs *come* out of the mouth of the dragon, and out of the mouth of the beast, and out of the mouth of the false prophet.
[14] For they are the spirits of devils, working miracles, *which* go forth <u>unto the kings of the earth and of the whole world</u>, to <u>gather them to the battle</u> of that great day of God Almighty.

Interestingly, "the earth" and "the whole world" seem to be two different places. It may be that the Antichrist will have full rule over "the earth," but not "the whole world." He would only influence the rest of the world through coercion if this were the case.

---

[114] MacDonald, W. (1995). *Believer's Bible Commentary: Old and New Testaments* (A. Farstad, Ed.; pp. 725–726). Thomas Nelson.

Chapter 9
Is Gog in Ezekiel 38-9 the Antichrist?

Ezekiel 38:2-3 (KJV)
[2] Son of man, set thy face against <u>Gog</u>, the land of Magog, <u>the chief prince</u> of Meshech and Tubal, and <u>prophesy against him</u>,
[3] And say, Thus saith the Lord GOD; Behold, I *am* against thee, O Gog, the chief prince of Meshech and Tubal:

Who is Gog, and where are the lands he comes from that are mentioned here? Those of us who take these verses literally want to know: When in time does this battle happen? Theologians for millennia have been struggling with and debating these questions without end. Because of recent Russian events, all sorts of people are shouting that Ezekiel 38-39 are coming true. I believe these chapters represent two different events and time periods. Therefore, "Gog" is a name that can represent more than one person.

Prophecy teacher Mark Hitchcock said:
"By far, the most controversial issue in Ezekiel 38–39 is the setting or timing of the invasion. The

specific time of the invasion in Ezekiel 38 is difficult to determine."[115]

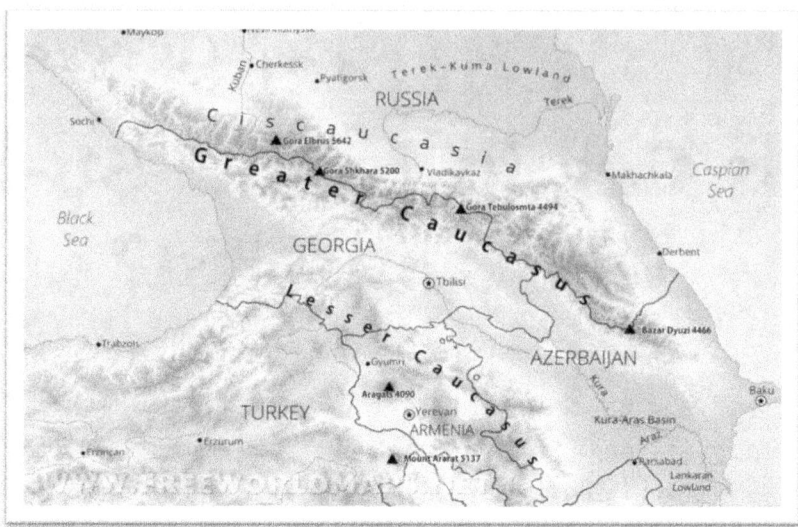

I believe these chapters explain who Gog is and for what period of time he exists. Magog was the general name of the country north of the Caucasus Mountains, which are between the Black and Caspian Seas.

But, where is Magog today?

"Most reference books, following Flavius Josephus, identify Tubal in Ezekiel's time as an area that is now in Turkey."[116]

According to Dake, the name "Gog" means "roof" or "mountain." Some translations interpret verse two as: "Gog, the land of Magog, prince of "Rosh (Russia), Meshech, and Tubal." Others translate it as "Gog from the land of Magog,

---

[115] Mark Hitchcock, Iran The Coming Crisis: Radical Islam, Oil, And The Nuclear Threat (Sisters, OR: Multnomah, 2006), p. 178.
[116] https://runyoncanyon-losangeles.com/blog/where-is-present-day-gog-and-magog/

chief prince of Meshech (Meshchovsk) and Tubal (Tobolsk)."
The difference being that "rosh" possibly means "chief," but
could be a proper name as the Septuagint uses and translates
this word as a proper name. [117]

Some say Rosh is today's Russia, and Magog is a group of
countries far north of Israel, but still mostly Russia- (see
map).[118]

Tom Constable on Ezekiel 38:1-3
  "The whole region would be what is now parts of
  southwestern Russia, Turkey, and Iran."

But notice the countries that are with him. All are
currently Muslim-majorities, and all share a hatred of Israel
today. Ethiopia is modern-day Sudan. Persia is modern-day

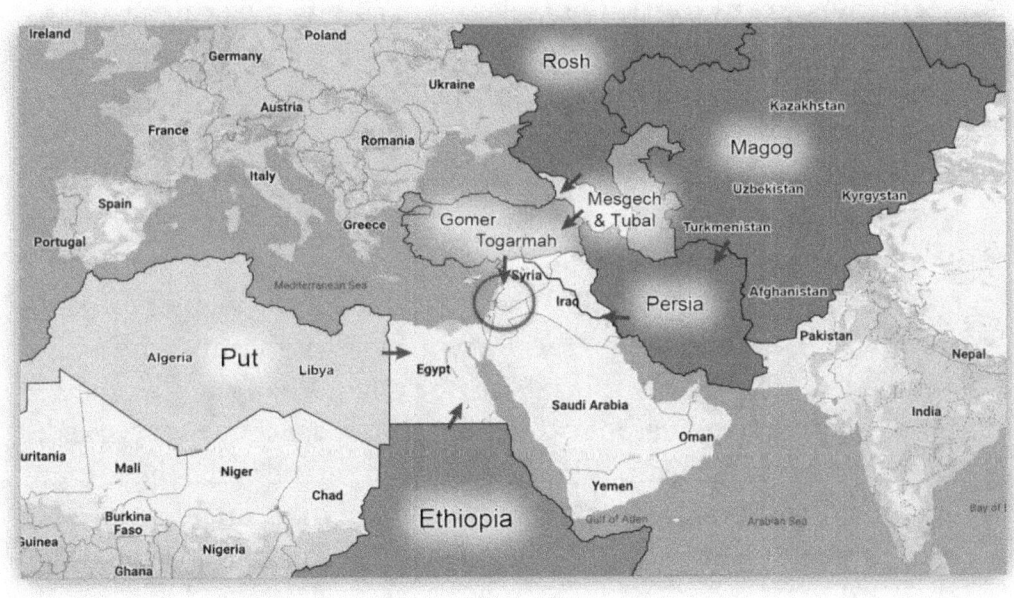

[117] Morris James C. Keys to Bible Prophecy. 2007 Holy Word Publishing Farmington Mo.63640,
P.90 footnote 33
[118] Taken from message by Dr. Jimmy Evans-
https://www.youtube.com/watch?v=7bHcvqDbySM

Iran. Put is northern African countries. Gomer and Togarmah are generally what Turkey is today.

Ezekiel 38:5-6 (KJV)
⁵ Persia, Ethiopia, and Libya with them; all of them with shield and helmet:
⁶ Gomer, and all his bands; the house of Togarmah of the north quarters, and all his bands: *and* many people with thee.

Let's just say the ruler of nations north of Israel will one day come against Israel, and this would include southern Russia, other parts of Russia and other countries connected to him. If we tried to apply this today, in 2023, Vladimir Putin would probably be called "Gog." But Ezekiel 38 is not necessarily prophetic for today's time. So in the last days, Gog will be over these countries and areas. Russia today is not ruling these areas, although it has influence in some of them.

Is "Gog" a Russian leader or another name for the Antichrist? I believe the answer can be found in the text. It seems whoever Gog is, controls much of what we call Russia today. There are so many different opinions about these chapters that it would make your head spin. Adam Clarke stated that Gog was probably Antiochus Epiphanes. "Chief prince of Meshech and Tubal—These probably mean the auxiliary forces, over whom Antiochus was supreme; they were the Muscovites and Cappadocians." [119]

When we are in the dark, we reach for improbabilities. If Gog was Antiochus, then God's word was not completely fulfilled, and we know this cannot be true. As a boy, I studied these chapters and came to the conclusion that they may speak of different wars against Israel. My main direction lately, after much study, leans toward Chapter 38 being the final battle mentioned in Revelation 20 *after* the millennial with "Gog and the land of Magog," and Chapter 39, "Gog," being the Antichrist and his demise at the end of the Tribulation.

---

[119] Adam Clarke, *Adam Clarke's Commentary*, (New York: Abingdon-Cokesbury Press, 1826), WORD*search* CROSS e-book, Under: "Ezekiel 38:2."

KEY:
Gog # 1 is the Antichrist and
Gog #2 is the millennial Gog.

Ez. 38:1-13	Gog^2 and Magog	Revelation 20 attack on Jerusalem
Ez. 38:14-23	Gog^2 & Gog^1	More likely the millennial Gog, and possibly both-Gog the Antichrist
Ez. 39	Gog^1	Antichrist at the end of the Tribulation

4 possibilities of when Gog attacks Jerusalem

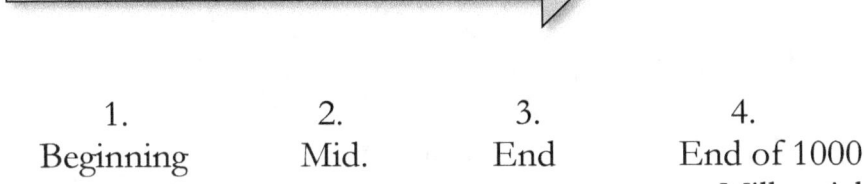

7 year Tribulation period

1.	2.	3.	4.
Beginning	Mid.	End	End of 1000 yr. Millennial

1. Before or at the beginning of the 7-year Tribulation, and then a treaty is signed for seven years.

2. In the middle of the 7 years, when Jesus and Paul prophesied about the abomination.

3. At the end of 7 years, when the Antichrist comes to destroy Israel.

4. At the end of the millennial reign, just before the Great White Throne Judgment

As we see, there are many theories about who Gog is and when he attacks. Some of my favorite Bible teachers disagree with each other.

Some believe this is an attack on Israel by Russia at the beginning of the Tribulation and not the Antichrist. This is John Walvoord's position:

> "Ezekiel was describing a battle that will involve Israel's remotest neighbors. They will sense their opportunity to attack when Israel feels secure under the false protection of her covenant with the Antichrist <u>sometime at the beginning of the seven-year period</u>. The nations involved in the attack will include the Soviet Union, Turkey, Iran, Sudan, Ethiopia, and Libya. Ezekiel first pictured the invasion by Gog and his allies (38:1–16)" [120]

But others disagree:

Harry Ironside believed this was the Antichrist at the close of the Tribulation:

> "It would seem, therefore, that these northern and eastern hordes must be included among the armies that will then invade Palestine, and therefore the onslaught depicted in this chapter will take place <u>toward the close of the great tribulation.</u>"[121]

---

[120] Dyer, C. H. (1985). Ezekiel. In J. F. Walvoord & R. B. Zuck (Eds.), *The Bible Knowledge Commentary: An Exposition of the Scriptures* (Vol. 1, p. 1300). Wheaton, IL: Victor Books.
[121] Ironside, H. A. (1949). Expository notes on Ezekiel, the prophet. (p. 265). Neptune, NJ: Loizeaux Brothers.

Thomas Constable considers it to probably be the Antichrist but also mentions the post-millennial possibility as found in Rev 20:

> "It is probably safe to say that "Gog" refers to the name or title of a ruler who will emerge in history while Israel is dwelling safely in her land (cf. v. 8). Perhaps Ezekiel referred to this unnamed future enemy of Israel as a dark figure (unknown and evil) calling him "Dark" much as we might refer to such a person as a new Hitler.[487] This may be the future Antichrist (cf. Dan. 11:40–45). I think it is, but Gog also represents another important eschatological figure." [122]

Finis Dake clearly believed this to be the Antichrist at the end of the Tribulation:

> "Gog is the same as the "little horn" of Dan. 7 and 8; "the prince that shall come" of Dan. 9; "the king of the north" of Dan. 11; the "man of sin," "the son of perdition," and "that wicked" of 2Th. 2; the "king of Babylon" of Isa. 13 -- Isa. 14; "the Assyrian" of Mic. 5; the "Antichrist" of 1Jn. 2; and "the beast" of Rev. 13. This is clear from a comparison of these passages with Ezek. 38 -- Ezek. 39. All these scriptures speak of a man who will come in the last days." [123]

---

[487] 487. Allen, *Ezekiel 20–48*, pp. 204–5.
[122] Constable, T. (2003). Tom Constable's Expository Notes on the Bible (Eze 38:1). Galaxie Software.
[123] Finis Jennings Dake, Dake's Annotated Reference Bible: Containing the Old and New Testaments of the Authorized or King James Version Text, (Lawrenceville, GA: Dake Bible Sales, Inc., 1997), WORDsearch CROSS e-book, Under: "Chapter 38."

"That Russia will invade Palestine before Armageddon. There is not the slightest proof of this in Ezek. 38-39, which passages deal exclusively with Gog leading many nations, including Russia, down from the north into <u>Palestine at the battle of Armageddon. Antichrist, not Russia, will make an invasion before this.</u> If Russia ever does invade Palestine before Armageddon, it will not be in fulfillment of any particular prophecy, especially not these two Chapters -- Ezek. 38-39." [124]

Albert Barnes seems to be saying this happens during the millennial reign after Israel is restored:

"38, 39. The last conflict of the world with God, and the complete overthrow of the former. <u>This section refers to times subsequent to the restoration of Israel</u>. As the Church (the true Israel) waxes stronger and stronger, more distant nations will come into collision and must be overthrown before the triumph is complete." [125]

Many of the older commentaries, like the *Pulpit Commentary* follow this interpretation: a past fulfillment, (some prior battle) and a future use of the name Gog, borrowed to mean any future enemy of Israel.

"Magog in Gen. 10:2 is mentioned among the sons of Japheth who were the ancestors of the

---

[124] Finis Jennings Dake, Dake's Annotated Reference Bible: Containing the Old and New Testaments of the Authorized or King James Version Text, (Lawrenceville, GA: Dake Bible Sales, Inc., 1997), WORDsearch CROSS e-book, Under: "Chapter 38."

[125] Barnes, A. (1879). *Notes on the Old Testament: Proverbs, Ecclesiastes, Song of Solomon, Jeremiah, Lamentations & Ezekiel* (F. C. Cook & J. M. Fuller, Eds.; p. 390). John Murray.

northern nations (cf. Ezek. 38:15 and 39:2). Hence the name *Magog* is used to denote the northern tribes, whose invasion of Palestine and adjoining parts took place about B.C. 630–600. From Ezek. 39 it seems that Gog was originally a leader among these tribes; and from Ezek. 38:17 it seems that Ezekiel took these names to be symbolical of all the foes of the people of God. Jewish tradition makes use of these names to indicate those nations who were expected to war against Jerusalem in the last days, and to be overthrown by the Messiah. Hence the employment of the terms here by St. John as denoting the ungodly people of the world, amongst whom Satan still exercises his power, though that power is limited to these, and he is completely bound as regards true believers.[126]

What a confusion of interpretation! As you see, there are many opinions. To see how four different preterists try to explain how Ezekiel 38-39 has *already* taken place, though none of them agree as to when it will, see the article *"Revelation 20: Four Views of Gog and Magog."* [127] None of these preterist views make sense to me, because I believe their fulfillment is in the future.

This future battle is specifically against Jerusalem but extends to all of Israel. Ezekiel Chapters 38-39 make the inference that the reason the "Gog" "prince of Rosh" in Chapter 38 is doing this is to "take treasure from them." This doesn't seem to follow the thinking behind the Antichrist building a worldly army, to only share in what he might take from Israel with other nations. His intention seems to be, at

---

126 Spence-Jones, H. D. M., ed. (1909). *Revelation* (p. 473). Funk & Wagnalls Company.
127 https://adammaarschalk.com/2010/04/05/revelation-20-four-views-of-gog-and-magog/

the end of the Tribulation: to utterly destroy Israel. This is an early clue that helps us understand that Gog is not the Antichrist in Chapter 38. Notice Gog's intent in verse twelve:

> **Ezekiel 38:12 (KJV)**
> ¹² <u>To take a spoil</u>, and to take a prey; to turn thine hand upon the desolate places *that are* <u>*now*</u> <u>inhabited</u>, and upon the people *that are* <u>gathered out</u> of the nations, <u>which have gotten cattle and goods, that dwell in the midst of the land</u>.

Israel seems to be in a normal state. These verses make more sense if they take place in the first part of the Tribulation or after the millennial reign. Israel seems prosperous in this verse and not desolate, as she surely would be at the end of the Tribulation.

To help rule out an end of the Tribulation interpretation, let's look at verses that are clearly about that time. These verses below, from Isaiah, Zechariah, and Revelation, are clearly about the Antichrist and the Day of the Lord, when the Antichrist does attack Israel and Christ in Israel. They show what state she is in at the end of the seven years. This will help us to set our Ezekiel 38 placement in the proper timeline.

The Day of the Lord at the end of the Tribulation verses

Isaiah 29:7 (KJV)
⁷ **And the multitude of all the nations that fight against Ariel** (LB- Ancient name for Jerusalem)**, even all that fight against her and her munition, and that distress her, shall be as a dream of a night vision.**

Isaiah 29:5-6 (KJV)
⁵ **Moreover the multitude of thy strangers shall be like small dust, and the multitude of the terrible ones *shall be* as chaff that passeth away: yea, <u>it shall be at an instant suddenly</u>.**

⁶ Thou shalt be <u>visited of the LORD of hosts</u> with thunder, and with earthquake, and great noise, with storm and tempest, and the flame of devouring fire.

Zechariah 14:1-3 (KJV)
¹ Behold, the day of the LORD cometh, and thy (LB-Jerusalem's) spoil shall be divided in the midst of thee.
² For I will gather all nations <u>against Jerusalem</u> to battle; and the city shall be taken, and the houses rifled, and the women ravished; and <u>half of the city</u> shall go forth into captivity, and the residue of the people shall not be cut off from the city.
³ Then shall the LORD go forth, and fight against those nations, as when he fought in the day of battle.

Zechariah 14:12 (KJV)
¹² And this shall be the plague wherewith the LORD will smite all the people that have fought against Jerusalem; <u>Their flesh shall consume away while they stand upon their feet, and their eyes shall consume away in their holes</u>, and their tongue shall consume away in their mouth.

Revelation 19:19 (KJV)
¹⁹ And I saw the beast, and the kings of the earth, and their armies, gathered together to make war against him that sat on the horse, and against his army.

The Antichrist will gather the nations of the world against Jerusalem and Israel to destroy them. He realizes he is facing Jesus Himself. His armies are not stopped in the mountains, and he enters Jerusalem and takes half of it. He hates the Jews because they are God's people. His main intent is not to take a spoil, although one will be taken. Jerusalem would not be have been at peace with him prior to this and would have been somewhat under his control from a prior attack. According to Jesus, in the middle of the seven years, the Antichrist will ravage Israel and attempt to kill them all. This will displace them once again, all over the world. How, after this point, could it be considered a peaceful time? So, the Gog and the Ezekiel 38 battle is probably not the Antichrist. Most of his armies will vaporize at the command of the Lord (see also Isaiah 11:4). The rest are consumed by the foul of the air.

This is the destruction of the Gog in Ezekiel 38, which seems to say he is destroyed in the mountains with great hailstones, and fire and brimstone. These verses do not match what we know of the Antichrist's demise.

Ezekiel 38:19-22 (KJV)
¹⁹ For in my jealousy *and* in the fire of my wrath have I spoken, Surely in that day there shall be a great shaking in the land of Israel;
²⁰ So that the fishes of the sea, and the fowls of the heaven, and the beasts of the field, and all creeping things that creep upon the earth, and all the men that *are* upon the face of the earth, shall shake at my presence, and the mountains shall be thrown down, and the steep places shall fall, and every wall shall fall to the ground.
²¹ And I will call for a sword against him <u>throughout all my mountains</u>, saith the Lord GOD: <u>every man's sword shall be against his brother.</u>
²² And I will plead against him with pestilence and with blood; and <u>I will rain upon him</u>, and upon his bands, and upon the many people that *are* with him, <u>an overflowing rain, and great hailstones, fire, and brimstone.</u>

Could these two Chapters be speaking of different time periods?

Notice each piece of these two chapters is separated by a phrase addressed to Ezekiel: "Son of man." This phrase denotes a change in thinking and maybe even a completely separate part of the prophecy. There are four sections: 38:1-13, 38:14-23, 39:1-16, and 39:17-29. To me, Chapter 38:1-13, is about the "Gog" who would come after the millennial reign (Rev. 20:8). Chapter 38:14-23 may be about both the postmillennial and the Antichrist but leans toward the

230

postmillennial Gog. It is not probable that both chapters are about the final Gog mentioned in Revelation 20.

Chapter 39:17-29 are fully and specifically about the time of the Antichrist and the end of the Tribulation, as we shall see. Maybe even the whole chapter, including verses 1-16. This would make it so much easier to understand these two chapters. Chapter 38 is about the final battle *after* the thousand-year reign of Christ, and Chapter 39 speaks of the Antichrist and the time at the end of the Tribulation period of seven years. They are two separate visions.

Ezekiel 39:7 (KJV)
⁷ So will I make my holy name known in the midst of my people Israel; and I will not *let them* pollute my holy name <u>any more</u>: and the heathen shall know that I *am* the LORD, the Holy One in Israel.

Ezekiel 39:7, which would probably be at the end of the Tribulation (because it is spoken in the 37ᵗʰ Chapter), declares that *after* this event the heathen will *never* be allowed to profane God's name there again. Why is this? Because Jesus now rules from His throne in Jerusalem. This does not mean that it couldn't possibly happen, but that from this point forward, "it would not be allowed." To me Verse 8 is the simplest proof that Ezekiel 38 is about the end of the Millennial.

Ezekiel 38:8 (KJV)
⁸ After many days thou shalt be visited: in the latter years thou shalt come into the land *that is* brought back from the sword, *and is* gathered out of many people, against the mountains of Israel, which have been always waste: but it is brought forth out of the nations, and they shall dwell safely all of them.

Could Russia and its Muslim allies one day attack Israel as a separate event? Of course, even today, in 2023, this scenario could very well be possible. Some believe this will happen before the Tribulation, and Israel will defeat Russia with the help of the Antichrist, which will begin a seven-year peace treaty. Many dispensationalists today teach this. Others teach slightly differently, saying that it will happen near the beginning of the Tribulation, after they have entered a peace treaty with the Antichrist, and God supernaturally delivers them, warning other nations to beware. Some say many will agree to a peace treaty out of fear of Israel.

However, it does not make the prophecy of Ezekiel 38-39 about that event. This would make "Gog" a Russian leader and not the Antichrist. Now, if, like in Daniel, this prophecy has two fulfillments according to a prophetic double reference, then maybe, in a roundabout way, some of these verses could be about a prior attack. I don't see anywhere in Scripture a clear statement of this. This is the best I can do after studying these chapters very carefully at face value. I would love to agree with all the modern prophecy teachers today, but I cannot. Prophecy teachers have been wrong a lot in the past because they tried to improperly interpret modern events by injecting themselves and current world events, into an ancient prophecy. For instance, many today say that the second gathering of Israel mentioned in Isaiah 11:11 is when Israel became a nation again in 1948, but the context of Isaiah 11 says the second re-gathering is when Christ comes back to the earth to rule (see v. 12).

Interpreting Ezekiel 38-39 as a whole single prophecy

A couple of verses make the interpretation that all of this prophecy is *only* about the Antichrist difficult for me. I believe that Chapter 38 is about another time and cannot be fully applied to the Antichrist.

There are four ideas in Chapters 38-39 that contradict this, namely:

1. Gog's attacks during a time of Israeli safety and "rest" (Ezekiel 38:11, 14),
2. The seven years of burning weapons afterwards (Ezekiel 38:9),
3. The Antichrist's burial (Ezekiel 39:4, 5, 11) and,
4. The attack on the city Jerusalem. There is no verse in Ezekiel 38-39 that says Gog comes into Jerusalem, but we know the Antichrist does this.

Let's look at these four points separately:

In Chapter 38- Gog's attack is during a time of Safety and Rest?

In this section of the prophecy, Gog is said to attack Israel when they are at rest and dwelling safely. Any Bible scholar will tell you this verbiage sounds like the one-thousand year millennial reign of Christ when Israel is promised peace and rest and is not likely a description of Israel today. One of my favorite dispensationalists, John Walvoord, suggests that this "rest" speaks of the time just *after* the peace treaty with the Antichrist, so that the seven years of burning weapons (39:9) would still fit. However, Israel might be *at peace* at this time but not *at rest*, which is spoken of here. Notice the similarity of these verses below that speak of the millennial reign and speak of the "rest" that comes in that dispensation of time.

Isaiah 11:10 (KJV)
[10] **And in that day there shall be a root of Jesse, which shall stand for an ensign of the people; to it shall the Gentiles seek: and his rest shall be glorious.**

233

Isaiah 14:5-7 (KJV)
⁵ The LORD hath broken the staff of the wicked, *and* the sceptre of the rulers.
⁶ He who smote the people in wrath with a continual stroke, he that ruled the nations in anger, is persecuted, *and* none hindereth.
⁷ The whole earth is at rest, *and* is quiet: they break forth into singing.

It seems to me that Chapter 38 is speaking of the time of the millennial, a time of REST. Also, this rings true because of the language of the previous Chapter 37, where it ends with Israel at the *beginning* of the millennial reign. It speaks of Israel reviving out of the graves and coming alive, and in Verse 22 it says, *"And I will make them one nation in the land upon the mountains of Israel; and one king shall be king to them all..."*, along with Verse 24: *"And David my servant shall be king over them; and they all shall have one shepherd..."* Here below are the last verses of Chapter 37. They are clearly about the time AFTER the Tribulation period. Israel is at rest when Christ himself makes a "covenant of peace" with them. So, one would assume that Chapter 38 would also be about the same time period going forward. Remember, men made the chapter numbers and placed them where they thought they should be. Chapter 37 ends at the beginning of the millennial reign. Let's continue to read in Chapter 37 to the last verse:

Ezekiel 37:24-28 (KJV)
²⁴ And David my servant *shall be* king over them; and they all shall have one shepherd: they shall also walk in my judgments, and observe my statutes, and do them. ²⁵ And they shall dwell in the land that I have given unto Jacob my servant, wherein your fathers have dwelt; and they shall dwell therein, *even* they, and their children, and their children's children for ever: and my servant David *shall be* their prince for ever.
²⁶ Moreover I will make a covenant of peace with them; it shall be an everlasting covenant with them: and I will place them, and multiply them, and will set my sanctuary in the midst of

them for evermore.
²⁷ **My tabernacle also shall be with them:** yea, I will be their
God, and they shall be my people.
²⁸ And **the heathen shall know** that I the LORD do sanctify
Israel, when my sanctuary shall be in the midst of them for
evermore.

The "rest" mentioned in Chapter 38 is the millennial
"rest." If 37 and 38 go together, we should be thinking about
the one-thousand-year reign as we cross the threshold of
Chapter 38. Now let's look at the three specific verses in
Chapter 38 that mention Israel being in a time of "rest and
safety."

Ezekiel 38:8 (KJV)
⁸ After **many days** thou shalt be visited: **in the latter years** thou
shalt come into the land *that is* brought back from the sword,
and is gathered out of many people, against the mountains of
Israel, which have been always waste: but it is brought forth
out of the nations, and **they shall dwell safely all of them.**

Ezekiel 38:11 (KJV)
¹¹ And thou shalt say, I will go up to the land of unwalled
villages; I will go to them that are **at rest, that dwell safely,** all
of them **dwelling without walls,** and having neither bars nor
gates,

Ezekiel 38:14 (HCSB)
¹⁴ **"Therefore prophesy, son of man, and say to Gog: This is
what the Lord GOD says: On that day when My people Israel
are dwelling securely, will you not know ⌊this⌋?**

Ezekiel 38:8 declares "after many days and "in the latter
years" in a time when Israel "shall dwell safely all of them," is
when this Gog attacks. In Verse 11 Gog says, "I will go to
them that are at rest." Maybe what is being said in Verse 14 is:
"Gog- do you know that Jesus has rule here with Israel and
that they are at peace?" "My people Israel are dwelling
securely." These verses sound millennial to me and would

make all of this flow with Revelation 20:8 about Gog and Magog there. If this time period is at the end of the Tribulation, wouldn't the Antichrist already have control of Israel? Would Israel be at peace and rest after the Antichrist makes war with them from the middle point on, as we see in Rev. 12:13-17? At the end of the Tribulation, the two witnesses have been in Jerusalem and have been murdered, raised from the dead, and raptured away. This is a cause for celebration in the world, even to the point of giving gifts to one another (Rev. 11:3-11). Maybe the true Israel, the remnant, is safe in Bozrah and Petra, hiding away, but not everyone in Israel is at rest. It just doesn't pan out that the "Gog" in Chapter 38 is the Antichrist.

Here are a few more speculative ideas to consider for Chapter 38. Could Gog be another force coming at the same time as the Antichrist and that be dealt with separately? Yes, this could be another possibility if he comes at the same time that the forces are at Megiddo and his forces come to attack Jerusalem from the north. However, based on our thinking, this would be inserted in Chapter 39 and not Chapter 38.

More improbable, this is a mid-Tribulation attack against the Antichrist, and Gog and all his armies fall in the mountains, and this is what the Antichrist uses to come into Jerusalem and sit in the temple. There are so many possibilities. As I said, most modern preachers teach that the rapture happens first, and then Russia will attack Israel *before* the Tribulation Period starts or just after.

Where are the other passages in the Bible about a pre-Trib. battle that fit these chapters? I cannot find them. I would not see a pre-Trib., nor a mid-Trib., battle in these verses, but would rather lean toward a future time after the millennial period mentioned in Revelation 20.

Revelation 20:7-9 (KJV)
⁷ **And when <u>the thousand years are expired</u>, Satan shall be**

loosed out of his prison,

⁸ And shall go out to deceive the nations which are in the four quarters of the earth, Gog and Magog, to gather them together to battle: the number of whom *is* as the sand of the sea.

⁹ And they went up on the breadth of the earth, and compassed <u>the camp of the saints about, and the beloved city</u>: and fire came down from God out of heaven, and devoured them.

A twofold prediction

Numbers 11:26-27 (KJV)

²⁶ But there remained two *of the* men in the camp, the name of the one *was* Eldad, and the name of the other Medad: and the spirit rested upon them; and they *were* of them that were written, but went not out unto the tabernacle: and they prophesied in the camp.

²⁷ And there ran a young man, and told Moses, and said, Eldad and Medad do prophesy in the camp.

Keep in mind Jewish tradition continues to believe Israel will be attacked in the last day by a ruler called Gog and Magog. Two men who prophesied during Moses's day, were mentioned in the Hebrew tradition. Notice that Adam Clarke's comments on Revelation 20:8, state that John repeated a hidden prophecy by these two men during Moses's day.

> **"Gog and Magog**—This seems to be almost literally taken from the Jerusalem Targum, and that of Jonathan ben Uzziel, on Numbers 11:26. I shall give the words at length: "And there were two men left in the camp, the name of the one was Eldad, the name of the other was Medad, and on them the spirit of prophecy rested. Eldad prophesied and said, 'Behold, Moses the prophet, the scribe of Israel, shall be taken from this world;

and Joshua the son of Nun, captain of the host, shall succeed him.' Medad prophesied and said, 'Behold quails shall arise out of the sea, and be a stumbling block to Israel.' Then they both prophesied together, and said, 'In <u>the very end of time</u> Gog and Magog and their army shall come up against Jerusalem, and they shall fall by the hand of <u>the King Messiah</u>; and for seven whole years shall the children of Israel light their fires with the wood of their warlike engines, and they shall not go to the wood nor cut down any tree.'" In the Targum of Jonathan ben Uzziel, on the same place, the same account is given; only the latter part, that is, the conjoint prophecy of Eldad and Medad, is given <u>more circumstantially, thus</u>: "And they both prophesied together, and said, 'Behold, <u>a king shall come up from the land of Magog in the last days,</u> and shall gather the kings together, and leaders clothed with armor, and all people shall obey them; and they shall wage war in the land of Israel against <u>the children of the captivity</u>, but the hour of lamentation has been long prepared for them, for they shall be <u>slain by the flame of fire</u> which shall proceed from under the throne of glory, and <u>their dead carcasses shall fall on the mountains of the land of Israel</u>; and all the wild beasts of the field, and the wild fowl of heaven, shall come and devour their carcasses; and <u>afterwards all the dead of Israel shall rise again to life,</u> and shall enjoy the delights prepared for them from the beginning, and shall receive the reward of their worlds.'"

This account seems most evidently to have been copied by St. John, but how he intended it to be applied is a question too difficult to be solved by the skill of man; yet both the account in the rabbins and in St. John is founded on Ezekiel, Ezekiel 38:1-39:29. The rabbinical writings are full of accounts concerning Gog and Magog, of which Wetstein has made a pretty large collection in his notes on this place. Under these names the enemies of God's truth are generally intended."[128]

According to Gotquestions.org, "The Targum (plural *Targumim*) is an Aramaic paraphrase/explanation/interpretation of the Hebrew text of the Jewish scriptures provided by the rabbis in the course of teaching." Jesus clashed with these teachings when they were taken above the word of God in Mark 7:8-13. The Jewish rabbis believed that these two men during Moses's day prophesied that Gog would come at the end of the seven years to fight against the "king Messiah."

It seems obvious and interesting to me that the predictions here are twofold. First, a Gog who would come in "the very end of time" against Jerusalem and the king Messiah (possibly the Millennial king) and would be destroyed by fire in their dead carcasses on the mountains. The second prophecy seems to describe a different person, a king from the land of Magog, in a different time period, who would fall in the "last days" against the "children of the captivity." To me, this prophecy plays on the position and timing of Israel coming out of the Tribulation period. Thus the statement, "Afterwards all the dead of Israel shall rise again to life." For it is at the end of the Tribulation that the righteous of Israel will arise to rule with Christ. So this prophecy speaks of two time periods, it seems, out of order of course. We only understand these predictions because of the verses in Revelation 20.

---

[128] Adam Clarke, *Adam Clarke's Commentary*, (New York: Abingdon-Cokesbury Press, 1826), WORD*search* CROSS e-book, Under: "Revelation20:8".

This is what Paul the Apostle said would happen concerning the *Day of the Lord* that ends the Tribulation for Israel: When the people of the world in the Tribulation are saying "peace and safety," the sudden destruction is upon them.

1 Thessalonians 5:2-3 (KJV)
² For yourselves know perfectly that the day of the Lord so cometh as a thief in the night.
³ For when they shall say, Peace and safety; then sudden destruction cometh upon them, as travail upon a woman with child; and they shall not escape.

"When *they* say," not "when the righteous of Israel" are saying this. Apparently, around the time of the "abomination of desolation" in the middle of the Tribulation, the rest of the world and unrighteous Jews will be saying "peace and safety." Jesus made this statement about the same time period at the end of the Tribulation:

Luke 17:28 (KJV)
²⁸ Likewise also as it was in the days of Lot; they did eat, they drank, they bought, they sold, they planted, they builded;

Jesus said that the world would act normally as if nothing were wrong, even after the Antichrist takes over. Some use this explanation to say that this battle happens in the middle of the Tribulation because Israel will be under a treaty of peace with the Antichrist up until the midpoint. Jesus said that after the middle point of seven years, the *abomination* that Daniel prophesied would happen-the Antichrist coming and sitting on the mercy seat in the Temple (2 Thess. 2:4). He then stated that "great tribulation" would come on Israel and that it would be worse than they have ever had (Matt. 24:15-21).

Matthew 24:21 (KJV)
²¹ For then (LB- after the desolation by the Antichrist) **shall be**

great tribulation, such as was not since the beginning of the world to this time, no, nor ever shall be.

There will be no peace and safety for them after the middle point until Christ comes back. I would contend that while the world might be declaring "peace and safety," it is not the "rest and security" mentioned in Ezekiel 38-39. These are two different things. Ezekiel 38:11, 14 clearly state that it is when *Israel* is "at rest and dwelling safely." This could only be speaking of the millennial era.

This is one person's explanation of the "peace and safety" at the end of the Tribulation. This person believed that Gog in Ezekiel 38 is the Antichrist:

Time of Sudden Destruction

"When Antichrist shall have conquered the 10 kingdoms inside the Roman Empire in the first 3 1/2 years of Daniel's 70th week (Dan. 7:23-24; Rev. 13 and Rev. 17), and by these kingdoms shall have conquered Russia and the other nations north and east of the Roman empire in the last 3 1/2 years of Daniel's 70th week (Dan. 11:40-45), it will be time for the world to be saying "Peace and safety." They will think that getting rid of Israel (Zech. 14) will mean no further wars. They will then look forward to a period of peace and prosperity, but the Lord will come suddenly when Jerusalem is half taken and sudden destruction will be upon all the nations at Armageddon (Zech. 14; Joel 3; Rev. 19:11-21)."[129]

---

[129] Finis Jennings Dake, Dake's Annotated Reference Bible: Containing the Old and New Testaments of the Authorized or King James Version Text, (Lawrenceville, GA: Dake Bible Sales, Inc., 1997), WORDsearch CROSS e-book, Under: "Chapter 5."

This statement above seems like a futile attempt to put Ezekiel 38 in the Tribulation Period timepiece. Most do this because Chapter 39 clearly is, so they put the two chapters together. I say again, it is a fact that the focus here is on *Israel* being safe *and* at peace, and not the rest of the world, in these verses in Ezekiel. The early verse here, in Verse 8, has nothing to do with the *world* feeling safe but with *Israel* being brought forth out of the nations and truly being safe in the earth. Gog attacks *after* Israel is completely safe in the millennium.

Ezekiel 38:8 (KJV)
[8] **After many days** thou shalt be visited: in **the latter years** thou shalt come into the land *that is* **brought back** from the sword, *and is* **gathered out** of many people, against the mountains of Israel, which have been always waste: but it is **brought forth** out of the nations, and **they shall dwell safely all of them.**

When does this prophecy in Chapter 38 happen?

1. After many days, … "in the latter years" (Ezekiel 38:8).
2. When Israel is **brought back** from the sword- When they return again from being cut off (Ezek. 37:21).
3. When Israel is **gathered out** of many people (Ezek. 37:21)
4. When Israel is **brought forth** out of the nations (Isaiah 66:19-20).
5. When all of Israel **dwells safely** (Ezekiel 37:24-25)

This alone proves to me that at least the first section of Chapter 38 is happening at the end of the Millennium period.

This verse is used by some people to say that this Ezekiel 38-39 war comes in before the final campaign of Armageddon and before the Tribulation starts because the description of

Israel here sounds like today. However, Israel does not dwell safely "without walls" (vs. 11) right now, as these verses point out. The problem is that Israel, even now, has many walls and is not currently living securely. In contrast, being "brought back from the sword" does describe Israel just *after the end* of the Tribulation period and entering the millennial reign, when they will finally, for the last time, be gathered from the world (called the *second* time in Isaiah 11:11; 66:19-20). She is relatively at peace now, but not fully so. So many countries hate her and want to destroy her today. Ask anybody who currently resides in Jerusalem, "Do you feel completely safe from an outside attack?" Of course, they do not. They live with a constant threat of danger.

While unlikely, I'm open to a possible double reference here, like in Daniel: that these passages are first to be used to describe the Antichrist or a Russian leader partially but not fully, and then also Gog one thousand years later. In Daniel, a future man named Antiochus IV is mentioned, but he did not fulfill all of Daniel's prophecies. We understand now that the complete prophecies refer to someone else, namely the Antichrist, who will one day fulfill all those verses. Here below is John's account of "Gog" after the thousand years of rest and peace for Israel and the world. He wrote of a future leader named "Gog" *with* "Magog" to gather "them" together who will come against Christ and the holy city.

Revelation 20:7-9 (HCSB)
7 When the 1,000 years are completed, Satan will be released from his prison
8 and will go out to deceive the nations at the four corners of the earth, Gog and Magog, to gather them for battle. Their number is like the sand of the sea.
9 They came up over the surface of the earth and surrounded the encampment of the saints, the beloved city. Then fire came down from heaven and consumed them.

Ezekiel 38:8 (AMPC)
⁸ After <u>many days</u> you shall be visited *and* mustered [for service]; in <u>the latter years</u> you shall go against <u>the land that is restored</u> from the ravages of the sword, where <u>people are gathered out of many nations</u> upon the mountains of Israel, which had been a continual waste; but its [people] are brought forth out of the nations and <u>they shall dwell securely</u>, all of them.

One verse could be bothersome to some, to interpret Ezekiel 38 as a post-one thousand-year statement, but never the less, it speaks of the last attack: Verse 21 says, "Every man's sword shall be against his brother."

Ezekiel 38:21 (KJV)
²¹ And I will call for a sword against him throughout all my mountains, saith the Lord GOD: every man's sword shall be against his brother.

This doesn't seem to be necessary at this time, for it is Christ himself who calls down fire from heaven to dissolve that attack on Jerusalem. Zech. 14:13 states this does happen during the last day of tribulation, in reference to the battle at Jerusalem. This battle confusion seems to have been common when a foe attacked Israel in the past. If this is post-millennial, it must refer to a final cleanup before judgment when believers once again root out all rebels.

So, a few more things are bothersome for me to interpret Ezekiel 38 as the Antichrist at the time of Armageddon:

1. The "time" of peace (obviously millennial; see Chapter 37:24-28, before that concludes with Christ reigning with a covenant of peace in Chapter 38).

2. Also, that God's name (YHWH) is mentioned so much in these verses, it makes me consider the

244

"Day of God," which comes at the end of the millennial period. The Apostle Peter says that *after* the thousands-years (2 Peter 3:8) finish, the "Day of God" occurs. This would happen just after the book of Revelation's "Gog and Magog" event. This time period is after all things are under Christ, and He subjects everything to God. Man will then walk with God like Adam did at first in the Garden of Eden.

Revelation 21:1-3 (KJV)
[1] **And I saw a new heaven and a new earth: for the first heaven and the first earth were passed away; and there was no more sea.**
[2] **And I John saw the holy city, new Jerusalem, coming down from God out of heaven, prepared as a bride adorned for her husband.**
[3] **And I heard a great voice out of heaven saying, <u>Behold, the tabernacle of God *is* with men</u>, and <u>he will dwell with them</u>, and they shall be his people, and <u>God himself shall be with them</u>, *and be* their God.**

2 Peter 3:12-13 (KJV)
[12] **Looking for and hasting unto the coming of the <u>day of God</u>, wherein the heavens being on fire shall be dissolved, and the elements shall melt with fervent heat?**
[13] **Nevertheless we, according to his promise, look for new heavens and a new earth, wherein dwelleth righteousness.**

3. I would also point out other nations are questioning Gog and asking, "Are you going to Israel to take spoil?" (38:13). The answer seems to be "yes." Now if this were the Antichrist, why would any nation question him if he were doing this during or at the end of the Tribulation? He would be the supreme ruler of the world, wouldn't he? According to

Zechariah and Revelation, he is gathering all the nations against Israel to utterly destroy her (Rev. 16:14; Zech. 14:2). This would be very clear to all nations, so why would they ask such a question?

The key to when in time this would be happening is found in Chapter 38

Let's continue our first point. Now we use a few verses in Chapter 39 to help us understand the timing of Chapter 38. As we have seen, it is a time when Israel "dwells safely." Finally, in Chapter 39:25-28, God tells us the exact period in time when Israel will "dwell safely" by speaking of the END of the Tribulation time period. It interprets for us *when* this prophecy in Chapter 38 will start to be fulfilled. It is the KEY to understanding these chapters.

Ezekiel 39:25-28 (KJV)
[25] **Therefore thus saith the Lord GOD; Now will <u>I bring again the captivity of Jacob</u>, and <u>have mercy upon the whole house of Israel</u>, and will <u>be jealous</u> for my holy name;**
[26] **<u>After</u> that <u>they have borne their shame</u>, and all their trespasses whereby they have trespassed against me, <u>when they dwelt safely in their land</u>, and none made *them* afraid.**
[27] **<u>When I have brought them again from the people</u>, and <u>gathered them</u> out of their enemies' lands, and <u>am sanctified in them</u> in the sight of many nations;**
[28] **Then shall they know that <u>I *am* the LORD their God</u>, which caused them to be led into captivity among the heathen: but <u>I have gathered them</u> unto their own land, and have <u>left none of them any more there</u>.**

Verses 25-28 declares when that they dwell safely-

1. AFTER God brings again the deliverance from captivity.
2. AFTER He has mercy on the whole house of Israel.
3. AFTER He becomes jealous for His people.
4. AFTER they have born their shame.
5. AFTER they are brought out of many people.
6. AFTER He is sanctified in them.
7. AFTER they know that the LORD (Jesus) is their God.
8. AFTER He has gathered them to their own land. And,
9. AFTER not one Jew is left anywhere in the world but in Israel.

Obviously, these verses make it clear that they are at rest and in peace *after the battle of Armageddon,* and Christ has come. Then all of Israel will return to their land and be at rest. Some try to teach that Ezekiel 38 could happen at any moment to start off the Tribulation period, but letting the passage itself tell us when this will happen makes it clear it would have to be AFTER the millennial period starts. So, this helps us understand that Chapter 38 is about the end of the millennial period, like Rev. 20 describes.

Let's look at my three other points.

Chapter 39- Seven years burning the weapons?

Ezekiel 39:1 (KJV)
¹ Therefore, thou son of man, prophesy against Gog, and say, Thus saith the Lord GOD; Behold, I *am* against thee, O Gog, the chief prince of Meshech and Tubal:

Now we are in the thirty-ninth chapter, and remember that I said that this chapter is probably entirely about the Antichrist and the battle at the end of the Tribulation. So I personally believe this burning of weapons begins on or around the first day of the one-thousand-year reign of Christ after that battle.

Ezekiel 39:9 (KJV)
⁹ And they that dwell in <u>the cities of Israel</u> shall go forth, and shall set on fire and burn the weapons, both the shields and the bucklers, the bows and the arrows, and the handstaves, and the spears, and they shall burn them with fire seven years:

At least four theories exist for when this action could happen. Namely, at the beginning of the Tribulation, in the middle of the Tribulation, at the end of the Tribulation, or at the end of the one-thousand-year reign of Christ. Some say this statement is too coincidental not to place this war at the *beginning* of the seven years of Tribulation. I'm not convinced yet that there would be a war against Israel to start off the Tribulation period. I don't see any other verse to support this theory. But this is what many teachers teach.

If this happened in the *middle* of the Tribulation, then it would mean that they would be burying bodies and bones found for seven years, going into the millennial period. But wouldn't this be stopped because of the war the Antichrist has on Israel at that time? It clearly states that the cities of Israel will be doing this.

If this is perhaps *after* the millennial period, then it would confirm that natural men will exist on earth after the one thousand years. This could be true, but we don't find this in Scripture here. Revelation 20-22 pictures what happens after the Millennium: first the Great White Throne Judgment, then the new heaven and earth.

> **Revelation 20:11 (KJV)**
> ¹¹ **And I saw a great white throne, and him that sat on it, from whose face the earth and the heaven fled away; and there was found no place for them.**

> **Revelation 21:1 (KJV)**
> ¹ **And I saw a new heaven and a new earth: for the first heaven and the first earth were passed away; and there was no more sea.**

Is there time between the post-millennial Gog event and the Great White Throne Judgment or the renewing of heaven and earth? At least seven years would be needed somewhere to burn the weapons. After the earth is recreated, there will be no need to bury bodies anymore. The renewing of heaven and earth happens after Gog and after the Great White Throne Judgment. To put seven years there makes no sense. Why would they be burying bodies after the thousand-year reign? These verses prove to me that Chapter 39, where this is recorded, is probably about the Antichrist and the end of the Tribulation and does not fit with the Chapter 38 scenario.

I believe the best option is that this burning of weapons happens at the beginning of the Tribulation. I believe Chapter 39:1 leads us into a different time period than Chapter 38. Now if we bump backwards in time to the end of the Tribulation, and we are speaking of the Antichrist here in this chapter, then the burning of the weapons would have to happen at the first seven years of the millennial. Let's look at Chapter 39 more closely.

If Chapter 39 would also still continue to speak about the post-millennial "Gog," then certain verses *would not fit*. Let's look at a few:

1. Chapter 39:2- Seems to say God allows a sixth part to survive or to stay in their countries. How would this be true of the group that comes up against Christ after the millennial? This also seems to be something new in reference to Armageddon. See my explanation about this later.

2. Chapter 39:7- "I will not let *them* pollute my Holy name ANYMORE." This refers to the time after Armageddon, but we know that thousands will attempt an attack once more at the end of the millennial period. Read this verse carefully; it declares that God will not allow *Israel* to pollute His name any longer. So this verse still fits as being about the Antichrist. Jesus will rule forever over Israel on the throne of David, and His people will be sanctified in Him.

Let's look at my next issue and point three about these chapters.

His burial in Chapter 39:

As we have seen in a previous chapter, the Antichrist is taken captive, judged, and killed by Jesus himself. In Ezekiel 39, the first section seems to say something different.

Ezekiel 39:4-5 (KJV)
[4] <u>Thou shalt fall upon the mountains of Israel</u>, thou, and <u>all thy bands</u>, and <u>the people</u> that *is* with thee: I will give thee unto the ravenous birds of every sort, and *to* the beasts of the field to be devoured.
[5] <u>Thou</u> (LB- all thy band, and people) <u>shalt fall upon the open field</u>: for I have spoken *it*, saith the Lord GOD.

Ezekiel 39:11 (KJV)
[11] **And it shall come to pass in that day,** *that* <u>I will give unto Gog a place there of graves in Israel,</u> **the valley of the**

passengers on the <u>east of the sea</u>: and it shall stop the *noses* of the passengers: and there shall <u>they bury Gog</u> and all his multitude: and they shall call *it* The valley of Hamongog.

"Gog" here seems to fall or die in the mountains, *and* the fields, and be buried in the Jezreel valley. Verse 4 lists three parts that are as one here: 1. "Thou" or Gog; 2. "All thy bands;" and 3. "the people" with Gog. So in verse 5, when it uses "thou," it is speaking of all of these antichrist groups falling in the mountains and the field. Keep in mind that the last "Gog" with his group in Rev. 20 dies entirely in the mountains. The vast number of the Antichrist army will fall in many places in Israel, from Bozrah to Jerusalem, the mountains, and the plains of Megiddo. Gog dies later, but according to Verse 11, he seems to be buried in Hamongog.

Isaiah 14 shows how the Antichrist will die.

Isaiah 14:19-20 (HCSB)
[19] But you are thrown out <u>without a grave</u>, like a worthless branch, <u>covered by those slain with the sword</u> and <u>dumped into a rocky pit</u> like a trampled corpse.
[20] You will not <u>join them</u> (LB- Your ancestors) <u>in burial</u>, because you destroyed your land and slaughtered your own people. The offspring of evildoers will never be remembered.

The Bible states in Ezekiel 39:11 that "Gog" *falls* in the mountains, *and* the field *and* is put into "graves." Obviously, "Gog" represents the entire group here. But it reads like he personally dies with his troops in the mountains. Isn't the Antichrist killed afterwards, when he is judged by Jesus himself and cast out with the others and not to be buried? This means that he is not buried in a kingly fashion with his people in a proper grave. We know from before that he is taken captive, and Christ destroys him and casts him (his spirit and body) into the fire at the judgment of the nations (Dan. 7:11; Rev. 19:20). If this "Gog" is the Antichrist, it seems that this verse bears out that he would be wounded in the mountains leading the attack, but be taken captive by Christ, judged, killed, and thrown into the pit of fire. Then all the bones, his included, will be put into giant graves for all the dead who died on the day of the Lord. Keep in mind that there is a giant ravine called Hinnom (or Kidron) also on the southeast side of Jerusalem that separates Jerusalem from the Mount of Olives, which will be used for the burning of dead bodies. All the bones then could be taken to Megiddo (see Joel 3:12-14). *So this chapter could match our Antichrist figure.* One person stated:

> "Probably means that multitudes of the enemy would be buried there, <u>not necessarily Gog personally</u> (cf. Rev. 19:20–21; 20:10). The slaughter would be so great that it would take a large valley to accommodate all the corpses. This valley would become known as "The Valley of the Multitude of Gog." This cemetery would be so large that travelers would not be able to pass through that part of the land. <u>Probably the Esdraelon Valley is in view since it is east of the</u>

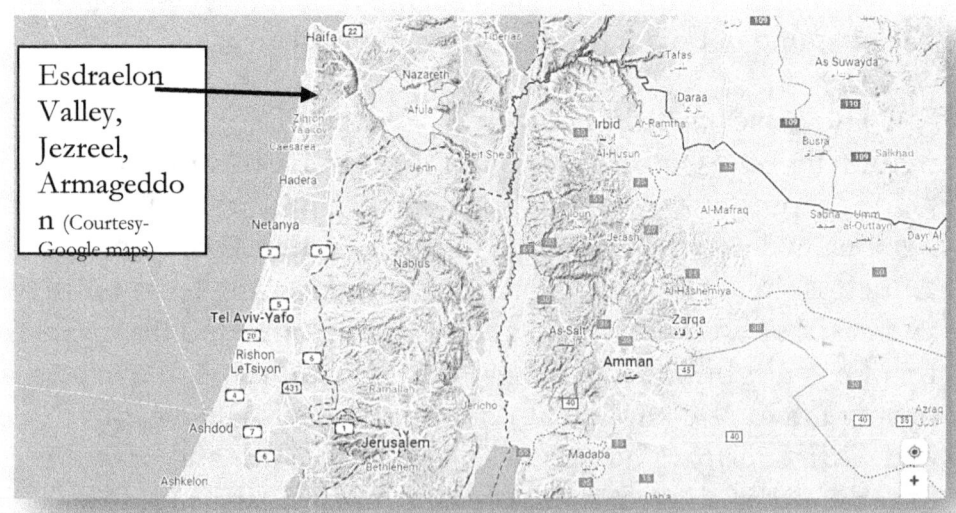

Esdraelon Valley, Jezreel, Armageddon (Courtesy- Google maps)

Mediterranean Sea and since many travelers normally passed and still pass through it. Furthermore it is the only major east west valley in Israel.[495] In biblical times a major highway connecting Egypt and Mesopotamia ran through this valley. The Apostle John identified this valley as the location of the battle of Armageddon (Rev. 16:13–16)." [130]

Next is my final point to look at in these chapters.

The city of Jerusalem is taken at the end of Tribulation

Another problem that exists for me in seeing both of these chapters as completely the work of the Antichrist is the recorded events at the end of the Tribulation period. According to Zachariah 12-14 and Zephaniah. 3, half of Jerusalem is taken during that day and recaptured by Jesus Himself. In Ezekiel 38-39 or Revelation 20:7-9, there is no mention of the enemy forces taking Jerusalem. In all those references, they only surround the city and die in the mountains.

Ezekiel 39:17-18 (KJV)
[17] And, thou son of man, thus saith the Lord GOD; Speak unto every feathered fowl, and to every beast of the field, Assemble yourselves, and come; gather yourselves on every side to my sacrifice that I do sacrifice for you, _even_ a great sacrifice upon the mountains of Israel, that ye may eat flesh, and drink blood.

---

[495] Some commentators argued for the valley being east of the Dead Sea, but that location seems unlikely.
[130] Constable, T. (2003). Tom Constable's Expository Notes on the Bible (Eze 39:11). Galaxie Software.

18 Ye shall eat <u>the flesh of the mighty, and drink the blood of the princes of the earth,</u> of rams, of lambs, and of goats, of bullocks, all of them fatlings of Bashan.

While Ezekiel 38 may be about the end of the millennial, Chapter 39 very well could be about the Antichrist and just does not mention the attack on Jerusalem specifically. Similar to Revelation 19, which is about Christ's return, we see birds feasting here on the dead bodies. Chapter 39:17, which says a great feast is upon the mountains of Israel of the princes of the earth and could very well include the mountains of Jerusalem. Verse 17 and 18 above sound very much like Revelation 19 and John's account of the slaughter at Megiddo at the end of the Tribulation. Let's research a little more about the battle that will happen in Jerusalem.

> **Zephaniah 3:14-15 (KJV)**
> **14 Sing, O daughter of Zion; shout, O Israel; be glad and rejoice with all the heart, O daughter of Jerusalem.**
> **15 The LORD hath taken away thy judgments, <u>he hath cast out thine enemy</u>: the king of Israel, *even* the LORD, *is* in the midst of thee: thou shalt not see evil any more.**

The battle at Jerusalem with the Antichrist- This happens just before Armageddon is judged

Two Invasions of Palestine by Gog?

Finis Dake taught that there would be *two* invasions by "Gog" in the last days upon Israel. One, in the middle of the Tribulation, with whom he refers to as the Antichrist with the ten-kings only. The second, is at the end of the Tribulation and describes it as Ezekiel 38-39, with the Antichrist ruling over

Russia and all the other countries.[131] I also believe this to be true, but I do not ascribe to him both Chapters of Ezekiel 38-39, as the Antichrist. Because Dake believes that Gog is specifically the Antichrist, he downplays the possibility that the "Gog" mentioned in Ezekiel could be the same as in Revelation 20:7-9. As I said before, the "Gog" in Chapter 38, probably is not the Antichrist of the Tribulation, but the time of the Antichrist is mentioned in the later part of Chapter 39. They both come to destroy Jerusalem, but they are probably two different people. They are both anti-Messiah.

The city will go into captivity, but Gog falls in the mountains

Zechariah prophesied specifically of the Day of the Lord when Christ comes back. He says that *the city will go into captivity* and terrible things will befall its inhabitants. So at the end of the Tribulation, an attack will happen upon Jerusalem by the Antichrist. Ezekiel makes no mention of Gog entering Jerusalem in Chapter 39, but only possibly dying in the mountains. This could be a problem for some. If the Gog here in Ezekiel 39 is the same as the one in Revelation 20, then it makes sense that he would not enter Jerusalem because Christ is already there, seated in his temple during the Millennium. We do not see it as such. The Antichrist will enter Jerusalem.

Herein lies our problem. If we separate the chapters into two different time periods, then we need to understand this distinction. In Chapter 38, Gog doesn't come close to taking the city, but in Chapter 39, while it does not say Gog enters the city, it implies he comes close. Zechariah says *half* of the city is taken, so this must mean that the Antichrist's forces inside the city already work against the people internally.

---

131 Finis Jennings Dake, Dake's Annotated Reference Bible: Containing the Old and New Testaments of the Authorized or King James Version Text, (Lawrenceville, GA: Dake Bible Sales, Inc., 1997), WORDsearch CROSS e-book, Under: "Chapter 38."

Maybe a small force comes in while the greater force falls in the mountains. We know they are all driven back by the Lord and the saints with him.

These verses below are also about the end of the Tribulation and the Antichrist.

> **Zechariah 14:1-5 (KJV)**
> [1] Behold, the day of the LORD cometh, and <u>thy spoil shall be divided</u> in the midst of thee.
> [2] For <u>I will gather all nations against Jerusalem to battle</u>; and <u>the city shall be taken</u>, and the houses rifled, and the women ravished; and <u>half of the city shall go forth into captivity</u>, and the residue of the people shall <u>not be cut off from the city</u>.
> [3] <u>Then shall the LORD go forth, and fight against those nations</u>, as when he fought in the day of battle.
> [4] And his feet shall stand <u>in that day</u> upon the mount of Olives, which *is* before Jerusalem on the east, and the mount of Olives shall cleave in the midst thereof toward the east and toward the west, *and there shall be* a very great valley; and half of the mountain shall remove toward the north, and half of it toward the south.
> [5] And ye shall flee *to* the valley of the mountains; for the valley of the mountains shall reach unto Azal: yea, ye shall flee, like as ye fled from before the earthquake in the days of Uzziah king of Judah: and the LORD my God shall come, *and* all the saints with thee.

> **Zechariah 14:14 (KJV)**
> [14] And <u>Judah also shall fight at Jerusalem</u>; and the wealth of <u>all the heathen</u> round about shall be gathered together, gold, and silver, and apparel, in great abundance.

> **Zechariah 14:16 (KJV)**
> [16] And it shall come to pass, *that* <u>every one that is left of all the nations</u> which came against Jerusalem shall even go up from year to year to <u>worship the King</u>, the LORD of hosts, and <u>to keep the feast of tabernacles</u>.

Zephaniah 3:11 (KJV)
[11] **In that day shalt thou** (LB-Jerusalem) **not be ashamed for all thy doings, wherein thou hast transgressed against me: for then <u>I will take away out of the midst of thee them that rejoice in thy pride,</u> and thou shalt no more be haughty because of my holy mountain.**

Isaiah 63:9 (KJV)
[9] **In all their affliction he was afflicted, and <u>the angel of his presence saved them</u>: in his love and in his pity he redeemed them; and he bare them, and carried them all the days of old.**

Isaiah 63:18 (KJV)
[18] **The people of thy holiness have possessed** *it* <u>**but a little while**</u>**: our adversaries have trodden down thy sanctuary.**

In the book of Joel, we see the events of the Day of the Lord unfold. Before Armageddon, a defense of Jerusalem is made by a supernatural army led by Christ.

Joel 2:1-10 (KJV)
[1] **Blow ye the trumpet in Zion, and sound an alarm in my holy mountain: let all the inhabitants of the land tremble: for <u>the day of the LORD cometh</u>, for** *it is* **nigh at hand;**
[2] <u>**A day of darkness and of gloominess, a day of clouds and of thick darkness,**</u> **as the morning spread upon the mountains: a great people and a strong; there hath not been ever the like, <u>neither shall be any more after it,</u>** *even* **to the years of many generations.**
[3] <u>**A fire devoureth before them**</u>**; and behind them a flame burneth: the land** *is* <u>**as the garden of Eden**</u> **before them, and behind them a desolate wilderness; yea, and nothing shall escape them.**
[4] <u>**The appearance of them** *is* **as the appearance of horses**</u>**; and as horsemen, so shall they run.**
[5] **Like <u>the noise of chariots</u> on the tops of mountains shall they leap, like the noise of a flame of fire that devoureth the stubble, as <u>a strong people set in battle array.</u>**
[6] **Before their face the people shall be much pained: all faces shall gather blackness.**
[7] **They shall run like mighty men; they shall climb <u>the wall</u> like**

men of war; and they shall march every one on his ways, and they shall not break their ranks:

[8] **Neither shall one thrust another; they shall walk every one in his path: and** *when* **they fall upon the sword, they shall not be wounded.**

[9] **They shall run to and fro** <u>in the city</u>**; they shall run upon** <u>the wall</u>**, they shall climb up upon the houses; they shall enter in at the windows like a thief.**

[10] **The** <u>earth shall quake</u> **before them; the** <u>heavens shall tremble</u>**: the sun and the moon** <u>shall be dark</u>**, and the stars shall withdraw their shining:**

This army is made up of the angels and saints that follow Christ from heaven, along with Israelis from the tribe of Judah. According to Revelation 19:14, we will be riding white horses. This is happening just after Jesus comes back physically to the earth. Notice that the city mentioned here in Joel 2:27 has walls, unlike the Millennial City in Ezekiel 38, where Israel is at peace and without walls. This is the case in millennial time. Verse 11 says this is *the Lord's* army and not the Antichrist's army, like so many try to say (Scofield agrees with this [132]). The Lord's army comes to deliver Jerusalem from destruction. Verse 8 says they will not hurt each other and cannot be wounded, even when injured by a sword. This is different from Ezekiel 38:21, where "every man's sword shall be against his brother."

1. There is an attack on the city.

2. The city has walls.

3. God's army with Christ comes to deliver Jerusalem.

4. This army cannot be hurt by anything.

---

[132] "To verse 10, inclusive the invading army is described; at verse 11, Jehovah's army. This "army" is described, Rev 19:11-18"

C.I. Scofield, ed., *The Holy Bible: Containing the Old and New Testaments*, WORD*search* CROSS e-book, Under: "Chapter 2"

5. They clean out the city of what remains of evil men who reside there (Luke 17:30-37).

Great repentance of the remnant of Israel, proceeds the Lord's return

Joel 2:11-21 (KJV)

[11] And <u>the LORD shall utter his voice before his army</u>: for <u>his camp</u> *is* very great: for *he is* strong that executeth his word: for <u>the day of the LORD</u> *is* great and very terrible; and who can abide it?

[12] Therefore also now, saith the LORD, turn ye *even* to me with all your heart, and with fasting, and with weeping, and with mourning:

[13] And <u>rend your heart</u>, and not your garments, and turn unto the LORD your God: for <u>he *is* gracious and merciful,</u> slow to anger, and of great kindness, and repenteth him of the evil.

[14] Who knoweth *if* he will return and repent, and <u>leave a blessing behind him</u>; *even* a <u>meat offering</u> and a <u>drink offering</u> unto the LORD your God?

[15] <u>Blow the trumpet in Zion</u>, sanctify a fast, call a solemn assembly:

[16] <u>Gather the people</u>, sanctify the congregation, <u>assemble the elders</u>, gather the children, and those that suck the breasts: <u>let the bridegroom go forth of his chamber, and the bride out of her closet.</u>

[17] Let <u>the priests, the ministers of the LORD, weep</u> between the porch and the altar, and let them say, Spare thy people, O LORD, and give not thine heritage to reproach, that the heathen should rule over them: wherefore should they say among the people, Where *is* their God?

[18] <u>Then will the LORD be jealous for his land, and pity his people.</u>

[19] Yea, the LORD will answer and say unto his people, Behold, I will send you corn, and wine, and oil, and ye shall be satisfied therewith: and I will no more make you a reproach among the heathen:

[20] But <u>I will remove far off from you the northern *army*</u>, and will drive him into a land barren and desolate, with his face

toward the east sea, and his hinder part toward the utmost sea, and <u>his stink shall come up</u>, and his ill savour shall come up, because he hath done great things.
[21] **Fear not, O land; be glad and rejoice: for the LORD will do great things.**

The picture in Joel after Israel's repentance is God's supernatural army defending Jerusalem against the northern army at the Day of the Lord. The last thing the Antichrist will do is come from the north toward Israel to utterly destroy them. Babylon (rebuilt, which is east of Jerusalem) has just been destroyed, but the Antichrist will not be there at that time (see Rev. 16:14). He draws all the nations together with him to assemble in the valley of Jezreel or Megiddo (where Mount Megiddo is on the western side). He or those who live there take half of Jerusalem temporarily with his forces (Zech. 14:1-2), and it is fought there by Judah (Zech. 12:1-9; Zech. 14:14), Ephraim, and the sons of Zion (Zech. 9:13). Also, finally, on that day, Christ and his armies from heaven come to fight this battle.

During this time, "nations from afar" attack Babylon and destroy her, according to Isaiah 13:3-6; 14:1-2. This is another group altogether. In any case, God sends a supernatural army to defend Israel and Jerusalem. In Verse 20, the invading army is called "the northern army." His armies will also stink like the Ezekiel Chapter 39 army because of the many people who die. We know Joel's passage is about Armageddon because of Verse 1, where it mentions the day of the Lord.

Micah 5:5-6 says "seven shepherds" and "eight principle men" will come against the Assyrian Antichrist. This prophecy has never been fulfilled as of yet. This may be what unseats the Antichrist from Babylon, but more so, he and the false prophet are out visiting nations to assemble a great army (Rev. 16:14). What triggers the swift return of the Lord to defend Israel is the repentance and cry of his people (Zech. 14:3). This is the last event before the second advent of Christ (Zech.

12:11; Joel 2). It seems Jesus hits the area of Selah (Petra) or the area of Bozrah, first in Edom (now in southern Jordan today- Isaiah 63:1-3), and saves those in the wilderness with a great battle that He alone fights. He bloodies his garment there and later appears at Armageddon (Jezreel), and in the city of Jerusalem with blood-red garments (Isaiah 34:6; Habakkuk 3:3-15; Rev. 19:13).

Then in Megiddo, millions who are gathered to fight will die by the words of Jesus' mouth and will die instantly. Thousands will drop dead all over the world (Ez. 39:6; Jer. 25:29-34; Matt. 13:37-43). Jesus defeats all the nations that have come against Israel and Himself and sets up a judgment seat in the Valley of Jehoshaphat (Joel 3:12-14). (See my "Prophetic Days of the Lord" study series and the campaign of the Lord for more details.)

The valley of Megiddo (Jezreel) from Mount Carmel- by Larry Booth

"Mt. Magedon (only at Rev. 16:16) is a Hebrew name for the place where the kings of the whole earth (16:14) will assemble under the direction of demonic spirits (16:13) for the final battle.[133]

"The Mount of Megiddo is located in the plain of Esdraelon or Jezreel, a valley fourteen by twenty miles in size located to the southwest of Nazareth. Here, it is thought by many, that the great final battle of Armageddon will be fought at the end of time."[134]

Revelation 19:11-21 (HCSB)

[11] Then I saw heaven opened, and there was a white horse. Its rider is called Faithful and True, and He judges and makes war in righteousness.

[12] His eyes were like a fiery flame, and many crowns were on His head. He had a name written that no one knows except Himself.

[13] He wore a robe stained with blood, and His name is the Word of God.

[14] The armies that were in heaven followed Him on white horses, wearing pure white linen.

[15] A sharp sword came from His mouth, so that He might strike the nations with it. He will shepherd them with an iron scepter. He will also trample the winepress of the fierce anger of God, the Almighty.

[16] And He has a name written on His robe and on His thigh: KING OF KINGS AND LORD OF LORDS.

[17] Then I saw an angel standing on the sun, and he cried out in a loud voice, saying to all the birds flying high overhead, "Come, gather together for the great supper of God,

[18] so that you may eat the flesh of kings, the flesh of commanders, the flesh of mighty men, the flesh of horses and of their riders, and the flesh of everyone, both free and slave, small and great."

[19] Then I saw the beast, the kings of the earth, and their armies

---

[133] Jeremias, J. (1964–). Ἀρ Μαγεδών. G. Kittel, G. W. Bromiley, & G. Friedrich (Eds.), *Theological dictionary of the New Testament* (electronic ed., Vol. 1, p. 468). Grand Rapids, MI: Eerdmans.
[134] http://www.battle-of-armageddon.org/

gathered together to wage war against the rider on the horse and against His army.
[20] But the beast was taken prisoner, and along with him the false prophet, who had performed the signs in his presence. He deceived those who accepted the mark of the beast and those who worshiped his image with these signs. Both of them were thrown alive into the lake of fire that burns with sulfur.
[21] The rest were killed with the sword that came from the mouth of the rider on the horse, and all the birds were filled with their flesh.

What a great battle it will be that day when the armies of heaven come to fight with Christ and take back Jerusalem. Ezekiel 39 could very well be about the Antichrist, but it seems this ruler, who is called Gog, falls just short of reaching Jerusalem. Jerusalem must be divided by those who live there or a small, advanced force. I previously thought that the Antichrist personally entered Jerusalem during those days. Maybe he does and is later drawn back by the news of Babylon falling. He is probably directing the attack just outside of Jerusalem.

Balaam saw that day

It is fitting here to remember the prophecy of Balaam toward Israel's favor against King Balak of Moab in Numbers 24. Remember, when the nation of Israel had left Egypt and was entering the Promised Land, the king of Moab asked a local prophet to prophesy against Israel, and he wouldn't. At his own peril, Balaam would not bring a curse against God's people. The Bible says that he went into a trance and saw Israel's future, including Christ coming to rule the world *and save the city.*

Numbers 24:17-19 (KJV)
[17] I shall see him, but not now: I shall behold him, but not

nigh: there shall come <u>a Star out of Jacob</u>, and a Sceptre shall rise out of Israel, and shall smite <u>the corners of Moab</u>, and destroy all <u>the children of Sheth</u>.
[18] And <u>Edom shall be a possession</u>, Seir also shall be a possession for his enemies; and Israel shall do valiantly.
[19] Out of Jacob shall come <u>he</u> that shall have dominion, and <u>shall destroy him that remaineth of the city.</u>

Is this the Antichrist that "remains in the city"? Interesting enough in this same prophecy he possibly calls the Antichrist "Asshur" or the "Assyrian," at least according to Arthur Pink in his book on the Antichrist.[135]

Numbers 24:21-24 (KJV)
[21] And he looked on the Kenites, and took up his parable, and said, Strong is thy dwellingplace, and thou puttest thy nest in a rock.
[22] Nevertheless the Kenite (LB- a branch of Midianites) **shall be wasted, until Asshur shall carry thee away captive.**
[23] And he took up his parable, and said, Alas, <u>who shall live when God doeth this!</u>
[24] And ships *shall come* from the coast of Chittim (LB- Cyprus gave their ships to the Greek conqueror Alexander the Great, for Greece to attack the Persian Empire who ruled Assyrian lands. Cyprus was ruled by Rome in Antiochus's day, but today is an independent republic associated with the E.U.), **and shall afflict Asshur** (the area of Syria today)**, and shall afflict Eber** (Heber the founder of the Hebrews)**, and he also shall perish for ever.**

Pink and Dake write to say this event is in the future and has not been fulfilled yet. Pink believes the mention of Asshur is the antichrist, and Dake believes that Cyprus represents the Antichrist here as a Greek force from which the Antichrist will

---

[135] "the name of "Asshur" (Numbers 24:22),—in future Chapters evidence will be given to prove that "Asshur" and the Antichrist are one and the same person." Arthur W. Pink, *The Antichrist*, (Swengel, PA: Bible Truth Depot, 1923), WORD*search* CROSS e-book, 10.

one day revive.[136] This is a big stretch for me to put the Antichrist here in either place. I could be wrong.

After all of these points, it is clear to me that Ezekiel 38 and these references to Gog are not the Antichrist.

If Gog is the Antichrist in Ezekiel 38

If Gog is the Antichrist in both Chapters 38 and 39, this is what we learn about him from these verses: (keep in mind that I personally do not believe this is the case for Chapter 38 although this Gog is anti-Jesus during the Millennium.)

1. God is personally against him (Ezek. 38:3).

2. God will turn him back (Ezek. 38:4). From what we are not sure.

3. God will put hooks in his jaws.

4. God will bring him forth, and all his armies, a great company.

5. His army will consist of horses, and horsemen clothed with all sorts of weapons.

---

[136] "Both the Assyrians and Hebrews will be afflicted by the Antichrist, and then he himself will be defeated to perish forever (Num. 24:24). According to Dan. 8:7-9,20-25; 11:35-45; Zech. 9:13; Rev. 13 and 17, the Grecian Empire will be revived by the Antichrist who will take over Assyria, Palestine, and many other lands, then fight against Jesus Christ at Armageddon, and at last, be cast into the lake of fire forever (Rev. 19:11-21; 20:10)." Finis Jennings Dake, *Dake's Annotated Reference Bible: Containing the Old and New Testaments of the Authorized or King James Version Text*, (Lawrenceville, GA: Dake Bible Sales, Inc., 1997), WORD*search* CROSS e-book, Under: "Chapter 24:24".

6. Persia, Ethiopia, Libya, Gomer and all his bands, the house of Togarmah and all his bands, and many people will be in the army (Ezek. 38:6). Rev. 16:14 says the whole world will be with the Antichrist.

7. After many days (the last days) he will be visited (Ezek. 38:8).

8. In the latter years he will come into the land that is brought back from the sword, and gathered out of many people.

9. He will come against the mountains of Israel, a people brought forth out of the nations and that dwell safely in their own land.

   Here is where some will put a future pre-Trib. war between Russia and Israel to kick off the Tribulation period. This concept wasn't so far-fetched during the writing of this book. Even as I type these words, Russian troops are invading Ukraine (Feb. 24, 2022) and expanding their kingdom. But then this would be a Russian leader and not the Antichrist.

10. He will ascend and come like a storm, and like a cloud to cover the whole land – "you and all your bands, and many people with you" (Ezek. 38:9).

11. At that time things will come into his mind, and he will think of an evil plan (Ezek. 38:10).

12. He will say, "I will go up to the land of unwalled villages that are at rest and that dwell safely, to take a spoil and a prey from the Jews that are gathered and are prosperous in their land" (Ezek. 38:12).

> "He would plan to invade the Israelites while they are at rest and to plunder them. Israel would seem to be completely defenseless relying on her God to protect her and not fortifying herself. <u>Israel has never in her past or present history enjoyed such an ideally peaceful situation</u>."— Tom Constable's Notes on the Bible

> "Never in history has there been a long period of peace, and most likely there never will be <u>until Christ does return to set up God's kingdom on earth.</u> Thus the commentators say that it is difficult to see how this battle could take place prior to Christ's return, for the earth has never known a period of extended peace under the rule of the human race." [137] - Leadership Ministries Worldwide Commentary.

To me, this rules out a battle today or tomorrow because Israel is walled in. Once again, this is why John Walvoord says that this battle happens after the Rapture and after some kind of peace treaty with the Antichrist- still at the beginning of the Tribulation period. For this to be true, Israel would have to pull down all of her walls and fortifications before this king attacks. This is not likely, because, as Joel states, there are still walls at the end of the Tribulation.

---

[137] Leadership Ministries Worldwide. (2007). Ezekiel (p. 300). Chattanooga, TN: Leadership Ministries Worldwide.

Today, Israel has walls to protect itself from other countries that wish to harm it. They do not dwell safely even as of 2023. Many walls exist around Israel today.[138] Below is a picture of the wall around Mount Zion.[139] This very thing helps us know these verses probably speak of a different time period in the future.

13. Sheba, Dedan, the merchants of Tarshish, with all the young lions thereof will say to you, "Are you come with a great company to take a spoil? To take a prey? To carry away silver, gold, cattle, goods, and a great spoil?" (Ezek. 38:13). If this were at the end of Trib. why would any nation speak to the Antichrist this way? An end of Trib. battle seems unlikely also.

---

[138] http://www.ipsnews.net/2012/07/israel-walls-itself-in/
[139] By Kyle Taylor from London, 84 Countries - Israel - Jerusalem - Mount Zion - 03, CC BY 2.0, https://commons.wikimedia.org/w/index.php?curid=38442663

14. In that day *when the people of Israel dwell safely* (LB- This is referring to the millennial reign. See above), he will come from his place in the north parts with many people riding horses, a mighty army (Ezek. 38:14-15). They are riding horses because of the rough mountainous terrain. But could it be because this is what resources they only have and are allowed during the millennial period?

15. He will come up against God's people Israel, as a cloud to cover the land (Ezek. 38:16).

16. It will be in the latter days.

17. God will bring him against His land, that the heathen may know God, when he will be sanctified in Gog, before their eyes.

18. At the same time when Gog comes against Israel, God's fury will come up in His face (Ezek. 38:18).

19. In that day there will be a great shaking in the land of Israel (Ezek. 38:19).

20. All men and beasts in the land will shake at God's presence (Ezek. 38:20).

21. The mountains will be thrown down. This here sounds like end of Trib. but could it not also be so at the end of the millennial?

22. The steep places will fall.

23. Every wall will fall to the ground. I thought they had no walls? So are these walls elsewhere?

24. God will call for a sword against him (Gog) throughout all My Mountains (Ezek. 38:21).

25. Every man's sword will be against his brother (This is not mentioned of Armageddon anywhere, although it could be true in Jerusalem during that time).

26. God will plead against him with pestilence and with blood (Ezek. 38:22).

27. God will rain upon him, and the many band with him, an overflowing rain.

28. God will rain on him great hailstones.

29. God will rain on him fire and brimstone.

30. God will magnify Himself (Ezek. 38:23).

31. God will sanctify Himself.

32. God will be known in the eyes of many nations, and they will know that He is Lord.

If Gog is the Antichrist in Ezekiel 39:1-17

Keep in mind that I do believe that this is probably all about the Antichrist. This does not mean the Antichrist is Russian or Turkish. It means the Antichrist rules there during the Tribulation period. Now, there is the possibility that the first section of this chapter spills over from the last chapter about the "Gog" at the end of the Millennium, and as I said before, this chapter could have a two-fold interpretation for both Gogs. Below is what we learn from this section.

1. God will turn Gog back (Ezek. 39:1-2). From where? Maybe as Daniel says the Antichrist has temporarily been distracted from news at Babylon and doubled back? (See Dan. 11:44.)

2. God will leave but a sixth part of them. This makes no sense. This is 166.667 men for every one million men. Why would God spare even one enemy at Armageddon? But this could be true for some who did not take the mark of the beast. There is a possible mistranslation in the KJV. Another explanation here is that this word was confused with the similar word *"shashah"* or "sixth," but the Hebrew word used here, *"shasha,"* means "annihilate," thus rightly translated: "I will annihilate you." Some work to keep the original KJV English word, and say this would be literally translated "I will six you."

One explanation of interest comes from the Preachers Homiletic Commentary:

"EXEGETICAL NOTES.—Ver. 2. **"I will leave but the sixth part of thee"**—I will six thee; *i.e.,* afflict thee with six plagues—pestilence, blood, overflowing rain, hailstones, fire, brimstone (chap. 38:22). Or, draw thee back with a hook of six teeth (chap. 38:4)—the six teeth being those six plagues. The rendering in the text supposes that the verb is derived from the Hebrew numeral six; but this rendering is not recognised by the LXX. or the Vulgate. The verb has an Ethiopic root, and the passage should be rendered—I will *lead thee along*—to thy ruin." [140]

3. God will cause him to come up from the north parts.

4. God will bring him against the mountains of Israel.

5. God will smite his bow out of his left hand (Ezek. 39:3).

6. God will smite his arrows out of his right hand. He has no weapon against God.

7. He will fall upon the mountains of Israel, he and all of his crowds of impending troupes (Ezek. 39:4).

8. God will give him unto the ravenous birds of every sort.

9. God will give him to the beasts of the field to be devoured.

10. He will fall upon the open field (Ezek. 39:5).

11. God will send a fire on Magog (Ezek. 39:6).

12. God will send a fire among them that dwell confidently in safety in the "isles" (this word could mean coast).

13. They will know that God has done this and that He is Lord.

14. God will make His holy name known in the midst of His people, Israel (Ezek. 39:7).

---

[140] Watt, D. G., Leale, T. H., & Barlow, G. (1892). *Ezekiel* (p. 414). New York; London; Toronto: Funk & Wagnalls Company.

15. He will not let them pollute His holy name <u>anymore</u>.

16. The heathen will know that God is Yahweh, the Holy One in Israel.

17. The judgment will be completed on Gog and his allies (Ezek. 39:8).

18. In that day God will give Gog a place of graves in Israel, the valley of passengers on the east of the sea (Ezek. 39:11).

19. The dead bodies will stink in the noses of passengers.

20. There to the East of the sea, they will bury Gog and all his multitude.

21. They will call it The Valley of Hamon-gog.

22. For seven months the house of Israel will be burying them, that they may cleanse the land (Ezek. 39:12).

23. All the people of the land will bury (Ezek. 39:13).

24. It will be to them a famous memorial day, the day that God will be glorified.

25. They will give men continual employment to pass through the land to bury those that remain upon the face of the earth to cleanse it (Ezek. 39:14).

26. At the end of seven months the burial program will be ended. Keep in mind this is during the one thousand years that proceed the Day of the Lord.

27. During the seven months, if travelers see a bone they will set up a sign by it, till the buriers have buried it in the valley of Hamon-gog (Ezek. 39:15).

28. The name of the city will be Hamonah. Thus they shall cleanse the land (Ezek. 39:16).

The Antichrist in Chapter 39:17-29

Chapter 39:17 and on are more specific about the time of the Antichrist and the end of the Tribulation. This is why many attribute all of 38-39 to him. I personally believe this to be a mistake. Notice the name "Gog" is not used in this section. This part certainly is not about the millennial reign period. Verses 22-29 rather prove this because they are speaking of finishing the Tribulation period and restoring Israel. This part can be confusing, but it seems Chapters 38 and 39:17 on contradict each other unless they are about two different time periods.

What we learn from these verses

1. Vs 17-20 the birds are called to a feast. Speak to every feathered fowl, and to every beast of the field, assemble yourselves, and come; gather yourselves on every side to "My sacrifices that I make for you upon the mountains of Israel." This is the same in Revelation 19:17-20.

   Revelation 19:17-18 (KJV)
   [17] And I saw an angel standing in the sun; and he cried with a loud voice, saying to all the fowls that fly in the midst of heaven, Come and gather yourselves together unto the supper of the great God;
   [18] That ye may eat the flesh of kings, and the flesh of

captains, and the flesh of mighty men, and the flesh of horses, and of them that sit on them, and the flesh of all *men, both* free and bond, both small and great.

2. God will display His glory among the Gentiles (Ezek. 39:21).

3. *All the heathen* will see God's judgment that He has executed upon the Antichrist and all his mighty armies, and His hand that is laid upon them.

4. The house of Israel will know that God is Yahweh their God from that day and forward (Ezek. 39:22). This is a key verse for timing, because this would not be a statement made at the end of the Millennium.

5. The heathen will know that the house of Israel went into captivity for their sins against God, and that He hid His face from them and gave them into the hands of their enemies to fall by the sword (Ezek. 39:23).

6. The heathen will know that God judged Israel according to their sins (Ezek. 39:24).

7. Now (after this battle of Armageddon is over and the judgment upon the Antichrist and his armies is complete) I will bring again the captivity of Jacob (Ezek. 39:25).

8. God will have mercy on *the whole house of Israel* (Zech. 12-14)

9. God will be jealous for His holy name.

10. After they have borne their shame and all their trespasses, when they dwell safely in their land with none making them afraid, when He has gathered them from all nations and has sanctified them in the sight of many nations, *then will they know* that He is the Lord their God, which *caused them* to be led away into captivity among the heathen: but have gathered *every one of them again* from the nations to their own land. (Ezek. 39:26-28).

11. If Ezekiel 38-39 is speaking of only *before* the Tribulation, then this above statement cannot be true, because in the middle of the Tribulation Israel will once again be laid siege by the Antichrist. This part is at least speaking of when the Tribulation is finished. Ezekiel 39:26-29 are *the key verses* for understanding Chapter 38 to know *when* the time of Israel's safety is, that Chapter 38 is speaking of.

12. God will never hide His face from *them again*, for He will pour out His Spirit upon the house of Israel (Ezek. 39:29).[141] This is definitely prophesied in many places to be at the end of the Tribulation for Israel.

This section seems to be more about the time of restoration for Israel than the Antichrist. Although, it does speak of the same time period, just after Armageddon.

---

[141] Adapted from Dake's list of "80 Eighty Predictions -- Unfulfilled:" Finis Jennings Dake, *Dake's Annotated Reference Bible: Containing the Old and New Testaments of the Authorized or King James Version Text,* (Lawrenceville, GA: Dake Bible Sales, Inc., 1997), WORD*search* CROSS e-book, Under: "Chapter 38."

So after all is said and done, my position for now is that these chapters are specifically speaking of two events in our future. First, in Chapter 38, it is the Revelation 20 event *after* the one thousand years of peace with Christ, which possibly *could have a double reference* to the end of the Tribulation scenario, but would not fulfill these verses entirely. Secondly, in Chapter 39, the end-of-Tribulation scenario with the Antichrist is described. Ezekiel 39:1-16 may be about the post-millennial event, but more likely it is about the Antichrist. Ezekiel 39:17 verses forward are definitely about the Antichrist.

Some commentators put both chapters together one way, say for a prophecy about the Antichrist altogether, and others feel like these chapters lean entirely toward a post-millennial time period fulfillment.

> "These two Chapters are unique. They describe an invasion of foreign powers against the people of God, even after the Messiah's reign of peace has begun." [142]

I'm taking the lesser road and seeing these two chapters as two different Gogs.

---

[142] Knowles, A. (2001). The Bible guide (1st Augsburg books ed., p. 335). Augsburg.

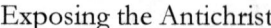

Chapter 10
The mark of the beast

So much has been said over the centuries about the mark of the beast; nevertheless, it is only fitting that remarks be made here concerning this in our study of the Antichrist.

Revelation 13:1 (KJV)
¹ And I stood upon the sand of the sea, and saw <u>a beast rise up out of the sea,</u> having seven heads and ten horns, and upon his horns ten crowns, and upon his heads the name of blasphemy.

We explained this chapter in detail previously. While this beast represents a political Antichrist *system* during the Tribulation period, it is most definitely a *man* also. Verses 5-10 are specifically about the person, i.e., the *mouth* of the beast system, the Antichrist. So the beast is a person, and he is a demonic system. Then in Verses 16-17, we see the first mention of the mark:

Name or Number

This mark is equal to the beast's name or *number* (13:17; 14:11). This mysterious number is announced in Rev. 13:18 as 666. But notice people may choose to have the "brand" of a number, or his (the Antichrist's) name, or possibly his kingdom's name, for his kingdom is also a "beast" system that is represented by a name. In today's language, we call this a "logo" or a "brand." Either of these could be imprinted on their right hand or forehead.

> **Revelation 13:16-18 (KJV)**
> [16] **And he** (LB- v. 11, the other beast who came up out of the earth, the false prophet) **causeth all, both small and great, rich and poor, free and bond, to receive a mark in their right hand, or in their foreheads:**
> [17] **And that no man might buy or sell, save he that had <u>the mark, or the name of the beast, or the number of his name.</u>**
> [18] **Here is wisdom. Let him that hath understanding count <u>the number of the beast:</u> for it is <u>the number of a man</u>; and his number *is* <u>Six hundred threescore *and* six.</u>**

Three brands are listed and one of these must be had to buy or sell.

Revelation 16:2 and 19:20 cite the "mark of the beast" as a sign or "mark" that identifies those who worship the beast, who emerge out of the sea of humanity in Revelation 13:1. Revelation 19:20 says they "received" (KJV) or "accepted" the mark willfully. The Greek is translated as the word "accepted" in English. It seems to infer that no one can be marked against their will. They will be deceived by the false prophet and freely accept the mark. This particularly indicates that they get the mark willfully first, worshipping this beast system, and then the false prophet deceives them with false signs and miracles. Those with the mark are told that they will be plagued with severely evil and painful ulcers. Could this be a biological result of this "mark"? They are also promised death during the time of Armageddon.

> **Revelation 16:1-2 (HCSB)**
> [1] **Then I heard a loud voice from the sanctuary saying to the seven angels, "Go and pour out the seven bowls of God's wrath on the earth."**
> [2] **The first went and poured out his bowl on the earth, and severely painful <u>sores broke out</u> on the people who had <u>the mark of the beast</u> and who worshiped his image.**

Revelation 19:20-21 (HCSB)
²⁰ But <u>the beast</u> was taken prisoner, and along with him <u>the false prophet,</u> who had performed the signs in his presence. <u>He deceived those who accepted the mark of the beast</u> and those who worshiped his image with these signs. Both of them were thrown alive into the lake of fire that burns with sulfur.
²¹ <u>The rest</u> were killed with the sword that came from the mouth of the rider on the horse, and all the birds were filled with their flesh.

I've never noticed this before, but there seem to be two groups of people represented here:

1. Those who worship the beast and his image out of their own free will.
2. Those who receive the mark willfully.

Revelation 14:11 (KJV)
¹¹ And the smoke of their torment ascendeth up for ever and ever: and they have no rest day nor night, who worship the beast and his image, and whosoever receiveth <u>the mark of his name</u>.

It is important to note that those with the mark are never able to rest. This and other physiological symptoms may be present in those who take the mark. This increases the possibility that insomnia and painful sores might be the result of some chemical or foreign body presented in the "mark." In whatever way, they will be the target of God's wrath because of this mark.

The mark

"Mark" here is the Greek word χάραγμα, *charagma*. According to *The Vine's Expository Dictionary:*

"from charasso, "to engrave" (akin to charaktēr, "an impress," RV, marg., of *Heb. 1:3*), denotes (a) "a mark" or "stamp," e.g., *Rev. 13:16, 17*; *Rev. 14:9, 11*; *Rev. 16:2*; *Rev. 19:20*; *Rev. 20:4*; *Rev. 15:2* in some mss.; (b) "a thing graven," *Acts 17:29.* [143]

"Charagma" is well proven to have been an "imperial seal" of the Roman Empire used on official documents during the first and second centuries. So here it means an engraving, stamp, or impression of the name. It sounds very much like what we call a "tattoo," but may not mean a tattoo at all. This seems to mean a *visible* impression or imprint on one's skin representing the beast system. The Greek word for a "tattoo" type of mark was a different word and would have been used here, but it wasn't. In the only other verse in which it is used except by the Book of Revelation, Acts 17:9, this *charagma* means an "engraved" piece of art.

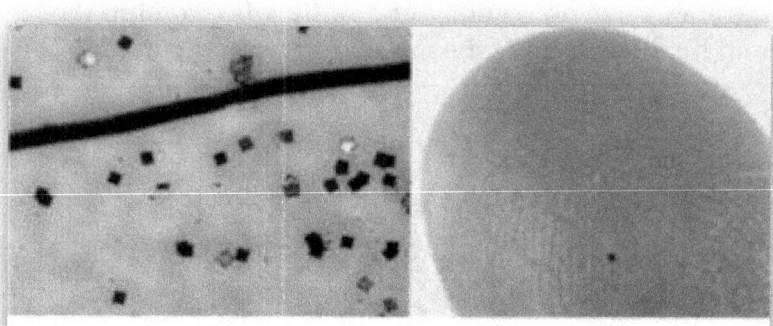

"These are made by Hitachi. They measure only.15X.15 mm each and have GPS capabilities! Sometimes called 'smartdust' as they can be sprayed on us and absorbed or taken in foods,drinks and even injected."

---

[143] William E. Vine, *Vine's Expository Dictionary of Old Testament and New Testament Words*, (Nashville, TN: Thomas Nelson, 1940), WORD*search* CROSS e-book, Under: "Graven."

So much lately has been said about the mark of the beast being a chip under the skin administered by a shot. Technology advances at almost lightning speed. Medical reports have led some to believe that some of these new "medical breakthroughs" come with the introduction of "gene-altering" abilities and have been found to include some form of nanite technology. This becomes dangerous territory when attempting to alter the human body. I believe these new technologies are leading to the process that will become the way a "mark" could be implemented in allowing purchases and sales. I image in the near future a machine that can create painlessly a permanent imprint on the skin of an individual. I do not believe the current series of "jabs" are the mark of the beast. While this is not the "mark," some of these "medical advancements" may prove to be more harmful than good.

"Nanochips and Smart Dust are the new technological means for the advancement of the human microchipping agenda. Due to their incredibly tiny size, both nanochips and Smart dust have the capacity to infiltrate the human body, become lodged within, and begin to set up a synthetic network on the inside which can be remotely controlled from the outside. Needless to say, this has grave freedom, privacy and health implications, because it means the New World Order would be moving from controlling the outside world (environment/society) to controlling the inside world (your body)." [144]

I personally have believed that this mark will be visible and worn proudly by those who worship the beast. This is the common understanding taught for years. I could be wrong.

[144] Article by Makia Freeman on NaturalBlaze.com. https://intothelight.news/files/2020-06-19-nanochips-smartdust.php. Photo same source.

Even though hidden technology will be present, a visible "mark" or impression seems to be what Revelation speaks of. This sounds totally bizarre for someone today to wear a mark on their forehead, but this will be a radical way of showing devotion to the Antichrist. It seems more like an "impression" type of mark than an ink mark. Below is the common view:

"The mark of the beast is evidently a brand-like mark, similar to a tattoo, which will identify beast-worshippers and will enable them to buy and sell. It probably connects with ancient customs. Domestic slave owners sometimes branded their slaves with their mark. Those bearing the mark of the beast show by their mark that they are his slaves. Sometimes Roman soldiers branded themselves with the mark of their general if they were particularly fond of him. Those devoted to the beast will take his mark. The same Greek word translated "mark" (*charagma*) also described the seal attached to legal documents that bore the name of the emperor and the date.

A less literal view understands the mark as, "John's way of symbolically describing authentic ownership and loyalty."[145]

CBN- Amazon's new hand scanner- 8/2022

"Amazon has created a new way for customers to make purchases with just their palm. The new hand recognition technology called "Amazon One" is currently available in two of its Amazon Go stores located in Seattle, Washington. By holding their palm above the device, patrons can

---

[145] Johnson, p. 532.— Tom Constable's Notes on the Bible Revelation 13:16

enter secure areas and pay for items without cash or credit card."[146]

All this scanner needs to do is read your unique palm print. So now technology has moved forward and taken one more step towards a way to implement the mark of the beast. This is still not the mark of the beast, but it's as close as you can get to it. In reality, this is remarkable technology to replace the use of cards to purchase goods. However, when technology like this is used against those refusing the mark of the beast, then it becomes devastatingly tragic. This article from CBN makes me wonder if I will ever get this book published before the Rapture of the Church and the "mark" are implemented.

Image Source: (Amazon via AP)

A less visible mark for Christians

---

[146] https://www1.cbn.com/cbnnews/us/2020/september/amazon-rolls-out-new-hand-scanner-and-its-already-being-compared-to-revelations-mark-of-the-beast

Revelation 7:3 (KJV)
[3] Saying, Hurt not the earth, neither the sea, nor the trees, till we have <u>sealed</u> the servants of our God in their foreheads.

Revelation 14:1 (KJV)
[1] And I looked, and, lo, a Lamb stood on the mount Sion, and with him an hundred forty *and* four thousand, having his <u>Father's name written in their foreheads.</u>

2 Corinthians 1:21-22 (KJV)
[21] Now he which stablisheth us with you in Christ, and hath anointed us, *is* God;
[22] Who hath also <u>sealed</u> us, and given the earnest of the Spirit in our hearts.

The Book of Revelation says that the 144,000 Jewish evangelists are "sealed" in their foreheads with a mark of Father God's name. Some argue that the 144,000 will have a *visible* mark. The Greek word used here is "*sphragizō*" which means to "stamp with a signet or private mark." *Strong's Concordance* defines it this way:

> 4972- "From <G4973> (sphragis); to *stamp* (with a signet or private mark) for security or preservation (literal or figurative); by implication to *keep secret*, to *attest* :- (set a, set to) seal up, stop."[147]

This mark may be visible or invisible to signify to the world that these men are chosen by God for His purpose. In either case, these and others are supernaturally protected because of this "seal." This is very much like those who are mentioned inside Jerusalem in Ezekiel's vision in Chapter 9. Perhaps this is how individuals are identified and protected by the Holy Spirit on the day of the Lord's wrath.

---

[147] James Strong, *Strong's Talking Greek & Hebrew Dictionary*, (Austin, TX: WORD*search* Corp., 2007), WORD*search* CROSS e-book, Under: "4972".

Ezekiel 9:6 (KJV)
⁶ Slay utterly old *and* young, both maids, and little children, and women: but come not near any man upon whom *is* the mark; and begin at my sanctuary. Then they began at the ancient men which *were* before the house.

There is something to be said about the false prophet initializing a "mark" and the 144,000 having some type of "seal" in their foreheads. Satan always tries to counterfeit the real with a fake. We don't know for sure during the Tribulation if their seal is visible, but it is probably not a visible mark because the same Greek work is used for the believer being stamped according to 2 Corinthians 1:22. We who are believers have this stamp or seal and this is not visibly seen. The 144,000 are sealed as well.

Even if this mark of the beast in the future is an invisible "tattoo" under the skin, those who take it, receive it, and accept it willfully will worship the Antichrist. People will be deceived, but not tricked. They will want the mark.

"A more common term for "mark" or "brand" is stigma [stivgma] in its noun and verb forms. Branding was practiced in the ancient world, and even in relation to religious concerns. Religious tattooing was observed (cf. Lucian, Syr. Dea 59; Herodotus 2.113). Third Maccabees 2:29 records an incident in which Jews were branded by Ptolemy Philopator I (217 b.c.) with the Greek religious Dionysian ivy-leaf symbol. The "mark" on Cain in Genesis 4:15 is rendered by semeion [shmei'on] in the Septuagint, the term for "sign." Paul's reference to his bearing in his body the "marks" of Jesus (Gal 6:17) utilizes stigma [stivgma], not charagma [cavragma]."[148]

---

[148] Edited by Gary T. Meadors. Baker's Evangelical Dictionary of Biblical Theology - Mark of the Beast. Mark of the Beast - Meaning & Definition - Baker's Bible Dictionary (biblestudytools.com)

This is from Baker's Evangelical Dictionary of Biblical Theology under "the mark of the beast"[149]:

"The interpretive difficulty in understanding the mark of the beast resides in identifying what response John expected by his challenge in Revelation 13:18 to calculate the number of the beast. The process of working from a number to a name was an ancient process called gematria in Hebrew and isopsephia in Greek. Many ancient languages utilized the letters of the alphabet for their numerical systems. The letter and number ratio was known by all. This existing process was used in enigmatic statements to conceal the identity of the person under consideration. An oft-quoted graffito from Pompeii (about a.d. 79) reads "I love her whose number is 545." Only those who knew the name or the pool of candidates could work out the riddle. The apocalyptic Sibylline Oracles used "888," the numerical equivalent of Iesous (Greek letters for Jesus), as an indirect reference to Jesus as the incarnate God. Therefore, John could have expected his audience to solve the riddle, but only if there was a shared pool of understanding concerning the enigmatic nature of the reference.

The history of interpretation concerning the correlation of a person with the number 666 has only resulted in endless speculations. One of the most prominent candidates has been the first-century Roman emperor Nero. A rare rendering of his name into Neron Caesar, transliterated into Hebrew as nrwn qsr, renders the number 666 (nun/50, resh/200, waw/6, nun/50, qof/100, samech/60, and resh/200 = 666). This rare

---

[149] © 1996 by Walter A. Elwell. Published by Baker Books, a division of Baker Book House Company, Grand Rapids, Michigan USA.

form of Nero's name was actually found in an Aramaic document from Qumran (cf. John's play on Hebrew words in the Book of Revelation at <u>9:11</u> and <u>16:16</u>). It is also noteworthy that a variant reading in Greek New Testament manuscripts exits that cites the number as "616" rather than "666." The transliteration of the normal Nero Caesar into the Hebrew nrw qsr, renders the number 616. <u>There was also a belief in a revived Nero as the antichrist from the first century</u> (cf. book 5 of the Sibylline Oracles) to the time of Augustine, who cites this idea in The City of God.

Irenaeus, however, wrote within a century of the apostle John and did not mention Nero. He proposed a number of options, including lateinos, meaning a Latin (30 + 1 + 300 + 5 + 10 + 50 + 70 + 200 = 666), and thus a Roman ruler, and teitan, a Roman name with which he was enamored (Contra Haereses 5.29-30). A few modern scholars have noted that the numbers can also argue for a connection with Babylon and Nimrod. The list is expanded with the creative use of numbers during times of modern crises (e.g., Hitler was a major candidate during World War II).

It is possible that John merely intended the number to be symbolic of what the beast and his followers represent: humankind in their ultimate rebellion against God, his Lamb, and the followers of the Lamb. John explains in 13:18 that the number 666 is the number of man. The number 7 is well established as a number of completeness or perfection. The number 6, being one less than 7, may symbolize humankind, which falls short of perfection. Irenaeus notes that the image set up by Nebuchadnezzar was 60 cubits high by 6 cubits wide. The number 666 could well personify the imperfection of man, even implying in the triple number the unholy trinity of the dragon, antichrist, and the false prophet. The identity of those who follow the Lamb or the beast is self-evident to the observer, whether it is the first century or the eschatological future. The vision calls John and his audience to discern the spirit of sinful humanity that accompanies the antichrist rather than to decode his identity."[150]

What we learn from these verses:

1. One must have a brand/mark of either *the name* of the beast or *the number* of his name to buy or sell some time during the Tribulation period.

2. This second beast from the earth, which probably denotes a lesser authority, is the false prophet, as he is called in Revelation 19:20, who initiates and forces the worship of the antichrist, and "brands" those who do so with the mark.

3. The mark of the Antichrist identifies those who worship him.
4. People will accept this mark willingly.

5. They are deceived by the false prophet.

6. The mark is equal to the beast's name or number.

7. The "mark" seems to be an impression or brand mark in the skin.

8. Those who have the mark will suffer painful sores during God's wrath.

---

[150] Edited by Gary T. Meadors. Baker's Evangelical Dictionary of Biblical Theology - Mark of the Beast. Mark of the Beast - Meaning & Definition - Baker's Bible Dictionary (biblestudytools.com) © 1996 by Walter A. Elwell. Published by Baker Books, a division of Baker Book House Company, Grand Rapids, Michigan USA.

Chapter 11

Will the Antichrist rule America?

This is a good question. Five years ago, I might have said that America in its present state would not be ruled by the Antichrist. I stated then that for this to happen, America would have to be weakened to the point that they could not or would not interfere with European affairs, even if they did not succumb to him in a complete way. I said that America would have to be destroyed financially for this to happen. My hope was that it wouldn't.

We all know that when millions of Christians depart from this earth all at once in the Rapture of the Church, it will leave countries reeling for leadership, which will be taken up by evil men. This could be the event that ruins America and brings her to the point of indifference. Now, five years later, we look through a different lens, and after 2020, we see what could devastate a country: a deadly virus possibly of evil human origin bringing the whole world to a halt and a country whose leaders seem bent on destroying its financial stability. I could have spoken too soon. If America is too weak to resist, at the very least they will not interfere.

Nations will successfully resist the Antichrist during the Tribulation

Did you know that there are nations who successfully resist the Antichrist during the tribulation period, even in the Middle East?

Daniel 11:41 (KJV)
[41] **He shall enter also into the glorious land, and many** *countries* **shall be overthrown: but these shall escape out of his hand,** *even* **Edom, and Moab, and the chief of the children of**

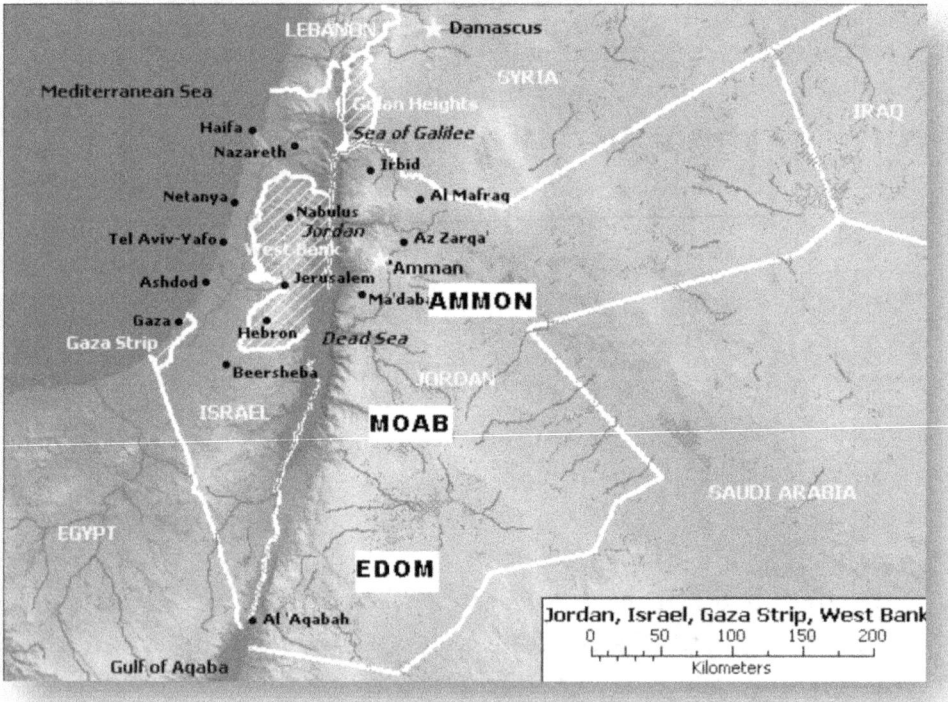

Ammon.

These are mostly Jordan and parts of Arabia. "Dake states, "If these countries escape Antichrist, these on the border of Palestine which does not escape him, then it is surely conceivable that many countries across the vast oceans will also escape him."

This is Finis Dake's 15 proofs why the Antichrist will not reign over America:

"Fifteen proofs Antichrist will not reign over America or be a worldwide dictator:

1. Four statements in Rev. 13 have led some to believe that Antichrist will literally rule the whole world and cause every man on earth to take a mark or be killed. They are:

(1) Power was given him over all kindreds, and tongues, and nations (Rev. 13:7)

(2) All that dwell upon the earth shall worship him (except Christians, Rev. 13:8)

(3) He causeth all, both small and great ... to receive a mark (Rev. 13:16)

(4) No man might buy or sell, save he that had the mark, name, or number (Rev. 13:17). On the surface it might seem that these statements prove Antichrist will be a world ruler, killing all on earth who do not take his mark, name, or number. But, the contrary is true because "all" in these passages is simply a figure of speech -- synecdoche -- in which a whole is put for a part, as we would say, "Everyone in town," or "the whole country." If the United States would make a law that "all men" of all nations, and tongues must register on a certain day or be killed, we would

naturally understand the law to apply only to all people of all nations and tongues who are under the government of the United States, not to the people of these nations and tongues who are under other governments. The word "all" is used in a limited sense hundreds of times in Scriptures (Gen. 6:17; Josh. 6:21-25; 2Sam. 6:5,15; 1Ki. 11:16-17; Mt. 3:5-6; Lk. 2:1-3; Rom. 1:8; 10:18; Col. 1:23; etc.).

2. Such terms as in Rev. 13 have been used of other rulers and kingdoms who did not literally rule the whole world. It was said of Nebuchadnezzar -- Wheresoever the children of men dwell ... hath made thee ruler over them ALL (Dan. 2:38). Of Greece -- Which shall bear rule over ALL the earth (Dan. 2:39). Of Rome -- Shall devour the WHOLE earth (Dan. 7:23-24). None of these kingdoms ruled the whole world.

3. Rev. 13 itself limits the kingdom of Antichrist to the 10 kingdoms that are yet to be formed inside the old Roman Empire territory (Dan. 7:23-24). The beast has only 10 horns, not 65, plainly teaching that a limited part of the earth will be under Antichrist (Rev. 13:1; 17:12-17).

4. Rev. 17:8-17 also limits the kingdom of Antichrist to the 10 kingdoms -- the 10 horns ... are 10 kings, which have received no kingdom as yet, but received power as kings with the beast ... these shall give their kingdom unto the beast.

5. In Dan. 7:7-8, 23-24 we have the definite location of the future 10 kingdoms. They are to be inside (out

of), not outside the old Roman Empire territory. America and many other lands were never a part of the old Roman Empire, so they will not be a part of the 10 kingdoms to be formed in the last days inside that empire. No country outside the 10 kingdoms will be ruled by Antichrist and no mark of the beast will be forced upon any man outside the kingdom of Antichrist.

6. In Dan. 9:27; 11:40-45 Antichrist breaks his 7-year covenant with Israel and takes over Palestine and many other countries, "but these shall escape out of his hand, even Edom, and Moab, and the chief of the children of Ammon," which would be modern Jordan and Arabia. If these countries escape Antichrist, these on the border of Palestine which does not escape him, then it is surely conceivable that many countries across the vast oceans will also escape him.

7. The nation of Israel escapes the Antichrist arriving safe in the wilderness of Edom and Moab where they are protected of God for 3 1/2 years, or during the time the whole world is supposed to be taking the mark of the beast (see pt. 10, The Sun-Clothed Woman)

8. In Dan. 11:44-45 it is stated that the countries north and east of the 10 kingdoms under Antichrist will make war on him. These countries too, then, are not ruled by him and are and are not therefore forced to take the mark.

9. In Rev. 16:13-16 we have 3 unclean spirits like frogs going forth working miracles through ambassadors thus seeking the cooperation of many nations to help Antichrist against Jesus Christ at Armageddon. These will not have been conquered by him or be under him or they would not have to be persuaded to help him at Armageddon. If he ruled them and they loved him enough to worship him and take his mark, such demonic ministries would be unnecessary.

10. In Rev. 13:4 we have proof that there are nations whom the Antichrist has not conquered. If there were no nations who were not under him it would be foolish to raise the question about who can conquer him.

11. In Rev. 14:9-11 it is stated that every man who does take the mark of the beast, or his name, or the number of his name, will be sent to eternal hell without exception. If, as some teach today, Antichrist will kill every man who does not take the mark of the beast, and if, as stated here, every man who does take it will be sent to eternal hell, there will not be one person left on earth to populate it in the Millennium and the New Earth. Thus, such a doctrine as Antichrist killing all on earth who do not take his mark and worship him is literally untrue.

12. The truth is that Antichrist will make a law that all in his 10 kingdoms must worship him and take his mark, but the law will not and cannot be literally enforced in such a vast territory in as short a time as 3 1/2 years. It would be impossible for one human

Antichrist to contact every man in the whole world and to see that every man is killed who does not take his mark. To say that, he could be virtually teaching that one man can do more in 3 1/2 years than what God, Christ, the Holy Spirit, angels, and all the redeemed people of over 1,900 years have been able to do. The gospel has been preached that long and still multiplied millions of people on earth have never heard the name of Jesus Christ. How could a new doctrine and a new religion of the beast be made known to all the world in 3 1/2 years? One reason why Antichrist cannot enforce such a law even inside the Roman Empire territory in 3 1/2 years is because of the wars between his 10 kingdoms and the many nations north and east of his empire (Dan. 11:44). These wars will keep him so occupied that he will not be able to pay full attention to the enforcement of his religious laws. Then, too, there will no doubt be ways of avoiding such laws in certain localities as there are concerning any other manmade law. Local officials, money, bribery, and many other things will enable some in his kingdom to escape literal compliance to such a law. Guerrilla warfare against Antichrist can be carried on in all parts of his kingdom, making it impossible to enforce such a law literally. Antichrist will come and go without millions of people in various parts of the earth knowing that he ever existed. This is true of Jesus Christ, and it will be true of Antichrist. Many peoples in the interior of certain lands do not yet know that there have been two world wars in a generation. Many do not know we have automobiles, airplanes, etc. The Bible teaches that in the Millennium Christ will be reigning in Jerusalem for some time before His agents contact certain peoples on earth and seek to bring them under His government (Isa. 2:2-4; 40:9; 52:7; 61:6; 66:18-21; Zech. 8:23; 14:16-21). So it will be in the days of Antichrist.

13. In Zech. 14:16-21 it is clear that many from every nation, even those that are under Antichrist, will be left alive on the earth in the Millennium. These will not take the mark of the beast. If so, they would be sent to eternal hell by Christ at His second coming. Since they are left to enter the Millennium, it is proof that every man on earth will not take the mark or be killed. For example, Egypt is spoken of in Dan. 11:40-45 as not escaping the Antichrist, but we find Egyptians left to enter the Milennium in Zech. 14:16-21. So it will be with many people of all the nations under Antichrist. Some will not take the mark or obey his law and yet escape death by him. Multitudes will be killed, but not all (Rev. 7:9-11; 14:13; 15:2-4; 16:2; 20:4-6).

14. In Mt. 25:31-46 we read of many of all nations that are called blessed of My Father who will inherit the millennial and eternal kingdom. These people will not take the mark of the beast or they would be sent to eternal hell, as stated in Rev. 14:9-11. The basis of the judgment of the nations here is their treatment of Israel. Such kind treatment of Israel could not be possible on the part of any nation if all were directly controlled by Antichrist.

15. The remnant of the woman in Rev. 12:17 escape the mark of the beast and the worship of Antichrist. This is made possible by new wars in the north and

east of his kingdom, forcing him to let them alone for the time being so as to conquer these new enemies. The ministry of the two witnesses helps protect them the last 3 1/2 years. Then when Antichrist conquers his enemies after nearly 3 1/2 years of war he gathers his forces against the Jews to destroy them. He is defeated by Jesus Christ at Armageddon before he even takes all of Jerusalem, which by some means has been suddenly delivered from Antichrist and is back in Jewish hands (Zech. 14:14-15).

Thus, we conclude that Antichrist will not rule America or be a worldwide dictator; that his kingdom will be limited to the old Roman Empire territory during the time he seeks to enforce the new beast worship; that he will be in constant wars with other nations during the whole 7 years he is here (Dan. 7:23-24; 9:27; 11:36-45); that multitudes of all nations will escape the mark of the beast and his worship; and that Antichrist will be defeated by Christ before he conquers all of Asia, Europe, Africa, the Americas, and all other parts of the world." [151]

Notice here that there are still kings during the last day, apart from the Antichrist. There are still countries with rulers, even though the Antichrist is ruling.

Why does the Antichrist go out to deceive if he has control of these nations?

---

[151] Finis Jennings Dake, *Dake's Annotated Reference Bible: Containing the Old and New Testaments of the Authorized or King James Version Text*, (Lawrenceville, GA: Dake Bible Sales, Inc., 1997), WORD*search* CROSS e-book, Under: "Chapter 13".

Revelation 16:13 proves that spirits come out of Satan, the Antichrist, and the false prophet, going out to deceive and prepare these kings to come to battle. These countries will still be sovereign during the Tribulation. They will have kings and presidents and parliaments and cabinets.

> **Revelation 16:13-14 (KJV)**
> [13] **And I saw three unclean spirits like frogs *come* out of the mouth of the dragon, and out of the mouth of the beast, and out of the mouth of the false prophet.**
> [14] **For they are the spirits of devils, working miracles, *which* go forth <u>unto the kings of the earth and of the whole world,</u> to <u>gather them to the battle</u> of that great day of God Almighty.**

The "earth" and the "whole world" seem to be two different areas

For whatever it is worth, notice that "the earth" and "the whole world" seem to represent two different places. Dake's points 1 & 2 are well taken, that when Scripture states a particular king ruled "the earth," his rule really was not over *all* the known world. It was probably the mass of *earth* that included Israel and the far reaching lands around it. Babylon, Greece, and Rome were all said to have ruled the entire earth but didn't. It may be that the Antichrist has full rule over "the earth," or his area of rule, but not "the whole world." He rules the territory he has conquered, but he would only influence the rest of the *world* through coercion if this were the case. Wouldn't the Antichrist just command these nations to come if he ruled over them and the whole world?

> "It explains how the kings of the earth, who are not under Antichrist, will be persuaded to cooperate with him at Armageddon (Rev.

16:13-16). Unclean spirits will inspire ambassadors and do miracles through them to convince the kings of the earth that the success of their future lies in the whole earth cooperating together to stop Christ from taking over the earth at His second coming. They will inspire the nations to fight against Christ, fulfilling Ps. 2." [152]

Psalm 2:2-3 (KJV)
2 The kings of the earth set themselves, and the rulers take counsel together, against the LORD, and against his anointed, *saying*,
3 Let us break their bands asunder, and cast away their cords from us.

Revelation 13:7-8 (KJV)
7 And it was given unto him to make war with the saints, and to overcome them: and power was given him over all kindreds, and tongues, and nations.
8 And all that dwell upon the earth shall worship him, whose names are not written in the book of life of the Lamb slain from the foundation of the world.

The Antichrist will have some power over those nations on earth. These powers are political, economic, and religious. To what extent this is true in each nation, we are unsure. It was said of other past kings in Scripture that they ruled the "world," but only ruled over the predominant kingdoms they were in.

---

[152] Finis Jennings Dake, Dake's Annotated Reference Bible: Containing the Old and New Testaments of the Authorized or King James Version Text, (Lawrenceville, GA: Dake Bible Sales, Inc., 1997), WORDsearch CROSS e-book, Under: "Chapter 16".

1. Nebuchadnezzar – "Wheresoever the children of men dwell ... hath made thee ruler over them ALL" (**Dan. 2:38**).

2. Greece – "Which shall bear rule over ALL the earth" (**Dan. 2:39**).

3. Rome – "Shall devour the WHOLE earth" (**Dan. 7:23-24**).

None of these kingdoms ruled the whole world in the sense that we see it today.

There are kings in the earth who will be allowed to rule after Jesus comes back?

In that day when Christ judges the Antichrist, some kings will be allowed to live under Christ for a season. They will probably live out their lives and die during the millennial reign. How could this be if they had been made to receive the mark of the beast? If they had all followed the Antichrist, would this be the case? This might be an indication that some kings on earth have not bowed the knee to the beast.

Daniel 7:11-12
[11] **"I watched, then, because of <u>the sound of the arrogant words the horn was speaking</u>. As I continued watching, <u>the beast was killed and its body destroyed</u> and given over to <u>the burning fire</u>.**
[12] **As for <u>the rest of the beasts, their authority to rule was removed</u>, but <u>an extension of life was granted</u> to them for <u>a certain period of time</u>.**

A "people" from the north, "a great nation," and "many kings" come to destroy the future city of Babylon

Did you know that a great nation and a group from afar will come and destroy the rebuilt city of Babylon during the reign of the Antichrist? Who are these people? Maybe a revived America? We don't know, but it could be possible.

The book of Revelation reveals that the destruction of the future city of Babylon will come in one literal day.

Revelation 18:8-9 (KJV)
8 Therefore shall her plagues come in one day, death, and mourning, and famine; and <u>she shall be utterly burned with fire</u>: for strong *is* the Lord God who judgeth her.
9 And the kings of the earth, who have committed fornication and lived deliciously with her, shall bewail her, and lament for her, when they shall see the smoke of her burning,

Jeremiah 50:41-43 (HCSB)
41 Look! <u>A people comes from the north</u>. <u>A great nation</u> and <u>many kings</u> will be stirred up from the <u>remote regions</u> of the earth.
42 They grasp bow and javelin. They are cruel and show no mercy. Their voice roars like the sea, and they ride on horses, lined up like men in battle formation against you, Daughter Babylon.
43 The <u>king of Babylon</u> has heard reports about them, and <u>his hands fall helpless</u>. <u>Distress has seized him— pain, like a woman in labor.</u>

Jeremiah Chapters 50-51 encapsulate the prophecy against a future Babylon. Some try to say that these were fulfilled by the Assyrians and Persians when they took Babylon. Some verses could only lightly apply. As we have stated before, only a future fulfillment is in view because the old Babylon never ceased to exist in one day, nor were its inhabitants ever completely removed. The ancient city just faded over time and ceased to exist. Jeremiah 50 and verses 39-40 are proof that these verses are about a future city of Babylon because the future destruction and judgment mentioned in these passages are that "no man would ever dwell there again" (see also vv. 3, 13, 39b-40; 51:29, 37, 43, 62). When the Persians, Greeks, and Romans came, the city continued to exist even with its citizens. Daniel was one of them who stayed when the Medes and later Cyrus the Great came.

Jeremiah 50:3 (KJV)
³ For out of the north there cometh up a nation against her, which shall make her land desolate, and <u>none shall dwell therein</u>: they shall remove, they shall depart, both man and beast.

Jeremiah states that a future "people" will come from the north, "a great nation," and "many kings" will be stirred up from "remote regions of the earth." These nations are gathered in the last part of the tribulation period to attack the Antichrist's capital city.

This prophecy in Jeremiah 50 has not been fulfilled in history yet. So we see here that a nation with other kings following it will be against the Antichrist. This helps us to prove that he may not rule the United States and other countries. This is my hope, even if we Christians are gone from the earth at this point. Even the Antichrist will have enemies.

So, for these reasons, we should have hope for America even after the believers leave. We personally believe revival will spread across the nations like it will in the future for Israel. In spite of all the evil that abounds, God's grace will also abound through many salvations during the tribulation period.

Chapter 12

Just the Facts

Next are the lists of names compiled from all these verses we used and all the facts about the Antichrist we also found. Keep in mind that not all of these names are proper names, but some are what the Antichrist is called based on his actions. Most of these are proper names, and some of these are descriptions of him.

38 Names that the Antichrist is called

1. Antichrist- 1 John 2:18

2. The king- Daniel 11:36

3. He- Daniel 9:27

4. The leader of the house of the wicked- Habakkuk 3:13

5. The horn- Daniel 7:11

6. The beast- Daniel 7:11; Rev. 13:4

7. The lawless one- 2 Thessalonians 2:8

8. The king of Babylon- Isaiah 14:4

9. The wicked one- Isaiah 14:5; 2 Thess. 2:8; Nahum 1:15

10. The man- Isaiah 14:16

11. The Assyrian- Isaiah 14:25; Micah 5:5; Isaiah 10:24, 31; Isaiah 30:31; Nahum 1:11-15

12. Another who will come in his own name- John 5:43

13. The liar- 1 John 2:22; John 8:44; 2 Thess. 2:11

14. The deceiver (Gr. imposter) 2 John 1:7

15. The subduer- Daniel 7:24

16. Another little horn- Daniel 7:8; 8:9

17. A king of fierce countenance; insolent- Daniel 8:23

18. The selfish king- Daniel 11:36

19. The last Syrian king, the king of the North- Daniel 11:40

20. The spoiler or powerful ravager- Isaiah 16:4

21. Terrible one or tyrannical mighty oppressor- Isaiah 29:20

22. Scorner or scoffer- Isaiah 29:20

23. Man of sin- 2 Thess. 2:3

24. The son of perdition/destruction- 2 Thess. 2:3

25. That wicked- 2 Thess. 2:8

26. Belial or the wicked one- Nahum 1:15

27. The bloody and deceitful man- Psalm 5:6

28. The man of earth- Psalm 10:18

29. The mighty man (immensely wealthy) man- Psalm 52:1

30. The northerner- Joel 2:20

31. Wicked counsellor- Nahum 1:11

32. A son of revived Greece?- Zech. 9:13-14

33. A foolish and idol-worthless shepherd- Zech. 11:15-17

34. The king of Sheshach or Babylon- Jer. 25:26

35. The prince of Tyre? Ezek. 28:2

36. A cruel lord and fierce king over Egypt- Isaiah 19:4, 26:13

37. The chief head or leader of the earth (part not whole- see Psalm 2:2)- Psalm 110:5-6

38. Gog the chief prince of Meshach and Tubal (Southwestern Russia, Eastern Turkey, Northern Iran- Not that he is from these, but during the Tribulation the Antichrist will rule these)- Ezek.39:1

286 Facts about the Antichrist, Compiled

2 Thess. 2:4, Dan. 9:27

1. He exalts himself above anything that is worshipped.

2. He sits in the sanctuary in Jerusalem, where no man is allowed defying Jewish law.

3. He publicizes that he is now God at this time.

4. This happens in the middle of the Tribulation period.

Habakkuk 3

5. Christ will crush or wound the leader of the house of the wicked.

6. He will be stripped from "foot to neck."

7. Christ will "pierce his head with his own spears." This could refer to his leaders or battlements, or that the Antichrist will be judged by his own words.

Dan. 7:9-12

8. The Ancient of Days takes his seat in glory.

9. The Antichrist, called the "horn" stands before Jesus.

10. He speaks arrogantly.

11. The "beast," another name for the Antichrist, is killed.

12. His body is destroyed and put in the fire.

2 Thess. 2:8

13. He sets himself apart from God's law and is wicked.

14. He will one day be revealed to the world.

15. He will be destroyed by the words of Jesus.

16. Nothing he will do will ever matter after Jesus returns.

Isaiah 14:7-11

17. He is called the king of Babylon, the future golden city (or city that requires tribute). This means that city will be rebuilt in the last days.

18. He is called the oppressor.

19. The golden city is ceased (comes to an abrupt end).

20. The Lord does the breaking of the staff and scepter.

21. He is called "the wicked" here corresponding with Paul in 2 Thess. 2:8.

22. He rules the nations.

23. He with his staff, struck people with unceasing blows.

24. He subdues the nations in rage with relentless persecution (HCSB).

25. He will be persecuted and will hinder no more.

26. At his defeat the whole earth will be at rest.

27. Trees will rejoice at his fall.

Isaiah 14:16-23

28. Those in Hell will narrowly look (examine to understand him) on him and stare.

29. They say "Is this the man?" and mock.

30. He made the earth to tremble with fear.

31. He made nations quake.

32. He made the inhabited world as a wilderness.

33. He destroyed (to pull down in pieces) its cities.

34. He will not have a normal grave like other kings.

35. He will go down into Hell below.

36. His physical body will not be buried, but will be a carcass thrown out with those thrust through with a sword to be stepped on, and dumped into a rocky pit (Gehenna).

37. He will not be buried *because* he has destroyed (ruined and caused to decay) his land and,

38. He slaughtered (smite with deadly intent, murdered) his own people.

39. He has "children" who are those who follow him.

40. God has prepared a place of slaughter for them.

41. The Lord will destroy Babylon and its descendants forever. (Vs. 21-23).

42. His offspring will be killed so he will never leave a heritage in the earth.

Jer. 50:39-43; Rev. 18;8-11

43. He is called the king of Babylon, she is called daughter.

44. A great country from afar and remote regions of the earth leads many other kings to battle the city.

45. He is not there when she is destroyed but hears reports.

46. His hands fall helpless to help Babylon.

47. He is greatly distressed when the city is destroyed.

John 5:43 (possibly about the false Jewish Messiah)

48. He will come in his own name or authority and not the Father's.

49. You (Israel) will receive him.

I John

50. Through Scripture and teaching the church has heard about a man called Antichrist.

51. Because (the spirit of the) antichrist exists now, we are in the last days.

52. He denies that Jesus is the Messiah.

53. He denies the Father and the Son.

54. He denies Jesus came in the flesh.

55. Even in John's day, antichrists were in the world.

56. They came out from among us (the apostles, the believers, the Jews?).

57. They are deceivers, therefore he is a deceiver.

58. They are liars, therefore he is the liar.

59. Antichrist is one who denies Jesus is the Messiah.

60. Antichrist is one who denies the Father and that Jesus is the Son of God.

Daniel 7:7-8

61. His kingdom begins at first as part of a fourth beast diverse and very different from the others: this is the Roman Empire. Rome being ruled as a republic was a very different way of ruling.

62. It then morphs into the 10 king coalition (this is future). Earlier Daniel says "out of the fourth."

63. A "little horn" comes up among them (not same as Daniel 8:9- Antiochus IV). This could mean insignificance in standing with the others, or a smaller country or weaker ruled position as compared to others, like an ambassador or vice president of a group.

64. It seems the little horn rips out three of the previous kingdoms by their roots.

65. The new king has "two eyes" (T. Constable suggests- "great intelligence") and a boastful mouth.

Daniel 7:19-27

66. An eleventh king (the Antichrist) will rise and subdue three of the ten.

67. He has "eyes" and the ability to see and speak great things.

68. His look is <u>more stout</u> than the others.

69. He will make war with the saints and prevail against them.

70. Until or up to the time Jesus comes back to reign.

71. Out of the fourth kingdom (within the Roman Empire) will come these 10 kings (a coalition formed before the little horn appears).

72. An eleventh king will rise up after and *different* from the 10 (vs. 8, 20).

73. He will put down and humble 3 of the kings to take full control (See Daniel 7:8; 11:43 three nations mentioned).

74. He will speak great words against God Himself.

75. He will "wear out" or mentally oppress the saints.

76. He will think to change times and laws.

77. The (Trib.) saints will be given into his hand for a period of 3 ½.

78. Then the court of judgment will convene- at the return of Christ.

79. Then the kingdom of all under heaven will be given to the people of the saints of the most high.

80. It will be an everlasting kingdom and all dominions shall obey and serve him- "Christ."

Daniel 8

81. Near the end of their kingdoms, when their rebellious *expansion* has reached full measure (Greece, Turkey, Syria/Babylon, and Egypt) an *insolent* king will come to the throne. These kingdoms exist today. Antiochus IV came through and ruled the Syrian quarter, which covered Iraq, Syria, and Palestine.

82. An insolent king in presence- fierce, mighty, strong and harsh.

83. He will be skilled in dark trickery, craftiness, puzzles and dark sayings- perhaps sciences.

84. His strength will be awesome bone breaking power, but it is not from his own power.

85. He succeeds in terrible corruption and destruction. AMP- "He shall corrupt and destroy astonishingly."

86. He will prosper in whatever he does.

87. He will destroy powerful nations and also the holy people Israel.

88. He will cause deceit to prosper by his knowledge and way of influence.

89. He will make himself great in his mind.

90. He will destroy many in a time that is peaceful.

91. He will stand against the prince of princes (Jesus).

92. He will be shattered not by human hands.

Daniel 9:25-27

93. The "he" here may have a possible connection to the Roman Empire or Titus himself (with the union of 10- The revised Roman Empire).

94. 69 weeks finished *before* Jesus died. There now is a great gap of time since then. This time marks the church age. Titus came 35 years later, not immediately or even 7 years later. The "end" for the nation of Israel came another 66 years later. Even now, the last seven years *have not been* fulfilled.

95. A covenant will be agreed upon with many for seven years, the last "week" (7 years) of Daniel. He will come at first with a false peace while nations submit to him. Rev. 6:1-2.

96. In the middle of the 7 years he will put a stop to sacrifice and offering. After Titus and 70 AD, John, in the book of Revelation at 95AD, was still prophesying about a future "beast" the Antichrist. So this last person in Daniel was not referring to Titus.

97. He will cause the abomination that makes desolate in the temple until he is destroyed.

98. What Antiochus IV Epiphanes did in 168 B.C. (before Christ) was an abomination, but Jesus said Daniel's prophecy is a future event (Matthew 24:14-16).

99. What Titus in 70 A.D. did (35 years after Jesus), was not the "abomination of desolation." He did not fulfill this literal last week. The Antichrist will do this.

Daniel 11:35-45

100. The time of the end an appointed time, is coming. But it also relates to this period of time.

101. God's people will also fall, be tried, and purified all the way up to the time of the end (70th week of years).

102. It appears by association that the Antichrist will be another Seleucid/Syrian (or possibly a Grecian-from the original territories of the old ¼ Grecian Empire- a king who rules over this same area of Iraq or Babylon). First, we connect him to the Roman union of 10 nations. Now specifically we see a connection with Antiochus' Seleucid Empire.

103. This king (the Antichrist) will do according to his will- whatever he wants to do- The opposite of that was the Seleucid king Antiochus IV, who was turned back from Egypt by Rome. The Roman Ambassador Popillias drew a circle in the sand around him and made him decide before he left the circle. He was forced to do something he obviously didn't want to do. So these verses are not about Antiochus IV.

104. Vs. 37- "He shall exalt himself and magnify himself above every god"- While Antiochus did stop official worship in Israel, he did not necessarily do this verse. He acted like he was Zeus/Jupiter in the flesh thus, the second name "Epiphanes," which meant "manifest god." However, he honored other gods.

105. He will say outrages things against the God of gods.

106. He will prosper until the indignation (Tribulation) be fulfilled (70th week of years).

107. Neither will he regard or "understand" the "gods" or "god" of his fathers or ancestors (Greek or Roman, Christian, Islam, Hindu?). "This king will abandon the religion in his past, whatever that religion may be."- Constable

108. He will not desire the delight of women, or the god that women desire after- (this according to Dake and the HCSB). NRSV reads: "to the one (LB-god) beloved by women." If connected to the previous statement then these versions would be correct. However, in the Hebrew it simply says: "or a woman's pleasant desire, or passion." Some teach that this means he will be gay or homosexual, while this may possibly be true, we know he will have offspring according to Isaiah 14:21.

109. He will not regard or understand any god including God Himself because he magnifies himself above all of them.

110. Instead, in his "office or stand," he will glorify or honor the "god of forces or fortresses" (Ashtoreth) with gold, silver, precious stones and riches. Because of the previous statements she would not be necessarily a god of his fathers. Maybe he will put his wealth into military might. See below for another possible explanation.

111. He will do this in the strongest fortresses with a foreign god. This verse sounds like he will create strong cities and appoint rulers over them with lands. This "foreign" god quite possibly is still Ashteroth.

112. He will honor those who know him and help him, with authority over peoples and gifts of land for a price.

113. At the time of the end- Egypt will push against him (the Antichrist is the king of the North-Syria Iraq, Iran), and the Antichrist will come down like a whirlwind with chariots and horsemen and ships and defeat him.

114. He will invade countries and sweep through them like a flood.

115. He will invade Israel and many will fall- at the 3 ½ year mark he will desecrate Israel and the Temple. Then and later just before Armageddon will he come to attack Jerusalem.

116. Edom, Moab and the prominent ones of Ammon will escape his powerful hand. Modern Jordan and parts of Arabia today.

117. He will extend his authority over nations including Egypt.

118. He will control the hidden treasures of Egypt: Silver, gold and all the riches.

119. Libya and Ethiopia will submit to him. Three subdued in Dan. 7:24?

120. Reports from the east and west will terrify him and he will go out with great fury to destroy.

121. He will move his headquarters to between the Dead Sea and Mount Moriah. This is probably referring to when he comes against Jerusalem the second time, at the very end and rifles Jerusalem (Zech. 14:2). Further proof of the latter would be the next reference that it is there where he will come to an end: in Jerusalem.

122. He will meet his end there with no one to help him.

Rev. 13:1-4

123. A beast or antichrist world system will come that incorporates 10 horns (kings) with seven heads (kingdoms), and all of the territories they covered. The seventh kingdom (one of the heads) will be greater than all the six before it, but it will cover the same areas and include a time of peace with Israel. (See explanation below in Rev. 17). The ten king coalition at the beginning of the Tribulation is the seventh kingdom. But this picture really is of the antichrist's eighth kingdom which is the final one that morphs from the sixth and seventh. This happens after the Tribulation is in full force.

124. Daniel's fourth kingdom, the Roman, with the iron legs, was the sixth kingdom in history to have ruled over Israel. It will later morph into the seventh and eighth kingdoms. In Revelation 13, what is pictured would be Daniel's fifth and sixth kingdoms, represented by the *ten-king* coalition and the Antichrist's kingdom. If God had pictured it as a beast for Daniel, this is what it would have looked like. What he did picture was the ten toes at the end of those iron legs, and he described the insolent king (see comparison chart).

125. This is the same as Revelation's seventh and eighth kingdoms, with the 10 crowned kings. This is why in Revelation 13:1-4 there are seven world kingdoms represented, and ten kings.

126. Daniel 7:44 proves that this kingdom will go into the last day and is marked by the union of the 10 kings. *This is when those in the world will know that they have entered this future seventh kingdom.* Ten kings from the original Roman Empire will be *united as one.* As the seventh kingdom and union of 10 kings, according to Daniel, the iron and clay do not mix, and will not work well together. This union, from its beginning, spans up to the first half of the Tribulation period.

127. In Revelation 13 the last kingdom is pictured like a leopard, with the feet of a bear and a mouth like a lion. See illustration. This might allude to a mixture of strengths of the Roman, Babylonian, Persian, and Grecian Empires. His terrible speech links him with Daniel's third kingdom and Antiochus IV. The body of the leopard says this system is the seventh and is similar to but different from all the rest. Perhaps a mixture of them.

128. His kingdom is swift, strong, loud, and is likened to a leopard. (Dan. 7:6 the Greek Empire- Dan. 8- Seleucid).

129. Another horn/king (the Antichrist, the 11th horn) must specifically at first, rule over three of the others nations- His and three more of the ten he conquers. HE IS THE "MOUTH" OF THIS BEAST.

130. All are united under one "name of blasphemy."

131. His power, reign and authority comes from the dragon himself (Satan).

132. One of the heads was wounded to death. Remember, that these represent kingdoms, not a person. The horns represent people. The angel explains this to John later in Chapter 17.

133. His deadly wound is healed and all the world marvels (the Babylonian/Assyrian/Greek Empire revived or he himself?) This relates specifically to the Antichrist area of rule which should include all the areas that Greece had ruled in Europe and the Middle East at the time of Antiochus IV.

134. This creates or merges into the *eighth* kingdom, the one the Antichrist controls fully in his possessed state.

135. This causes them to worship Satan and the beast.

136. Saying, "who is like this beast?"

137. Saying, "Who is able to make war with him?" This would include all nations.

Rev. 13:4-10

138. People will worship the dragon (Satan) and the beast system.

139. "Who is able to make war with *him*?" implies no nation dares to.

140. Now (after 42 months) the beast is given a "mouth"- who is the antichrist. Now he is given the ability to

speak powerfully and hypnotically of blasphemous things.

141. Power is given to him by the 10 kings, and then he rises as all powerful with his kingdom the eighth, and to continue 42 months.

142. He speaks against God, His name, His tabernacle, and those raptured and already in heaven.

143. He is given the motivation demonically to "war" against the saints (Israel and the Tribulation saints).

144. To "overcome" the saints.

145. The *legal right to rule* was given to him over all offshoot tribes, peoples, those with different languages, and nationalities (races).

146. *All that dwell on the earth* whose names are not in the book of life, shall worship him.

Rev. 17
147. There is a woman who is called a harlot who rides the beast system for a time.

148. She comes out of a large group of nations and peoples- V.15.

149. She is "drunken" with the blood of saints and Christian martyrs (historically before *and* during the Tribulation).

150. John marvels at her (possibly because she *appears* to be Christian and is spectacular like Rome and the Vatican

are even today, (or perhaps a whole different religion that he had never seen before like Islam) and the angel asked "why are you admiring her?"

151. The "beast" here has seven heads and ten horns (seven kingdoms and ten kings).

152. It will arise out of the bottomless pit and go into destruction and ruin.

153. This beast (worldly kingdom of the Antichrist) was, and is not, and yet is, and the world will marvel at its return.

154. The woman is seated not only on the beast, but also sits on seven "mounts," which could mean hills or the seven kingdoms that are mentioned next. This could mean she has had influence over the last *seven* kingdoms.

155. The seven heads are seven kings/mountains (mountains/kingdoms: demonic principality/king ruled- "kingdoms"). Five are fallen, one is now in John's day in operation (the sixth- was the old Roman), and the seventh is not yet here (the revised Roman).

156. When the seventh comes it only last a short time- Revised Roman Empire.

157. The eighth kingdom that rises is most likely one of the first five kingdoms revived, (if the phrase "was and is not" is referring to the statement of the seventh kingdom lasting a short time before ending, and then morphing into the eighth).

158. Daniel's prophecies pinpoint the sixth and revised seventh (what he called the *fourth* beast) kingdom to be *Roman,* by stating "of the people of the prince" in Daniel 9:27. The prince to come, spoken of there, was the Roman Titus, who would destroy the temple in 70 A.D. Then Daniel describes the future Antichrist by saying "he" would stop the sacrifices in the middle of the week of seven years left to come for Israel. This connects the Antichrist to the future revised *Roman* Empire.

159. Daniel also pinpoints his *third* kingdom in his vision (the fifth worldly kingdom) around a future "type" of Antiochus IV., who was of the Grecian Empire. He described him in detail but ended up speaking about the Antichrist, and revealing things about him that Antiochus did not fulfill. (Dan. 11:36-45). *This kingdom was likened to a leopard and would produce a future oppressor of Israel who would be destroyed by the Messiah Himself.* Daniel 7:6 correlated with Revelation 13:2 gives us a clue as to why we believe the eighth and final kingdom will be Grecian/Babylonian. *They both are likened to a leopard.* So the Antichrist would be out of the Roman (Middle East/and Europe), but specifically ruling over the same Greek area like Antiochus did, which was the Syrian/Babylonian and part of Europe. It was called the Seleucid (312-63 BC).

160. The ten horns are ten kings on the Roman beast who during John's day had no real kingdoms.

161. They all agree and will give their strength and authority to the "beast," the Antichrist's eighth kingdom.

162. They will war with Jesus, and He will overcome them.

163. That kingdom will destroy the harlot in the future.

164. The woman separate from the beast not only sits on the beast, but is on, or over multitudes of people and nations and languages.

165. The ten kings eventually hate the harlot and *destroy her* by stripping her, eating her "flesh," and finally by burning her.

166. God originates this judgment to fulfill what He wants to happen. Even in the fact of them giving their kingdom (the seventh) to the beast. This fulfills more than one word from God.

167. The woman is THAT great city, (one that exist in John's day-probably Rome, this could not be Mecca or New York, for they had not existed yet) which reigns over kings of the earth.

Rev. 13:11-17- Here, the False Prophets role becomes clear.

168. He comes out of the earth (peoples, he is a man possessed by a demon).

169. Two horns like a lamb. He appears to be peaceful like a lamb

170. Spoke as a dragon, or with authority.

171. He stands in place of, and with the same authority as the Antichrist.

172. The kingdom/Antichrist has a deadly wound that is miraculously healed.

173. He does great wonders.

174. Causes fire to come down from the sky to the earth in plain sight.

175. Doing miracles in front of the Antichrist, he deceives those on earth.

176. During the time of the kingdom/Antichrist's wound being healed, he makes men to make an image of the Antichrist.

177. He brings to life this image that people are worshiping.

178. This image speaks and murders those who do not worship him.

179. He causes all to receive a mark in their right hand or forehead.

180. No one is allowed to buy or sell unless he has the mark, or the name of the Antichrist, or the number of his name on them.

181. He is not only possessed by devils, but directs demon spirits in other men, as ambassadors to other countries to work miracles.

182. The false prophet is used to gather men to Armageddon.

183. On the day of the Lord they will be taken alive and cast into Hell. KJV- the Lake of Fire.

Isaiah 16:1-4

184. He is a gangster like ravager who violently takes from others. Isaiah 16:4

185. He is one who squeezes and oppresses people. Isaiah 16:4

Isaiah 29:20

186. He is the terrible one, in the Hebrew it means "tyrannical mighty oppressor." To come upon one suddenly to terrorize.

187. He is a "scorner" The word "scorner" means: *to speak barbarously, to deride, to mock* any one.

2 Thess. 2:3-4- The second coming will not happen until:

188. The departure (I believe this means the Rapture) happens first (departure from what? is debated).

189. The man of sin be uncovered as the son of destruction (doom, perdition). Antichrist.

190. He opposes and elevates himself above anything godly.

191. He sits himself *in the temple* as if to say he were god, in the middle of the 7 years (Daniel 9:27; Matt. 24:15, Rev. 13:5). Some say that he will do this at the dedication of the new temple in Jerusalem.

2 Thess. 2:7-10

192. The mysterious working of the Antichrist was already working in Paul's day.

193. The Holy Spirit will take the church out of the way first, and then the Antichrist will be uncovered.

194. He works just like Satan with all his energy, with powerful lies and signs and wonders.

195. He is called "the wicked," possibly a reference to Isaiah 11:4; Psalm 9:17, 10:2, 4, Jeremiah 30:14, 23.

196. He comes with supernatural manifestations.

197. With extreme deception toward the lost- They will believe a lie-Extremely charismatic.

198. Jesus will kill him with the breath of His mouth.

199. Jesus will destroy all that he has done and is "by His appearing at His coming-" AMP.

Psalm 5:6
200. Bloody and deceitful man.

Psalm 10:18
201. Oppressive Man of the earth.

Psalm 52:1
202. The Mighty (immensely wealthy) Man.

Joel 2:20
203. He attacks Israel like others, from the North thus he is called the "northerner."

204. The Antichrist is attacking at the same time the remnant is repenting.

205. The "army" of the Lord lays everything waste.

206. The Antichrist has factions all over attacking from different sides.

207. He is defeated on all sides (the North, the wastelands, the Dead Sea, and the Mediterranean Sea.).

Isaiah 10, 30, 14:25, Micah 5:5-6, Nahum 1- The Assyrian

208. He will set up his headquarters for battle in Nob. Nob was about ten miles north of Jerusalem, and that is where the high priest resided.

209. His anger is directed at Jerusalem.

210. The voice of the Lord will defeat him one day.

211. He will smite (to strike quickly) Israel with a rod (the rod was used for protection and also used as an instrument for either remedial or penal punishment.),[153] like Pharaoh did in Egypt.

212. He will lift up his staff, (He. *natah* (: אנ, 5186), "to stretch forth, spread out, stretch down, turn aside." This verb also occurs in Arabic, late Aramaic, and postbiblical Hebrew. The Bible attests to it in all periods and about 215 times.[154]) against them like it

---

[153] Waltke, B. K. (1999). 2314 שׁבט. R. L. Harris, G. L. Archer Jr., & B. K. Waltke (Eds.), *Theological Wordbook of the Old Testament* (electronic ed., p. 897). Chicago: Moody Press.
[154] Vine, W. E., Unger, M. F., & White, W., Jr. (1996). Vine's Complete Expository Dictionary of Old and New Testament Words (Vol. 1, p. 248). Nashville, TN: T. Nelson.

was in Egypt. This could mean he exercises authority over them improperly, like Pharaoh did in Egypt.

213. He would only oppress them for a little while.

214. This will mark the end of the age and God's anger toward Israel.

215. The Lord will stir up "Hebrew- wake up" a whip (scourge) against him like he did against Median when Gideon called for help in Judges 7:25 and the tribe Ephraim came out to fight, and <u>took the two princes</u> and killed them.

216. The Lord will raise up his staff like he did in Egypt, with plagues and disasters.

217. The burden and yoke of bondage shall be destroyed by the anointed one-Messiah.

218. The Assyrian will be broken on the mountains of Israel, and the Lord will tread him under foot.

219. Again his burden and yoke will be broken.

220. When he comes to tread in Israel's palaces (these verses have never happened in history), Israel will raise up seven shepherds (Leaders) and eight principle men. There will be plenty of leaders to help with the transition.

221. These leaders will destroy what is left of "Nimrod" or Assyria where the Antichrist hails from.

Daniel 9:27; Rev. 17:3-14

222. He is mentioned with Rome and assumed to be somehow connected, but not necessarily so.

223. He will establish a covenant with many nations for seven years.

224. He will desecrate the Jewish temple.

225. He is associated with the Harlot of Rome.

Zech. 9:13-14

226. A son of revived Greece or Babylon?

Ezekiel 28:2-10- Like the Prince of Tyre

227. He says I am God; I sit in the seat of God.

228. He fixes it in his heart that he is God.

229. With his wisdom, he has amassed great personal wealth.

230. With his expertise in trade, he has increased his wealth immensely.

231. He is full of pride because of his great wealth.

232. God will bring strangers from the outside who will wage war against him.

233. They will be fierce men from other nations.

234. They will destroy your bright splendor (city?).

235. He will die at a stranger's hands.

236. You will die the death of the uncircumcised.

237. You will go down into the "pit" like someone drowning in the sea.

Isaiah 19:4; Daniel 11:42
238. He will rule as a fierce king over Egypt.

Ezekiel 39:1-16
239. God will turn Gog back (Ezek. 39:1-2). From where? Maybe as Daniel says the Antichrist has temporarily been distracted from news at Babylon and doubled back? See Dan. 11:44.

240. God will leave but a sixth part of them. This makes no sense. This is 166.667 men for every one million men. Why would God spare even one enemy at Armageddon? But this could be true for some who did not take the mark of the beast. There is a possible mistranslation in the KJV. Another explanation here is that this word was confused with the similar word "*shashah*" or "sixth," but the Hebrew word used here, "*shasha,*" means "annihilate," thus rightly translated: "I will annihilate you." Some work to keep the original KJV English word, and say this would be literally translated "I will six you."

241. God will cause him to come up to Jerusalem from the north parts.

242. God will bring him against the mountains of Israel.

243. God will smite his bow out of his left hand (Ezek. 39:3).

244. God will smite his arrows out of his right hand. He has no weapon against God.

245. He will fall upon the mountains of Israel, he and all of his crowds of impending troupes (Ezek. 39:4).

246. God will give him unto the ravenous birds of every sort.

247. God will give him to the beasts of the field to be devoured.

248. He will fall upon the open field (Ezek. 39:5).

249. God will send a fire on Magog (Ezek. 39:6).

250. God will send a fire among them that dwell confidently in safety in the "isles" (this word could mean coast).

251. They will know that God has done this and that He is Lord.

252. God will make His holy name known in the midst of His people Israel (Ezek. 39:7).

253. He will not let them pollute His holy name anymore.

254. The heathen will know that God is Yahweh, the Holy One in Israel.

255. The judgment will be completed on Gog and his allies (Ezek. 39:8).

256. In that day God will give Gog a place of graves in Israel, the valley of passengers on the east of the sea (Ezek. 39:11).

257. The dead bodies will stink in the noses of passengers.

258. There to the East of the sea, they will bury Gog and all his multitude.

259. They will call it The Valley of Hamon-gog.

260. For seven months the house of Israel will be burying them, that they may cleanse the land (Ezek. 39:12).

261. All the people of the land will bury (Ezek. 39:13).

262. It will be to them a famous memorial day, the day that God will be glorified.

263. They will give men continual employment to pass through the land to bury those that remain upon the face of the earth to cleanse it (Ezek. 39:14).

264. At the end of seven months the burial program will be ended. Keep in mind this is during the one thousand years that proceed the Day of the Lord.

265. During the seven months, if travelers see a bone they will set up a sign by it, till the buriers have buried it in the valley of Hamon-gog (Ezek. 39:15).

266. The name of the city will be Hamonah. Thus they shall cleanse the land (Ezek. 39:16).

Ezekiel 39:17-23

267. Vs 17- the birds are called to a feast. Speak to every feathered fowl, and to every beast of the field, assemble yourselves, and come; gather yourselves on every side to "My sacrifices that I make for you upon the mountains of Israel." This is the same in Revelation 19:17-20.

268. God will give His glory among the Gentiles (Ezek. 39:21).

269. All the heathen will see God's judgment that He has executed upon the Antichrist and all his mighty armies, and His hand that is laid upon them.

270. The house of Israel will know that God is Yahweh their God from that day and forward (Ezek. 39:22). This would not be stated at the end of the Millennium.

271. The heathen will know that the house of Israel went into captivity for their sins against God and that He hid His face from them, and gave them into the hands of their enemies to fall by the sword (Ezek. 39:23).

272. The heathen will know that God judged Israel according to their sins (Ezek. 39:24).

273. Now (after this battle of Armageddon is over and the judgment upon the Antichrist and his armies is complete) I will bring again the captivity of Jacob (Ezek. 39:25).

274. God will have mercy on the *whole house* of Israel (Zech. 12-14).

275. God will be jealous for His holy name.

276. After they have borne their shame and all their trespasses, when they dwell safely in their land with none making them afraid, when He has gathered them from all nations and has sanctified them in the sight of many nations, *then will they know* that He is the Lord their God, which *caused them* to be led away into captivity among the heathen: but have gathered *every one of them again* from the nations to their own land. (Ezek. 39:26-28).

277. If Ezekiel 38-39 is speaking of only *before* the Tribulation, then this statement above cannot be true, because in the middle of the Tribulation Israel will once again be laid siege by the Antichrist. This part is at least speaking of when the Tribulation has finished. Ezekiel 39:26-29 are the *key verses* for understanding Chapter 38 to know *when* the time of Israel's safety is, that Chapter 38 is speaking of.

278. God will never hide His face from *them again*, for He will pour out His Spirit upon the house of Israel (Ezek. 39:29).[155] This is definitely prophesied in many places to be at the end of the Tribulation for Israel.

Revelation verses about the Mark of the Antichrist-

279. One must have a brand/mark of either the name of the beast or the number of his name to buy or sell during the Tribulation period.

---

[155] Adapted from Dake's list of "80 Eighty Predictions -- Unfulfilled:" Finis Jennings Dake, *Dake's Annotated Reference Bible: Containing the Old and New Testaments of the Authorized or King James Version Text,* (Lawrenceville, GA: Dake Bible Sales, Inc., 1997), WORD*search* CROSS e-book, Under: "Chapter 38."

280. This second beast from the earth, which probably denotes a lesser authority, is the false prophet, as he is called in Revelation 19:20, who initiates and forces the worship of the antichrist, and "brands" those who do so with the mark.

281. The mark of the Antichrist identifies those who worship him.

282. People will accept this mark willingly.

283. They are deceived by the false prophet.

284. The mark is equal to the beast's name or number.

285. The "mark" seems to be an impress or brand mark in the skin.

286. Those who have the mark will suffer painful sores during God's wrath.

I hope this has been a good study for you! Maybe instead of trying to find out who the Antichrist is in the world and naming names, we should be studying who he is in Scripture. So when he does appear on the world scene, we will recognize him. I believe that it won't matter so much for the Church, because we will be gone when he is revealed to the earth.

Maybe you are reading this book during the Tribulation period and wish to know how to accept Jesus, who will soon be coming back to judge this world? Repent that you are a sinner and are lost without a remedy. Jesus loves us so much that He came, and upon Him was laid the judgment we deserved. He paid the ultimate price for our sins. Ask the Lord to forgive you of all your sins. Say that: "Lord, forgive me of all my sins."

The Bible says that you must believe in your heart that Christ Jesus came, and died, and arose from the grave. Because of this, He is the Messiah and Lord. Say that out loud: "I believe, Lord Jesus that you came, and died for my sins, and arose from the dead on the third day." The Bible says that if you pray and believe that, then you are now a Christian and are saved! Trust in Jesus; have faith that he will bring you through. I hope to see you in Heaven!

Romans 10:9 (HCSB)
[9] **If you confess with your mouth, "Jesus is Lord," and believe in your heart that God raised Him from the dead, you will be saved.**

For free lessons, study guides, audios, and video teachings go to:

www.JoyfulHM.org

You can write us at:

Joyful Harvest Ministries
P.O. Box 367 Ironton Mo. 63650